HAMLYN ALL COLOUR VEGETARIAN COOKBOOK

HAMLYN
ALL COLOUR
VEGETARIAN
COOKBOOK

HAMLYN

Front cover shows, left to right: *Wholewheat pasta salad (recipe 137), Potato and cashew curry (recipe 65), Melon and grapefruit cocktail (recipe 13).*

Title page shows, from left: *Iced orange cups (recipe 225), Fruit tartlets (recipe 253).*

Back jacket shows, clockwise from top left, *Tomato roulade (recipe 201), Leek and chickpea chowder (recipe 1), Derby and lentil loaf (recipe 37), Caerphilly bean salad (recipe 105), Cheese and semolina bake (recipe 169).*

The publishers would like to thank the following for supplying photographs: Batchelors 1, 212; Edward Billington (Sugar) Ltd 229, 246, 259, 262; Birds Eye Wall's Limited 20, 78, 115, 156; British Cheese 18, 37, 105, 106, 107, 108, 160, 205; Butter Information Council 86, 154, 194; California Raisin Advisory Board 230, 240, 241, 260; Concentrated Butter 202, 243, 249, 250; Danish Dairy Board 10, 24, 28, 35, 36, 71, 81, 83, 87, 113, 155, 189, 224, 207, 209, 211, 233, 236, 237, 247, 255, 256, 265, 267; Egg Marketing 235, 253; Fresh Fruit and Vegetable Information Bureau 72, 101, 116, 124, 201, 228, 252; The Kellog Company of Great Britain Ltd 2, 7, 118, 200, 251, 254, 258, 268; Mushroom Growers' Association 11, 12, 19, 21, 23, 25, 73, 74, 76, 102, 114, 119, 121, 122, 223; Pasta Information Centre 157; Potato Marketing Board 6, 67, 68, 69, 70, 104; St Ivel 8, 17, 27, 42, 57, 66, 75, 82, 90, 109, 151, 153, 183, 198, 206, 235, 242, 263, 264, 269, 271; Sun Pat Peanut Butter 111; Tabasco 39, 175, 177; Twining's Information Service 261; U.S. Rice Council 47, 140, 141, 143; U.S.A. Peanuts Information Service 40, 89, 117, 133, 142, 231, 257; John West Foods 15, 110, 227, 248, 266

First published in Great Britain in 1988
by Hamlyn, an imprint of Reed Consumer Books Limited
Michelin House, 81 Fulham Road, London SW3 6RB
and Auckland, Melbourne, Singapore and Toronto

Copyright © 1988, 1992 Reed International Books Limited

Revised edition 1992
Reprinted 1992, 1993 (twice), 1994

Additional photography by Chris Crofton, Philip Dowell, Laurie Evans, James Jackson, David Jordan, Graham Kirk, Chris Knaggs, Vernon Morgan, Norman Nichols, Ian O'Leary, Roger Phillips, Charlie Stebbings, Clive Streeter, Paul Williams
Line drawings by Roberta Colegate-Stone and Gay John Galsworthy

A CIP catalogue record for this book is available from the British Library

ISBN 0 600 57528 4

Produced by Mandarin Offset
Printed and bound in China

OTHER TITLES IN THIS SERIES INCLUDE

Hamlyn All Colour Entertaining
Hamlyn All Colour Salads
Hamlyn New All Colour Cookbook
Hamlyn All Colour Indian Cookbook
Hamlyn All Colour Chinese Cookbook

CONTENTS

USEFUL FACTS AND FIGURES

NOTES ON METRICATION

In this book quantities are given in metric and Imperial measures. Exact conversion from Imperial to metric measures does not usually give very convenient working quantities and so the metric measures have been rounded off into units of 25 grams. The table below shows the recommended equivalents.

Ounces	Approx g to nearest whole figure	Recommended conversion to nearest unit of 25	Ounces	Approx g to nearest whole figure	Recommended conversion to nearest unit of 25
1	28	25	9	255	250
2	57	50	10	283	275
3	85	75	11	312	300
4	113	100	12	340	350
5	142	150	13	368	375
6	170	175	14	396	400
7	198	200	15	425	425
8	227	225	16(1lb)	454	450

Note

When converting quantities over 16 oz first add the appropriate figures in the centre column, then adjust to the nearest unit of 25. As a general guide, 1 kg (1000 g) equals 2.2 lb or about 2 lb 3 oz. This method of conversion gives good results in nearly all cases, although in certain pastry and cake recipes a more accurate conversion is necessary to produce a balanced recipe.

Liquid measures

The millilitre has been used in this book and the following table gives a few examples.

Imperial	Approx ml to nearest whole figure	Recommended ml	Imperial	Approx ml to nearest whole figure	Recommended ml
¼	142	150 ml	1 pint	567	600 ml
½	283	300 ml	1½ pints	851	900 ml
¾	425	450 ml	1¾ pints	992	1000 ml (1 litre)

Spoon measures

All spoon measures given in this book are level unless otherwise stated.

Can sizes

At present, cans are marked with the exact (usually to the nearest whole number) metric equivalent of the Imperial weight of the contents, so we have followed this practice when giving can sizes.

Oven temperatures

The table below gives recommended equivalents.

	°C	°F	Gas Mark		°C	°F	Gas Mark
Very cool	110	225	¼	Moderately hot	190	375	5
	120	250	½		200	400	6
Cool	140	275	1	Hot	220	425	7
	150	300	2		230	450	8
Moderate	160	325	3	Very hot	240	475	9
	180	350	4				

NOTES FOR AMERICAN AND AUSTRALIAN USERS

In America the 8 fl oz measuring cup is used. In Australia metric measures are now used in conjunction with the standard 250 ml measuring cup. The Imperial pint, used in Britain and Australia, is 20 fl oz, while the American pint is 16 fl oz. It is important to remember that the Australian tablespoon differs from both the British and American tablespoons; the table below gives a comparison. The British standard tablespoon, which has been used throughout this book, holds 17.7 ml, the American 14.2 ml, and the Australian 20 ml. A teaspoon holds approximately 5 ml in all three countries.

British	American	Australian
1 teaspoon	1 teaspoon	1 teaspoon
1 tablespoon	1 tablespoon	1 tablespoon
2 tablespoons	3 tablespoons	2 tablespoons
3½ tablespoons	4 tablespoons	3 tablespoons
4 tablespoons	5 tablespoons	3½ tablespoons

AN IMPERIAL/AMERICAN GUIDE TO SOLID AND LIQUID MEASURES

Imperial	American	Imperial	American
Solid measures		**Liquid measures**	
1 lb butter or margarine	2 cups	¼ pint liquid	⅔ cup liquid
		½ pint	1¼ cups
1 lb flour	4 cups	¾ pint	2 cups
1 lb granulated or caster sugar	2 cups	1 pint	2½ cups
		1½ pints	3¾ cups
1 lb icing sugar	3 cups	2 pints	5 cups
8 oz rice	1 cup		(2½ pints)

NOTE: WHEN MAKING ANY OF THE RECIPES IN THIS BOOK, ONLY FOLLOW ONE SET OF MEASURES AS THEY ARE NOT INTERCHANGEABLE.

INTRODUCTION

THE HAMLYN ALL COLOUR VEGE-
TARIAN COOKBOOK provides an in-
valuable collection of recipes for aspiring
vegetarian cooks as well as for cooks look-
ing for fresh ideas to enlarge their reper-
toire of vegetarian dishes. The wonderful
variety of recipes in this book offers con-
vincing proof that following a vegetarian
diet need not limit your choice of ingredients to eggs, cheese and lentils.

A colour photograph illustrates each
recipe, so that you can see the result you
are aiming for. Those important finishing
touches are highlighted in the photographs
as well. In addition, much useful dietary
and food preparation information is pro-
vided in the Cook's tips which appear
below each recipe, many of them illus-
trated with a line drawing to give further
clarification of a particular technique, ingredient, or decoration. Every recipe is
calorie-counted to assist in health and
weight-conscious meal planning.

Preparation and cooking times are
clearly given before the recipe method, so
that you can see at a glance whether you
have time to cook a particular dish. And of
course, when planning a special meal in
advance, it is simple to leaf through selecting a starter, main course and dessert, cal-
culating the best combination to achieve
infallible timing.

The chapter sequence is helpful for
menu planning, opening with soups and
starters, following with pulse-based dishes,
vegetable dishes and salads. Rice and pasta
offer further main course options, while
recipes for suppers and snacks and for
special occasions give a great variety of
ideas, for both speedy and more elaborate
dishes. Irresistible desserts and delicious
baking recipes conclude this book.

As many cheeses contain animal rennet, recipes using cheese indicate a vegetarian variety, if one is available. Ask at your
local supermarket or health food shop for
cheeses containing a vegetarian rennet.

Parmesan cheese is not vegetarian, but
Pecorino is a suitable substitute. Of Danish
cheeses, only Danish Blue and Danish
Mozzarella have vegetarian alternatives,
which have been used in recipes. There is
no vegetarian alternative at present for
Danish Dania or Havarti, or for German
smoked cheese. Among English cheeses,
there are no vegetarian alternatives for
Derby or sage Derby. Strict vegetarians
may wish to avoid recipes containing these
cheeses or to experiment with their own
alternatives.

Vegetarians will generally use only
free-range eggs in dishes, avoiding battery
or barn varieties. The seaweed product
agar-agar can be used in place of gelatine.
Butter is suitable for vegetarians, but
because of its high saturated fat content, a
healthier vegetable variety, such as sunflower margarine, may be used. Dishes
suitable for vegans have been indicated
throughout the book.

Choose from over 250 recipes to find
the right one for every occasion.

SOUPS

Choose a soup to complement the courses which follow, in both texture and flavour, and even colour if possible. Light, tangy, Mulligatawny soup or delicately flavoured Tomato and carrot soup make good appetizers for a substantial main course. If the course to follow is light, consider serving a protein- and fibre-rich pulse-based soup, such as Bean and pasta soup. But don't confine soup to a permanent position of first course – extend its status to that of a nourishing snack or lunch.

1 LEEK AND CHICK PEA CHOWDER

Preparation time:
10 minutes

Cooking time:
25 minutes

Serves 4

Calories:
235 per portion

Suitable for Vegans

YOU WILL NEED:
100 g/4 oz leeks, sliced
1 small onion, chopped
2 tablespoons oil
1 teaspoon ground cumin
1 teaspoon ground coriander
350 g/12 oz potatoes, diced
1 × 415 g/14½ oz can chick peas
750 ml/1¼ pints vegetable stock or water
salt and pepper

Sauté the leeks and onion in the oil until soft. Sprinkle over the cumin and coriander and cook for a further minute. Add the potatoes and turn them thoroughly in the mixture. Stir in the drained chick peas with 450 ml/¾ pint stock or water. Bring to the boil, cover and cook gently until the potatoes are soft, about 15 minutes. Add the remaining stock or water with seasoning to taste. Serve hot as a chowder or liquidize to make a smooth thick soup. Accompany with crusty bread.

2 BEAN AND PASTA SOUP

Preparation time:
5 minutes

Cooking time:
25 minutes

Serves 4-6

Calories:
215-145 per portion

YOU WILL NEED:
1 large onion, sliced
1.2 litres/2 pints vegetable stock
75 g/3 oz pasta shapes
2 tablespoons tomato purée
salt and pepper
50 g/2 oz All-Bran cereal
1 × 275 g/10 oz can red kidney beans
100 g/4 oz canned broad beans
1 tablespoon chopped parsley (optional)

Simmer the onion in the stock in a large covered saucepan for 10 minutes. Add the pasta and tomato purée and cook for 10 minutes. Add the salt and pepper, cereal, kidney and broad beans and cook gently for a further 5 minutes. Pour into soup bowls and sprinkle with parsley, if you like.

■ COOK'S TIP

Buy ready-ground spices and store them in an airtight jar ready for use. Alternatively, coriander seeds grind easily in a small pestle and mortar to give fragrant results.

■ COOK'S TIP

All-Bran cereal is a versatile store-cupboard item – use it to add texture and valuable fibre to plain cake, pastry or bread mixtures. Combine it with unsweetened crumble *mixture and grated cheese to make a tasty savoury topping for vegetables and pulses. Combine it in nut loaves, vegetable burgers and terrines for added flavour.*

3 MULLIGATAWNY SOUP

Preparation time:
5 minutes

Cooking time:
1 hour

Serves 6

Calories:
95 per portion

Suitable for Vegans

YOU WILL NEED:
1 apple, chopped
1 large carrot, chopped
2 tablespoons oil
25 g/1 oz plain flour
1 tablespoon curry powder
1.2 litres/2 pints vegetable stock
1 tablespoon mango chutney
25 g/1 oz sultanas
pinch of sugar
salt and pepper
2 teaspoons lemon juice or wine or
    cider vinegar

Cook the apple and carrot in the hot oil for 2 minutes. Stir in the flour and curry powder to make a paste. Gradually stir in the stock, bring to the boil and cook until thickened. Add the chutney, sultanas, sugar, a little salt and pepper, and the lemon juice, wine or vinegar. Cook very gently for 45 minutes – 1 hour or until the vegetables are very soft.

   Cool slightly and either press through a sieve or blend until smooth in a liquidizer. Pour the purée into the rinsed pan. Taste and adjust seasoning, if necessary. Reheat gently before serving.

4 PEA SOUP

Preparation time:
10 minutes, plus
overnight to soak

Cooking time:
1¼-1½ hours

Serves 4

Calories:
210 per portion

Suitable for Vegans

YOU WILL NEED:
225 g/8 oz dried split peas
1.2 litres/2 pints vegetable stock
2 medium onions, chopped
1 medium carrot, chopped
1 small turnip, chopped
salt and pepper
1 sprig of mint
1 teaspoon sugar

Cover the split peas with water and soak them overnight. Drain well. Place in a large saucepan with the stock, onions, carrot, turnip, a little salt and pepper, and the mint. Bring slowly to the boil, then simmer for 1¼-1½ hours or until the peas are very soft. Cool slightly and either press through a sieve or blend until smooth in a liquidizer. Pour the purée back into the rinsed pan, add sugar to taste and adjust the seasoning. Reheat very gently and serve hot.

■ COOK'S TIP

Try serving a basket of crisp cooked poppadoms with this soup. Look out for these flavoured with chilli, cumin seeds and other spices as well as the plain variety.

Instead of frying them, cook them under the grill, keeping them away from the hot element.

■ COOK'S TIP

Swirl a little soured cream, natural yogurt or plain fromage frais into this soup before serving – delicious!

5 CHESTNUT SOUP

Preparation time:
35 minutes

Cooking time:
35 minutes

Serves 4-6

Calories:
360-240 per portion

YOU WILL NEED:
450 g/1 lb chestnuts
1 large onion, sliced
40 g/1½ oz butter
1 medium potato, chopped
3 celery sticks, chopped
1.4 litres/2½ pints vegetable stock
salt and pepper
15 g/½ oz plain flour
½ teaspoon light brown sugar
pinch of dried mixed herbs
300 ml/½ pint milk
1 tablespoon dry sherry
FOR THE GARNISH
croutons (optional)
1 tablespoon chopped parsley
(optional)

Slit the hard shell of each chestnut. Put the chestnuts into a pan of boiling water and simmer for 20 minutes. Remove the hard shells, rub off the brown skins and roughly chop the chestnuts.

Put the onion and half of the butter into a pan and gently cook until soft. Add the potato, celery, chestnuts, stock, salt and pepper, and bring to the boil. Cover and simmer until the chestnuts are soft. Press through a sieve, or liquidize.

Melt the remaining butter, work in the flour and cook for 2 minutes. Stir in the sugar, herbs and chestnut purée, and heat through gently. Add the milk and reheat, but do not boil. Stir in the sherry and serve, garnished as shown, if you like.

■ COOK'S TIP

If you have a garden, then try drying some herbs for the winter. For example, sage, thyme and tarragon can be tied in bunches and hung in a cool, dry place.

6 WINTER WARMER

Preparation time:
5 minutes

Cooking time:
40 minutes

Serves 4

Calories:
355 per portion

YOU WILL NEED:
25 g/1 oz butter
450 g/1 lb onions, chopped
675 g/1½ lb potatoes, chopped
900 ml/1½ pints vegetable stock
1 × 280 g/10 oz can creamed
    sweetcorn
pinch of mace or nutmeg
2 bay leaves
¼ teaspoon celery salt
pepper
1 × 170 g/6 oz can evaporated milk or
    single cream
1 tablespoon chopped fennel, to
    garnish (optional)

Heat the butter in a large saucepan, add the onions and cook over moderate heat until golden, about 8 minutes. Add the potatoes, stock, sweetcorn, mace or nutmeg, bay leaves, salt and pepper. Bring to the boil, stirring, cover and simmer for 30 minutes or until the potatoes are very soft. Remove the bay leaves. Stir in the evaporated milk or cream, check seasoning, heat through gently and serve in warmed individual bowls. Garnish with fennel, if using.

■ COOK'S TIP

A delicious accompaniment for soup: clean potato peelings, dipped in a thin batter and deep fried until crisp and golden.

7   CARROT SOUP

Preparation time:
15 minutes

Cooking time:
35 minutes

Serves 4

Calories:
145 per portion

YOU WILL NEED:
450 g/1 lb carrots, diced
900 ml/1½ pints vegetable stock
25 g/1 oz All-Bran cereal
175 g/6 oz onion, chopped
100 g/4 oz potatoes, diced
1 celery stick, chopped
1 tablespoon chopped parsley
salt and pepper
½ teaspoon caraway seeds
150 ml/¼ pint single cream (optional)

Put all the ingredients, except the cream, into a large pan and bring gently to the boil. Cover and simmer for 30 minutes, or until the vegetables are soft. Allow the soup to cool slightly and then purée in a food processor or a liquidizer until smooth and thick. Alternatively, press the soup through a sieve.

Return the soup to the pan and reheat when required, stirring in the cream just before serving. Accompany with Caraway rolls (see recipe 268).

8   TOMATO AND CARROT SOUP

Preparation time:
25 minutes

Cooking time:
42 minutes

Serves 6

Calories:
160 per portion

YOU WILL NEED:
100 g/4 oz carrots, peeled and sliced
1 small onion, chopped
1 garlic clove, chopped
2 tablespoons oil
450 g/1 lb tomatoes, peeled and
    chopped
600 ml/1 pint vegetable stock
salt and pepper
a little grated nutmeg
25 g/1 oz tomato purée
300 ml/½ pint single cream
1 tablespoon chopped parsley
additional parsley, to garnish

Cook the carrots, onion and garlic in the oil over gentle heat for about 10 minutes, without browning. Stir in the tomatoes and stock. Season well with the salt and pepper and nutmeg, then stir in the tomato purée. Bring to the boil, reduce the heat and simmer for 30 minutes.

Blend the soup in a food processor or a liquidizer, return to the pan and stir in the cream and parsley. Heat gently, without boiling, then serve garnished with a sprinkling of fresh chopped parsley.

■ COOK'S TIP

If you have a food processor, then simply roughly chop all the vegetables, using the knife attachment. Do not over-process them.

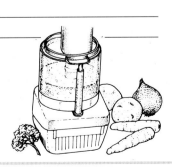

■ COOK'S TIP

Flavour this soup with the grated rind and juice of 1 orange if you like. Add to the soup with the tomatoes and stock.

9 CREAMY ONION SOUP

Preparation time:
10 minutes

Cooking time:
55 minutes

Serves 4

Calories:
325 per portion

YOU WILL NEED:
50 g/2 oz butter
3 large onions, chopped
1.2 litres/2 pints vegetable stock
450 g/1 lb potatoes, peeled and
  chopped
2-3 teaspoons soup seasoning
2 teaspoons paprika
½-1 tablespoon tomato purée
150 ml/¼ pint single cream
fried onion rings, to garnish

Melt the butter in a pan and fry the onions until soft. Add the stock, potatoes, soup seasoning, paprika and tomato purée.

Simmer for about 45 minutes. Sieve or blend the soup and reheat. Stir the cream into the hot soup and heat through very gently. Garnish with fried onion rings and serve.

10 LEEK AND POTATO SOUP

Preparation time:
15 minutes

Cooking time:
40-45 minutes

Serves 4

Calories:
220 per portion

YOU WILL NEED:
25 g/1 oz butter
2 medium leeks, thinly sliced
350 g/12 oz potatoes, thinly sliced
750 ml/1¼ pints vegetable stock
salt and pepper
¼ teaspoon ground nutmeg
2-4 tablespoons milk or water
  (optional)
75-100 g/3-4 oz vegetarian Danish
  Blue cheese
chopped chives, to garnish (optional)

Melt the butter in a large pan and add the leeks. Cover and cook gently, stirring occasionally, for 8-10 minutes, until soft. Reserve a few rings for garnish. Add the potatoes to the pan with the stock, seasoning and nutmeg. Bring to the boil, cover and simmer for 25-30 minutes, until the potatoes are soft.

Cool slightly then rub the soup through a sieve, or liquidize in a blender until smooth. Return to the pan and reheat, adding a little milk or water if the soup is too thick. Just before serving, crumble in the Blue cheese and stir until melted. Garnish with the reserved leek rings and chopped chives, if using.

▪ COOK'S TIP

Serve this soup cold as a smooth summer starter. Chill the sieved soup and add the cream just before serving. Omit the onion rings and float a spring onion curl on top of each portion instead (see Cook's Tip 211).

▪ COOK'S TIP

Vegetable stock: fry 2 each chopped onions, potatoes, and celery sticks. Stir in 1 each sliced parsnip and turnip, add 1.2 litres/2 pints water and herbs. Simmer 1 hour.

11 CREAM OF MUSHROOM SOUP

Preparation time:
10 minutes

Cooking time:
25-30 minutes

Serves 4

Calories:
135 per portion

YOU WILL NEED:
1 tablespoon sunflower oil
1 medium onion, chopped
450 g/1 lb mushrooms, finely chopped
600 ml/1 pint vegetable stock
1 tablespoon chopped parsley
salt and freshly ground white pepper
2 teaspoons cornflour
150 ml/¼ pint single cream
croutons, to garnish

Heat the oil and cook the onion gently until soft, about 5 minutes. Add the mushrooms and cook, stirring, for 3-4 minutes. Stir in the stock, parsley and seasoning; bring to the boil, cover and simmer gently for 15 minutes. Blend the cornflour with a little cold water and stir into the soup, cooking for a further 2-3 minutes until thickened. Stir in the cream and serve at once with croutons.

12 COUNTRY MUSHROOM SOUP

Preparation time:
15 minutes

Cooking time:
20 minutes

Serves 6

Calories:
105 per portion

YOU WILL NEED:
2 tablespoons oil
1 onion, finely chopped
1 garlic clove, crushed
2 teaspoons ground coriander
225 g/8 oz flat mushrooms, finely chopped
1.2 litres/2 pints vegetable stock
grated rind of 1 lemon
3 tablespoons chopped parsley
100 g/4 oz fresh wholewheat breadcrumbs
salt and pepper
FOR THE GARNISH
2 tablespoons soured cream
1 tablespoon chopped parsley

Heat the oil and cook the onion gently until just soft, about 5 minutes. Stir in the garlic and coriander and cook for a minute to bring out the flavours. Add the mushrooms and cook for a further 3-4 minutes. Stir in the stock, lemon rind and parsley. Bring to the boil, cover and simmer for 10 minutes. Stir in the breadcrumbs and seasoning to taste and cook for 1 minute longer. Remove from the heat and swirl through the soured cream. Sprinkle with parsley and serve the soup at once.

■ COOK'S TIP

Pale button mushrooms give the best colour and a delicate flavour when making soup, but you will find that open, darker mushrooms offer a fuller flavour and are more suitable for hearty soups than creamy ones.

■ COOK'S TIP

To freeze vegetable stock (see recipe 10): leave it to cool, then fill plastic bags, supporting them in a basin, freeze, then remove the basin when hard.

STARTERS

Starters are designed to stimulate the taste buds, making them receptive to the courses which follow. When selecting a starter for a main meal, consider the menu as a whole and pick and choose from the recipe ideas in this chapter. A juicy, fruity starter like Melon and grapefruit cocktail with a fresh mint garnish will sharpen the appetite, and the unusual Crunchy Brie, served with the colourful and contrastingly flavoured cherry sauce will create enthusiastic anticipation of things to come.

13 MELON AND GRAPEFRUIT COCKTAIL

Preparation time:
10 minutes, plus 1
hour to chill

Serves 4

Calories:
104 per portion

YOU WILL NEED:
1 ripe honeydew melon, halved and seeded
2 grapefruit, peeled
3-4 tablespoons clear honey
4 mint sprigs

Scoop out the melon flesh, using a melon baller, and place in a bowl.

Cut between the segments of the grapefruit, removing the pith and pips, and catch any juice from the fruit by working over a plate. Mix the grapefruit segments and juice with the melon, and trickle over the honey. Add the sprigs of mint to the fruit and chill thoroughly.

Serve the cocktail in glasses, carefully removing the mint to use as a garnish.

14 GRAPEFRUIT AND AVOCADO SALAD

Preparation time:
20 minutes

Serves 6

Calories:
165 per portion

Suitable for Vegans

YOU WILL NEED:
2 avocados, halved, peeled and stoned
2 grapefruit
2 oranges
½ teaspoon sugar
2 tablespoons olive oil
1 tablespoon chopped mint
salt and pepper
6-10 lettuce leaves, washed and torn into bite-sized pieces, or 2 heads of chicory, washed

Cut the avocado flesh into thin slices. Spread the slices out in a shallow bowl.

Holding a grapefruit over the bowl (so that the juice will go over the avocado slices), peel it with a sharp knife. Using a sawing action, cut round the fruit down to the flesh and remove all the white pith. Cut each segment of fruit away from the inner white skin. When all the segments have been removed from the grapefruit, squeeze the remaining juice from the skin over the avocado slices. Repeat this with the other grapefruit and the oranges, putting the segments on a plate.

Turn the avocado slices in the juice. Drain off any excess juice into a small bowl and add the sugar, oil, mint and salt and pepper to make a dressing.

To assemble the dish, cover individual plates with lettuce or chicory leaves, then arrange segments of grapefruit, orange and avocado on top, dividing them between the plates. Spoon a little dressing over each salad.

■ COOK'S TIP

For special occasions, frost the tops of the glasses by dipping the rims lightly in beaten egg white, then in sugar.

■ COOK'S TIP

Sprinkling the avocado slices with the citrus fruit juices prevents them from discolouring.

The watercress sprigs and sprinkling of herbs shown in *the photograph give additional colour to the salad.*

15 GRAPEFRUIT SORBET

Preparation time:
10 minutes, plus
several hours to
freeze

Cooking time:
7-8 minutes

Serves 6

Calories:
50 per portion

YOU WILL NEED:
25 g/1 oz honey
300 ml/½ pint water
2 × 540 g/1 lb 3 oz cans grapefruit
   segments in natural juice
150 ml/¼ pint lemon juice
grated rind of 2 lemons
2 egg whites
mint sprigs, to decorate

Bring the honey and water gently to the boil and simmer for 5 minutes. Cool slightly. Use one can of grapefruit to make the sorbet; reserve the second can for serving. Drain the grapefruit juice from the segments in one can and add to the honey liquid with the lemon juice and rind. Cool and freeze until half frozen.

Whisk the egg whites until stiff and fold into the mixture. Freeze again until firm. Serve the sorbet on a bed of grapefruit segments, reserving a few for decoration. Top with mint sprigs.

16 PEARS WITH MUSTARD CREAM MAYONNAISE

Preparation time:
30 minutes, plus 1
hour to chill

Serves 4

Calories:
175 per portion

YOU WILL NEED:
2 ripe eating pears
1 tablespoon lemon juice
4 tablespoons mayonnaise
1 tablespoon Dijon mustard
2 tablespoons double cream, whipped
FOR THE GARNISH
flaked almond
lettuce leaves

Peel the pears, keeping them in good shape. Using a teaspoon, scoop out the seeds and core. Brush each pear with the lemon juice to prevent from discolouring.

Whisk the mayonnaise with the mustard and whipped double cream, adding 1 teaspoon of boiling water if the consistency is too thick to coat the pears smoothly. Toast the almonds under the grill until golden brown. Cool.

To serve, place a few lettuce leaves on four small plates. Place a pear half, cut side down, on each plate and coat with mustard mayonnaise. Sprinkle with the toasted almonds. Chill before serving.

▓ COOK'S TIP

Crystallized mint leaves make an attractive decoration for sorbets. Dip clean leaves in egg white, then in caster sugar. Dry on a wire rack.

▓ COOK'S TIP

Watch the almonds closely. It takes only a few seconds for beautifully golden nuts to become burnt offerings.

17 SAVOURY PEAR MOUSSE

Preparation time:
20 minutes, plus 1-2 hours to set

Cooking time:
15 minutes

Serves 8

Calories:
95 per portion

YOU WILL NEED:
2 pears, peeled and chopped
1 small onion, chopped
120 ml/4 fl oz water
pinch of chilli powder
pinch of turmeric
4 juniper berries, crushed
salt and pepper
175 g/6 oz vegetarian low-fat soft
    cheese
4 tablespoons double cream
100 g/4 oz button mushrooms, finely
    chopped
2 teaspoons agar-agar
cress and capers, to garnish
TO SERVE
Melba tost
2 hard-boiled eggs, sliced
2 tomatoes, cut into wedges

Place the pears and onion in a small pan with 2 tablespoons of the water, the chilli, turmeric, juniper berries and seasoning. Cover and cook gently for about 15 minutes, or until tender.

When the pears are soft, drain, blend in a liquidizer or press through a sieve. Add the soft cheese, cream and mushrooms and blend until smooth. Dissolve the agar-agar in the remaining cold water in a small saucepan, then bring to the boil, stirring constantly. Stir into the mousse. Pour into individual dishes and chill to set. Garnish with cress and capers, serve as shown.

■ COOK'S TIP

To make Melba toast, toast medium-thick bread slices, cut off the crusts and slice through to give very thin pieces – work quickly before the toast cools.

Lightly toast the second side of each piece.

18 TOMATO COUPE

Preparation time:
10 minutes, plus 1 hour to set

Cooking time:
10 minutes

Serves 6

Calories:
95 per portion

YOU WILL NEED:
1 × 397 g/14 oz can tomatoes
grated rind of ½ lemon
1 bay leaf
1 garlic clove, crushed
3 tablespoons white wine
2 teaspoons agar-agar
150 ml/¼ pint water
salt and pepper
½ teaspoon sugar
100 g/4 oz vegetarian Cheddar cheese,
    grated
6 spring onions, thinly sliced
brown bread and butter, to serve

Pour the tomatoes and their juices into a saucepan, add the lemon rind, bay leaf and garlic. Chop the tomatoes roughly, bring to the boil, cover and simmer for 10 minutes. Press the tomato mixture through a sieve into a measuring jug and add the wine. Dissolve the agar-agar in the cold water in a small saucepan, bring to the boil, stirring constantly, then add to the tomato and wine mixture. Add more boiling water if necessary to make 600 ml/1 pint. Stir in salt, pepper and sugar to taste. Cool. Pour into 6 individual ramekins or coupé glasses and refrigerate until set.

Mix together the cheese and spring onions and top each coupé with the mixture. Serve chilled with brown bread and butter.

■ COOK'S TIP

If you like, set the tomato mixture in one large mould, then turn it out before serving. Offer the cheese and spring onions in a separate dish.

19 GREEK MUSHROOM SALAD

Preparation time:
10 minutes, plus 1
hour to chill

Cooking time:
15 minutes

Serves 6

Calories:
30 per portion
180 per piece of
pitta bread

YOU WILL NEED:
2 garlic cloves, crushed
3 tablespoons tomato purée
3 tablespoons lemon juice
150 ml/¼ pint water
1 teaspoon oregano
½ teaspoon basil
225 g/8 oz button mushrooms
450 g/1 lb cauliflower florets
12 black olives, roughly chopped
salt and pepper
pitta bread, to serve

Suitable for Vegans

Place the garlic, tomato purée, lemon juice and water in a
large saucepan and mix well. Stir in the herbs, mushrooms
and cauliflower. Cover and bring to the boil, then reduce the
heat and simmer gently for 10 minutes, stirring frequently.
Stir in the olives and seasoning to taste. Transfer to a serving
bowl and leave until cold.

   This is best served chilled, accompanied with warm pitta
bread cut into fingers.

20 SAVOURY STUFFED TOMATOES

Preparation time:
10 minutes

Serves 4

Calories:
50 per portion

YOU WILL NEED:
4 large firm tomatoes
75 g/3 oz vegetarian cream cheese,
   softened
½ teaspoon finely chopped chives or
   onion
1 tablespoon mayonnaise
salt and pepper
100 g/4 oz frozen peas, cooked
parsley or watercress sprigs, to garnish

Slice the tops off the tomatoes and scoop out the pulp with a
teaspoon. Beat the cream cheese with the chives or onion and
mayonnaise and season well. Stir in the peas and fill the tomatoes with the mixture, replacing the top of each. Garnish with
sprigs of parsley or watercress.

■ COOK'S TIP

If you prefer, mix tomatoes
with the mushrooms in this
salad instead of the
cauliflower. Cook the
mushrooms as above, then
add 6 peeled and quartered
tomatoes at the end of the
cooking time.

■ COOK'S TIP

For best results, when you
have scooped out the
tomatoes, leave them to
drain on double-thick
absorbent kitchen paper.

21 MUSHROOMS INDIENNE

Preparation time:
10 minutes, plus 30
minutes to chill

Serves 4

Calories:
100 per portion

YOU WILL NEED:
150 ml/¼ pint soured cream or
  natural yogurt
1-2 teaspoons curry paste
1 tablespoon sieved mango chutney
salt and pepper
1 dessert apple, peeled, cored and
  chopped
175 g/6 oz button mushrooms
Chinese leaves, shredded
4 lemon slices, to garnish

Mix together the cream or yogurt and curry paste according to taste. Add the chutney, seasoning, apple and mushrooms and mix well. Chill for at least 30 minutes before serving.

Pile each portion on to a bed of shredded Chinese leaves and garnish with a twist of lemon.

22 PEANUT DIP WITH CRUDITES

Preparation time:
15-20 minutes

Cooking time:
5 minutes

Serves 6

Calories:
190 per portion

YOU WILL NEED:
2 tablespoons sunflower oil
1 onion, finely chopped
2 garlic cloves, crushed
½ teaspoon chilli powder
1 teaspoon ground cumin
1 teaspoon ground coriander
6 tablespoons crunchy peanut butter
6 tablespoons water
1 teaspoon shoyu
1 teaspoon lemon juice
FOR THE CRUDITES
1 small cauliflower
1 bunch of radishes
1 red pepper, seeded
6 celery sticks
6 carrots

Heat the oil in a small saucepan, add the onion and fry for a few minutes until softened. Add the garlic and spices, stir and cook for 1 minute. Mix in the peanut butter, then gradually blend in the water, stirring until thickened. Add the shoyu and lemon juice, stir well and leave to cool.

Break the cauliflower into florets and halve the radishes if large. Cut the remaining vegetables into long thin pieces.

Turn the dip into a small dish, place on a large plate and surround with the crudités.

▮ COOK'S TIP

*Instead of the curry paste,
you can use curry powder
but halve the quantity.
Cook the powder in a little
butter for 3 minutes before
adding to the cream.*

▮ COOK'S TIP

*Wholemeal grissini – Italian
breadsticks – make excellent
dippers, much favoured by
children. If serving the dip
for a child's party, eliminate
the spices.*

23 MUSHROOM AND AVOCADO STARTER

Preparation time:
15 minutes, plus 30 minutes to chill

Serves 4

Calories:
100 per portion

YOU WILL NEED:
225 g/8 oz button mushrooms, sliced
3 tablespoons lemon juice
4 spring onions, chopped
1 tablespoon sunflower seeds, toasted
salt and pepper
1 ripe avocado

Suitable for Vegans

Put the mushrooms in a mixing bowl with 2 tablespoons lemon juice, the spring onions, sunflower seeds and seasoning. Mix well and chill for at least 30 minutes.

Just before serving, remove the stone and peel the avocado, slice the flesh and sprinkle with the remaining lemon juice. Arrange the avocado slices on individual serving plates with the mushroom salad at the side.

24 CHEESE CROUSTADES

Preparation time:
15 minutes

Cooking time:
24 minutes

Oven temperature:
200 C, 400 F, gas 6

Makes 12

Calories:
110 per croustade

YOU WILL NEED:
25 g/1 oz butter, melted
12 slices medium-sliced bread
FOR THE FILLING
225 g/8 oz small button mushrooms
25 g/1 oz butter
125 g/4½ oz Danish Dania cheese, plain
½ teaspoon cornflour
2 tablespoons chopped parsley
salt and pepper
FOR THE GARNISH
paprika
parsley sprigs

Brush a 12-hole bun tin with a little of the melted butter. Cut the crusts off the bread and flatten each slice with a rolling pin. Cut out an 8.5 cm/3½ inch circle from each piece of bread, then press into the tins. Brush with the remaining melted butter and bake for 15 minutes.

To make the filling, wipe and quarter the mushrooms. Melt the butter and cook the mushrooms, covered, for 5 minutes. Remove the rind from the cheese, and add the cheese to the mushrooms, stirring until melted.

Mix the cornflour to a smooth paste with a little water, stir into the mushroom mixture and bring just to boiling point to thicken, still stirring. Lower heat, add half the parsley and salt and pepper and heat for 30 seconds.

Divide the mushroom mixture between the warm croustades and sprinkle with paprika. Add a sprig of parsley.

■ COOK'S TIP

To remove the stone easily from a halved avocado, pierce it with the point of a knife, then pull it out.

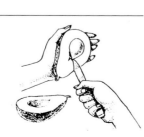

■ COOK'S TIP

Croustades lend themselves perfectly to lots of different fillings. Try ratatouille, sautéed vegetables or Leeks au gratin (Recipe 94), adding the filling of your choice just *before serving to prevent the croustades becoming soggy.*

25 MUSHROOM PUFFS WITH SPICY SAUCE

Preparation time:
15 minutes

Cooking time:
20-30 minutes

Serves 4

Calories:
230 per portion

YOU WILL NEED:
225 g/8 oz mushrooms
FOR THE SAUCE
1 tablespoon oil
1 small onion, finely chopped
½ garlic clove, crushed
1 teaspoon dark soft brown sugar
2 teaspoons lemon juice
1 tablespoon tomato purée
1 × 227g/8 oz can tomatoes
1 tablespoon mushroom ketchup
salt and pepper
parsley sprigs, to garnish
FOR THE BATTER
50 g/2 oz plain flour
salt and pepper
4 tablespoons lukewarm water
1 egg white
oil for frying

First make the sauce: heat the oil in a pan, add the onion and garlic and cook until tender. Add the remaining ingredients and boil, season and keep warm. For the batter, place the flour and seasoning in a bowl, then beat in the water and fold in the stiffly-beaten egg white. Heat the oil for deep frying to 190 C/375 F. Dip the mushrooms in the batter, then deep fry until golden. Drain on absorbent kitchen paper, garnish with parsley sprigs and serve with the sauce.

26 MUSHROOM PATE

Preparation time:
15 minutes plus 1-2 hours to chill

Cooking time:
20 minutes

Serves 4

Calories:
190 per portion

YOU WILL NEED:
75 g/3 oz butter
2 shallots or small onions, finely sliced
1 garlic clove, crushed (optional)
225 g/8 oz flat mushrooms, sliced
25 g/1 oz fresh wholewheat
   breadcrumbs
100 g/4 oz vegetarian cottage cheese
pinch of grated nutmeg
pinch of ground mace
salt and pepper
FOR THE GARNISH
1 tablespoon chopped parsley
lemon wedges

Melt 25 g/1 oz butter in a saucepan and cook the shallots or onions and garlic gently for 3 minutes. Add the mushrooms, cover and cook for 15 minutes. Remove the lid, turn up the heat and reduce the liquid until the mushrooms are just moist. Add a further 25 g/1 oz butter.

Cool slightly, then put the mushrooms, breadcrumbs, cheese, nutmeg, mace, salt and pepper and remaining butter in a liquidizer or food processor and blend until smooth.

Adjust the seasoning, and spoon the pâté into a small dish. Cover and chill for 1-2 hours. Just before serving sprinkle the top with parsley and garnish with lemon wedges.

■ COOK'S TIP

When deep frying, make sure that the food absorbs the minimum of fat: have the oil hot before cooking, then drain the food on absorbent kitchen paper.

■ COOK'S TIP

A useful vegetarian spread. Tasty with chopped watercress as a sandwich filling, or served with warm Granary bread and butter.

27 CHEESE BALLS

Preparation time:
30 minutes, plus 1
hour to chill

Serves 6

Calories:
280 per portion

YOU WILL NEED:
225 g/8 oz vegetarian low-fat hard
    cheese, finely grated
75 g/3 oz butter
salt and pepper
1 tablespoon milk
cayenne pepper
2 teaspoons sherry
100 g/4 oz walnuts, finely chopped

Mix all the ingredients together, except the walnuts, adding a little cayenne to taste. Take small spoonfuls of the cheese mixture and roll them into balls. Coat each with chopped walnuts. Chill for at least an hour before serving.

28 CRUNCHY BRIE

Preparation time:
15 minutes, plus 30
minutes to chill

Cooking time:
5-6 minutes

Serves 4

Calories:
385 per portion

YOU WILL NEED:
150 g/5 oz vegetarian Blue Brie cheese
15 g/½ oz plain flour
1 egg, beaten
40 g/1½ oz fresh white breadcrumbs
oil for deep frying
dill sprigs, to garnish
FOR THE SAUCE
1 × 220 g/7¾ oz can pitted black
    cherries
1½ teaspoons arrowroot
2 teaspoons caster sugar

Cut the cheese into four equal wedges. Dip each into the flour and shake off the excess. Dip in the egg, allow excess to run off, then coat completely in the breadcrumbs. Re-coat in egg and breadcrumbs. Place on a plate, cover and refrigerate for at least 30 minutes.

Meanwhile make the sauce. Drain the juice from the cherries and reserve the fruit. In a small saucepan blend the arrowroot to a smooth paste with a little of the juice. Add the remaining juice and bring to the boil, stirring all the time, until thickened. Sweeten to taste, add the cherries and heat through gently. Pour into a sauceboat.

Heat the oil in a deep pan to 180 C/350 F, or until a day-old bread cube browns in 60 seconds. Lower the cheese portions into the hot oil, two at a time, and fry for 30-60 seconds, until the coating is golden. Remove from the pan and drain on absorbent kitchen paper. Cook the remaining cheese portions, garnish with dill and serve with the cherry sauce.

▨ COOK'S TIP

Serve these tasty cheese
balls as a cocktail snack.
For a first course, arrange a
few balls on shredded
lettuce on individual plates
and garnish with tomato.

▨ COOK'S TIP

This unusual dish can be
served as a savoury at the
end of a meal or even at a
cheese and wine party for a
change. Prepare the cheese
earlier in the day ready to

be cooked just before
serving.

29 GLAMORGAN SAUSAGES

Preparation time:
20 minutes

Cooking time:
5-7 minutes

Serves 4

Calories:
520 per portion

YOU WILL NEED:
1 medium onion, finely chopped
175 g/6 oz vegetarian Cheddar cheese, grated
275 g/10 oz fresh breadcrumbs
pinch of dried sage
pinch of mustard powder
2 egg, separated
salt and pepper
fresh breadcrumbs for coating
oil for frying

Mix together the onion, cheese, breadcrumbs, sage, mustard, egg yolks, and salt and pepper. Divide the mixture into 12 pieces and roll each portion into a small sausage shape.

Lightly beat the egg whites in a shallow bowl. Place the breadcrumbs on a large plate. Coat each sausage shape with egg white and then press on a coating of crumbs.

Heat about 2.5 cm/1 inch of oil in a large saucepan. Fry the 'sausages' for 5-7 minutes or until golden, turning once. Drain on absorbent kitchen paper. Serve hot.

30 AVOCADO AND CHEESE MOUSSE

Preparation time:
15 minutes, plus 2 hours to chill

Serves 4

Calories:
180 per portion

YOU WILL NEED:
1 large ripe avocado
75 g/3 oz vegetarian cream cheese
1 garlic clove, crushed
juice of 1 lemon
salt and pepper
2 tablespoons single cream
watercress sprigs, to garnish

Halve the avocado, remove the stone and scoop out the flesh into a bowl. Mash and mix with the cream cheese, garlic and lemon juice. Season well and stir in the cream.

Spoon the mixture into individual glasses and chill for up to 2 hours. Serve garnished with watercress and accompany with Melba toast (see recipe 17).

▌ COOK'S TIP

Try using other types of cheese in these delicious savouries: Edam or Cheddar with chives, Sage Derby, or blue Stilton for a rich flavour.

▌ COOK'S TIP

Do not prepare this mousse more than about 2 hours in advance as it tends to discolour.

31 GARNISHED ARTICHOKE HEARTS

Preparation time:
10 minutes, plus 20
minutes to chill

Serves 4

Calories:
245 per portion

YOU WILL NEED:
2 × 90 g/3½ oz packets vegetarian
    soft cream cheese
1 garlic clove, crushed
1 egg yolk
6 tablespoons double cream, lightly
    whipped
pinch of paprika
2 tablespoons chopped herbs (e.g.
    sage, parsley, thyme)
salt and pepper
1 × 400 g/14 oz can artichoke hearts
    in brine, drained
FOR THE GARNISH
shredded lettuce
red pepper slices

Beat the cream cheese with the crushed garlic, egg yolk,
cream, paprika, herbs and salt and pepper to taste. Spoon into
a piping bag fitted with a star-shaped nozzle and pipe swirls
of the mixture on to the artichoke hearts. Chill the artichoke
hearts lightly before placing on a bed of lettuce on a serving
plate. Garnish with red pepper slices.

■ COOK'S TIP

*Garnished artichoke hearts
make a delicious party
snack, or hors d'oeuvre.
Serve with garlic bread and
a light dry red wine.*

32 VEGETABLE PATE

Preparation time:
15 minutes

Cooking time:
1 hour 25 minutes

Oven temperature:
160 C, 325 F, gas 3

Serves 6

Calories:
210 per portion

YOU WILL NEED:
2 tablespoons olive oil
1 onion, thinly sliced
350 g/12 oz courgettes, sliced
1 × 225 g/8 oz carton vegetarian curd
    cheese
50 g/2 oz fresh white breadcrumbs
2 teaspoons chopped fresh basil or 1
    teaspoon dried basil
2 teaspoons chopped fresh marjoram
    or 1 teaspoon dried marjoram
salt and pepper
1 egg, beaten
2 tablespoons melted butter
350 g/12 oz spinach, cooked and
    chopped
½ teaspoon fresh grated nutmeg
blanched courgette slices, to garnish

Heat the oil in a frying pan and cook the onion and courgettes
until softened. Drain and purée, then dry out in a saucepan
over low heat (2-3 minutes). Beat in the curd cheese, breadcrumbs, basil, marjoram, seasoning and egg.

Spoon half the courgette mixture into a lined and well-
buttered, 450 g/1 lb loaf tin. Season the spinach, add the nutmeg and spread in an even layer over the courgettes. Cover
with the remaining courgette mixture and press down firmly.
Cover with buttered foil, place in a bain-marie and cook in a
moderate oven for 1¼ hours. Cool and chill overnight. Turn
out and serve garnished with courgette slices.

■ COOK'S TIP

*A bain-marie is a suitable
vessel filled with hot water.
Containers of food are sat
in the water to ensure they
do not overheat during
cooking.*

33   CLASSIC GREEK SALAD

Preparation time:
15 minutes, plus
30-60 minutes to
stand

Serves 4

Calories:
125 per portion

YOU WILL NEED:

1 medium onion, sliced and separated
   into rings
1 tablespoon olive oil
1 tablespoon wine vinegar
salt and pepper
4 tomatoes, thinly sliced
½ cucumber, peeled and diced
10-12 black olives (optional)
100 g/4 oz vegetarian feta cheese or
   other white, crumbly cheese, diced

Put the onion into a bowl with the oil, vinegar and a little salt and pepper. Mix well, then leave to stand for 30-60 minutes to allow the onion to soften slightly. Stir occasionally.

Add the tomatoes, cucumber, olives and cheese, mixing gently to distribute all the ingredients. Serve at once.

34   SMOKED CHEESE AND NUT SALAD

Preparation time:
15 minutes

Serves 6

Calories:
270 per portion

YOU WILL NEED:

50 g/2 oz hazelnuts, coarsely chopped
6 tablespoons vegetable oil
2 tablespoons wine vinegar
salt and pepper
pinch of cayenne
½ teaspoon prepared English mustard
½ teaspoon sugar
1 crisp lettuce, shredded
1 head radicchio, separated into leaves
2 dessert apples
1 tablespoon lemon juice
150 g/5 oz German smoked cheese,
   cut into 1 cm/½ inch cubes
watercress, to garnish

To make the dressing, toast the chopped hazelnuts under a medium grill until evenly browned. Cool. Put oil, vinegar, salt and pepper, cayenne, mustard and sugar into a screwtop jar, add the hazelnuts and shake for 1 minute until well mixed.

Arrange the lettuce and radicchio on 6 individual plates. Cut the apples into 1 cm/½ inch cubes, toss in the lemon juice and arrange with the cubes of cheese on top of the salad. Spoon the dressing over the cheese and apple just before serving and garnish with sprigs of watercress.

▓ COOK'S TIP

*Instead of the feta cheese,
you can use another mild,
crumbly cheese such as
Cheshire. For a creamy
texture, try mozzarella.*

▓ COOK'S TIP

*An unusual colourful starter
using radicchio. The same
quantities will serve 2-3 as a
main meal salad.*

35 SPEEDY PARTY DIP

Preparation time:
5 minutes, plus 1
hour to chill

Serves 4-6

Total calories:
1075 (270-180 per
portion)

YOU WILL NEED:
*225 g/8 oz vegetarian full-fat soft
   cheese with garlic*
150 ml/¼ pint natural yogurt
*½ small green pepper, seeded and
   finely shredded*

Beat the cheese to soften, add the yogurt and beat until
smooth. Stir in the pepper and mix well. Turn into a serving
dish and chill.

   Serve with a selection of small pieces of raw carrot, courgette, celery, pepper, broccoli and cauliflower, and crisp
savoury biscuits.

36 BLUE CHEESE DIP

Preparation time:
10 minutes, plus 30
minutes to chill

Serves 4-6

Total calories:
1100 (275-185 per
portion)

YOU WILL NEED:
*100 g/4 oz vegetarian Danish Blue
   cheese*
2 tablespoons mayonnaise
150 ml/¼ pint whipping cream
freshly ground black pepper
FOR THE GARNISH
cucumber slices
parsley sprigs

Mash the blue cheese with a fork or electric mixer. Beat in the
mayonnaise until smooth. Lightly whip the cream and fold
into the cheese mixture. Add pepper to taste and turn into a
serving bowl to chill. Garnish with cucumber and parsley
before serving.

   Offer cucumber sticks, olives, breadsticks, tomato
wedges and other savoury snacks as dippers.

▮ COOK'S TIP

*This dip also makes a
delicious topping for baked
potatoes.*

▮ COOK'S TIP

*Blue cheese is easier to
mash when at room
temperature. For a variation
to the dip, try adding half a
green pepper, seeded and
finely chopped, or 25-50 g/*

*1-2 oz finely chopped
walnuts.*

BEANS & PULSES

In a vegetarian diet versatile dried peas and beans provide valuable sources of protein and fibre. Many people will be familiar with the delicious dhals – made from lentils, chick peas and mung beans, among others – that are an integral part of an Indian meal, but may not have experimented at home to make the most of the huge variety of pulses available. There are many good ideas here.

37 DERBY AND LENTIL LOAF

Preparation time:
20 minutes

Cooking time:
1½ hours

Oven temperature:
180 C, 350 F, gas 4

Serves 4-6

Calories:
240-360 per portion

YOU WILL NEED:
225 g/8 oz red lentils, soaked overnight
1 vegetable stock cube
1 onion, chopped
100 g/4 oz Derby or sage Derby cheese, grated
150 ml/¼ pint tomato juice
2 eggs, beaten
2 slices wholemeal bread, made into crumbs
2 teaspoons mixed herbs
pinch of salt
cucumber slices, to garnish

Drain water from soaked lentils and put them in a saucepan with fresh water to cover. Add the vegetable stock cube; bring slowly to the boil. Cover and simmer for 20-30 minutes or until the lentils are tender. Drain away any surplus water.

Add the chopped onion and grated cheese to the lentils. Mix well. Add the tomato juice, beaten eggs, breadcrumbs, herbs and salt and stir the mixture thoroughly. Spoon the mixture into a greased 450 g/1 lb loaf tin and bake for 1 hour. Turn out the cooked loaf and serve hot or cold, garnished with cucumber.

38 LENTIL MOUSSAKA

Preparation time:
10 minutes

Cooking time:
40-45 minutes

Oven temperature:
200 C, 400 F, gas 6

Serves 4

Calories:
205 per portion

YOU WILL NEED:
100 g/4 oz red lentils
1 × 397 g/14 oz can tomatoes
1 garlic clove, crushed
½ teaspoon dried oregano
pinch of ground nutmeg
1 vegetable stock cube
150 ml/¼ pint boiling water
1 tablespoon oil
225 g/8 oz aubergine, sliced
1 onion, chopped
FOR THE CHEESE TOPPING
1 egg
150 g/5 oz vegetarian low-fat soft cheese
pepper
nutmeg

Put the lentils in a large saucepan with the tomatoes, garlic, oregano and a generous pinch of nutmeg. Crumble in the stock cube and then pour in the boiling water. Simmer for 20 minutes.

Heat the oil and lightly cook the aubergine slices with the onion. Layer them with the lentil mixture in an ovenproof dish. Beat the egg and cheese, seasoning and nutmeg. Pour over the moussaka and cook in a moderately hot oven for about 20-25 minutes.

COOK'S TIP

Although the lentils are soaked in this recipe, it is not always essential to do so. For a quick supper, just simmer them for about 30 minutes. Serve with soured cream.

COOK'S TIP

Low-fat soft cheese is an excellent ingredient to use in cooking since it gives a rich flavour without being too runny. Look out for varieties flavoured with herbs and garlic to create an interesting flavour.

39 LENTIL AND VEGETABLE BAKE

Preparation time:
10 minutes

Cooking time:
40 minutes

Serves 4

Calories:
405 per portion

YOU WILL NEED:
2 tablespoons oil
1 large onion, chopped
2 medium carrots, chopped
2 celery sticks, chopped
175 g/6 oz red lentils
1 teaspoon mixed herbs
a few drops of Tabasco sauce
600 ml/1 pint vegetable stock
2 tablespoons tomato purée
salt and pepper
100 g/4 oz mushrooms, sliced
2 small courgettes, diced
1 tablespoon sunflower seeds
25 g/1 oz chopped nuts
50 g/2 oz fresh wholewheat
    breadcrumbs
50 g/2 oz vegetarian Cheddar cheese,
    grated

Heat the oil in a large saucepan, add the onion and cook for 5 minutes until softened. Add the carrots and celery and cook for 2 minutes. Stir in the lentils, herbs, Tabasco, stock, tomato purée and salt and pepper and bring to the boil. Cover and simmer for 20 minutes or until the lentils are soft. Stir in the mushrooms and courgettes and cook for a further 10 minutes. Pour the mixture into a shallow ovenproof dish. Mix the seeds, nuts, breadcrumbs and cheese and sprinkle evenly over the top. Cook under a hot grill until golden and crisp.

COOK'S TIP

To freeze breadcrumbs for future use, reduce a whole loaf to crumbs in a liquidizer or food processor, then pack loosely in large freezer bags.

40 LENTIL AND PEANUT LAYER

Preparation time:
20 minutes

Cooking time:
45-55 minutes

Serves 4

Calories:
570 per portion

YOU WILL NEED:
2 tablespoons groundnut oil
1 onion, chopped
2 carrots, diced
2 celery sticks, chopped
175 g/6 oz red lentils
1 teaspoon dried mixed herbs
1 tablespoon soy sauce
300 ml/½ pint vegetable stock
1 × 397 g/14 oz can tomatoes
100 g/4 oz salted peanuts, chopped
salt and pepper
675 g/1½ lb potatoes
50 g/2 oz vegetarian Cheddar cheese,
    grated

Heat the oil in a large saucepan, add the onion and fry for 5 minutes until softened. Add the carrots and celery and cook for 2 minutes more. Add the lentils, herbs and soy sauce and mix well. Stir in the stock and tomatoes and bring to the boil. Cover and simmer gently for 20-30 minutes, adding more stock if necessary, until the lentils are cooked and the mixture thickened. Stir in the peanuts and seasoning. Simmer for 5 minutes more.

Meanwhile, boil the potatoes in their jackets, drain, skin and slice thinly. Place the lentil mixture in an ovenproof dish and cover with the sliced potato. Sprinkle with the cheese and place under a hot grill for 6-8 minutes, until the cheese has melted and the potatoes are golden brown.

COOK'S TIP

When red lentils are used in a recipe, you can substitute green ones. They need longer cooking – about 40-45 minutes – and you may have to add extra liquid.

41 WALNUT AND LENTIL LOAF

Preparation time:
10 minutes

Cooking time:
1 hour 25 minutes

Oven temperature:
190 C, 375 F, gas 5

Serves 6

Calories:
245 per portion

YOU WILL NEED:
1 tablespoon oil
1 onion, chopped
1 garlic clove, crushed
2 celery sticks, sliced
175 g/6 oz green lentils
450 ml/¾ pint water
100 g/4 oz walnuts, ground
50 g/2 oz wholewheat breadcrumbs
2 tablespoons chopped parsley
1 tablespoon shoyu
1 egg, beaten
salt and pepper
thyme sprigs, to garnish

Heat the oil in a saucepan, add the onion and fry for a few minutes until softened. Add the garlic, celery, lentils and water and bring to the boil. Cover and simmer for 30-40 minutes, until the lentils are tender, stirring occasionally and removing the lid for the last 10 minutes to allow the moisture to evaporate.

Stir in the walnuts, breadcrumbs, parsley, shoyu, egg and salt and pepper to taste, and mix thoroughly.

Line a 450 g/1 lb loaf tin with foil to cover the bottom and along the sides. Brush with oil. Spoon the mixture into the tin, cover with foil and bake in a moderately hot oven for 45-50 minutes.

Leave in the tin for 2 minutes, then loosen with a knife and turn out on to a warmed serving dish. Garnish with thyme. Serve with a tomato sauce (recipe 154) or tomato mayonnaise.

■ COOK'S TIP

If you do not have a food processor or liquidizer, then you will find a rotary grater useful for grinding nuts.

42 LENTIL CROQUETTES

Preparation time:
15-20 minutes, plus 1 hour to chill

Cooking time:
30-35 minutes

Serves 4-6

Calories:
565-375 per portion

YOU WILL NEED:
225 g/8 oz red lentils, rinsed
600 ml/1 pint water
1 tablespoon oil
175 g/6 oz vegetarian low-fat hard
   cheese, grated
50 g/2 oz peanut butter
50 g/2 oz fresh wholewheat
   breadcrumbs
2 tablespoons chopped parsley
juice of 1 lemon
1-2 teaspoons yeast extract
salt and black pepper
FOR THE COATING
1 egg, beaten
50-75 g/2-3 oz wholewheat
   breadcrumbs
2-3 tablespoons oil for cooking

Place the lentils in a pan with the water and simmer, covered, for 30 minutes, until the water is absorbed and the lentils form a purée. Add the oil, cheese, peanut butter, breadcrumbs, parsley, lemon juice, yeast extract to taste and seasoning. Mix well. Cool, then chill lightly.

Shape large spoonfuls of the mixture into croquettes. Coat each with egg and breadcrumbs. Chill again. Fry the croquettes in the oil, turning once until golden all over. Drain on absorbent kitchen paper and serve with a salad.

■ COOK'S TIP

Dry, uncooked breadcrumbs are best for coating food before frying. Make the fresh crumbs, then dry them out in a very cool oven until crisp. For a fine texture put them through the liquidizer or food processor once more. If thoroughly dried they store well in an airtight container in a cool place.

43 LENTIL PATTIES

Preparation time:
15 minutes

Cooking time:
1 hour 20 minutes

Serves 4

Calories:
320 per portion

Suitable for Vegans

YOU WILL NEED:
175 g/6 oz lentils, rinsed
450 ml/3/4 pint cold water
1 large onion, finely chopped
4 tablespoons wholemeal flour
*2 tablespoons mixed fresh herbs,
  chopped*
salt and pepper
freshly grated nutmeg
oil for shallow frying
FOR THE GARNISH
watercress sprigs
tomato wedges

Place the lentils and water in a saucepan and bring to the boil. Reduce the heat, cover the pan and simmer gently for 30-40 minutes until all the water has been absorbed. Remove from the heat and allow to cool.

Mix the onion into the lentils, and stir in the flour, herbs, seasoning and nutmeg. Shape the mixture into eight patties, about 10 cm/4 inch in diameter, on a floured board.

Shallow fry the patties slowly in oil until golden brown, then turn them over and brown the second side. Drain, then serve, garnished with watercress sprigs and tomato wedges.

44 SPICED LENTIL DHAL

Preparation time:
5 minutes

Cooking time:
35 minutes

Serves 4-6

Calories:
110-70 per portion

Suitable for Vegans

YOU WILL NEED:
100 g/4 oz red lentils
*225 g/8 oz frozen onion slices, or 2
  small fresh onions, chopped*
450 ml/3/4 pint boiling vegetable stock
3 garlic cloves, crushed
1/2 teaspoon ground turmeric
1 teaspoon paprika
1 teaspoon ground coriander
1 teaspoon ground cumin

Place all the ingredients in a large saucepan, bring to the boil, then reduce heat and simmer for about 30 minutes or until cooked. The dhal should be thick and the lentils should be soft and still retain their shape. Serve the dhal as an accompaniment to an Indian main dish.

■ COOK'S TIP

These patties are delicious served with mayonnaise or soured cream, accompanied by baked potatoes and a green salad.

■ COOK'S TIP

Cool the dhal, pack into a rigid container, label and freeze. Use within 3 months. Reheat from frozen in a moderately hot oven (200 C, 400 F, gas 6) for about 20

minutes or cook on high in the microwave for 10-15 minutes.

45 CRISPY PEA CROQUETTES

Preparation time:
20 minutes

Cooking time:
8-10 minutes

Serves 4

Calories:
320 per portion

YOU WILL NEED:
450 g/1 lb cooked peas
100 g/4 oz vegetarian cream cheese
  with herbs and garlic
100 g/4 oz fresh wholewheat
  breadcrumbs
2 eggs
1 teaspoon ground coriander
1 teaspoon chopped mixed herbs
salt and pepper
75 g/3 oz dry breadcrumbs
oil for deep frying
dill sprig, to garnish (optional)
FOR THE GARNISH
1 tomato, quartered
chopped parsley
watercress sprigs

Mash the cooked peas to a purée with the cream cheese. Mix in the breadcrumbs, 1 egg, coriander, herbs and salt and pepper to taste to make a fairly stiff paste.

Shape into croquettes, about 2.5 cm/1 inch in diameter and 7.5 cm/3 inch long. Beat the remaining egg and dip the croquettes first into beaten egg, then into breadcrumbs.

Heat the oil for deep frying to 190 C/375 F, and fry the croquettes quickly, in 2-3 batches, until crisp and golden. Serve hot or cold, garnished as shown.

COOK'S TIP

For a light lunch party, serve these crisp croquettes with Creamed lentils (Recipe 64) and ratatouille.

46 PROVENCAL BEANS

Preparation time:
15 minutes, plus
overnight to soak

Cooking time:
2 hours 15 minutes

Serves 4

Calories:
355 per portion

Suitable for Vegans

YOU WILL NEED:
350 g/12 oz haricot beans or pinto
  beans, soaked overnight
salt and pepper
2 tablespoons olive oil
2 onions, sliced
1 red pepper, seeded and sliced
1 green pepper, seeded and sliced
2 garlic cloves, crushed
1 × 397 g/14 oz can chopped
  tomatoes
2 tablespoons tomato purée
1 teaspoon chopped marjoram
1 bouquet garni
50 g/2 oz black olives, halved and
  stoned
2 tablespoons chopped parsley

Drain the beans, place in a medium saucepan and cover with cold water. Bring to the boil, boil rapidly for 10 minutes, then cover and simmer for 1-1¼ hours, until almost tender, adding a pinch of salt towards the end of cooking. Drain, reserving 300 ml/½ pint of the liquid.

Heat the oil in a medium saucepan, add the onions and fry until softened. Add the peppers and garlic and fry gently for 10 minutes. Add the tomatoes with their juice, tomato purée, herbs, beans, reserved liquid, and salt and pepper to taste. Cover and simmer for 45 minutes, adding the olives and parsley 5 minutes before the end of the cooking time. Remove the bouquet garni and serve.

COOK'S TIP

For a fresh bouquet garni, tie a bay leaf, parsley sprig, thyme sprig, rosemary sprig and a few chives together. Vary the herbs according to taste and season.

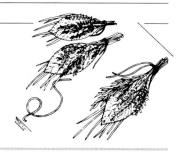

47 BEAN AND RICE CASSEROLE

Preparation time:
15 minutes, plus
overnight to soak

Cooking time:
2 hours

Oven temperature:
180 C, 350 F, gas 4

Serves 4

Calories:
370 per portion

Suitable for Vegans

YOU WILL NEED:
175 g/6 oz haricot beans, soaked
    overnight
900 ml/1½ pints vegetable stock
salt and pepper
1 tablespoon vegetable oil
1 large onion, sliced
225 g/8 oz courgettes, sliced
1 red pepper, seeded and sliced
1 green pepper, seeded and sliced
1 aubergine, halved and sliced
150 ml/¼ pint dry cider
175 g/6 oz long-grain brown rice

Drain the beans and place in a flameproof casserole with the stock and seasoning. Bring to the boil, cover and simmer for 1 hour, until the beans are tender but retain their shape.

Heat the oil and fry the onion, courgettes and peppers for 2 minutes. Add the aubergine slices a few at a time and cook for a further 5 minutes. Transfer the vegetables to the bean casserole together with the cider and rice. Cover and cook in a moderate oven for 45 minutes, or until the rice is tender and the liquid absorbed. Season to taste before serving.

48 SWEET AND SOUR BUTTER BEANS

Preparation time:
10 minutes

Serves 4

Calories:
140 per portion

Suitable for Vegans

YOU WILL NEED:
100 g/4 oz pineapple pieces, canned or
    fresh
1 × 415 g/14½ oz can butter beans
1 medium carrot, cut into matchsticks
175 g/6 oz fresh beansprouts
1 tablespoon oil
1 garlic clove, crushed
1½ teaspoons cider or white wine
    vinegar
fresh marjoram, to garnish

Drain the pineapple pieces, if canned. Drain the butter beans. Combine the pineapple, beans, carrot and bean sprouts in a bowl. Mix the oil, garlic and vinegar, pour over the fruit and vegetables, chill and serve. Garnish with sprigs of marjoram.

■ COOK'S TIP

To freeze: cool quickly and transfer to foil containers. Cover, seal and freeze. To serve, defrost then reheat, covered, in a moderate oven (180 C, 350 F, gas 4) for 30 minutes or until heated through.

■ COOK'S TIP

Sprout beans in a jar covered with muslin kept in place with an elastic band. Rinse the beans daily until the sprouts are long enough.

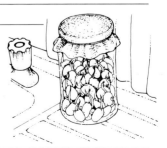

49 BUTTER BEANS IN SESAME SAUCE

Preparation time:
20 minutes

Cooking time:
25-30 minutes

Serves 4

Calories:
575 per portion

Suitable for Vegans

YOU WILL NEED:
100 ml/4 fl oz oil
1 teaspoon cumin seeds
1 large onion, chopped
100 g/4 oz sesame seeds, finely ground
1 tablespoon ground coriander
1 × 397 g/14 oz can chopped
   tomatoes
salt
2 teaspoons sugar
1 teaspoon chilli powder
1 teaspoon ground turmeric
2 × 425 g/15 oz cans butter beans,
   drained
1 tablespoon chopped coriander, to
   garnish

Heat the oil in a pan, add the cumin seeds and fry until they begin to crackle. Add the onion and fry until soft and transparent.

Add the ground sesame seeds and fry for 3-5 minutes, then add the ground coriander and fry for a further minute. Stir in the tomatoes, salt to taste, the sugar, chilli powder and turmeric. Mix well and cook the sauce for 3-5 minutes.

Add the drained beans and stir carefully until well coated with the sauce. Simmer until the beans are thoroughly hot. Sprinkle with chopped coriander.

■ COOK'S TIP

For textural contrast and a good protein mix, combine this curry with a crunchy salad, such as Fruit coleslaw (recipe 116) or Crunchy cabbage salad (recipe 117).

50 BEAN CURRY

Preparation time:
10 minutes, plus
overnight to soak

Cooking time:
1 hour 10 minutes

Serves 4

Calories:
345 per portion

Suitable for Vegans

YOU WILL NEED:
350 g/12 oz red kidney beans, soaked
   overnight
2 tablespoons oil
1 garlic clove, crushed
1 × 2.5 cm/1 inch piece fresh root
   ginger, grated or finely chopped
1 medium onion, chopped
2 carrots, diced
2 celery sticks, sliced
100 g/4 oz mushrooms, sliced
¼ teaspoon chilli powder
2 × 397 g/14 oz cans tomatoes
450 ml/¾ pint water
salt
2 tablespoons chopped coriander
   leaves (optional)

Drain the beans and bring them to the boil with enough water to cover them by at least 2.5 cm/1 inch. Boil vigorously for 10 minutes, reduce heat, cover and simmer for about 1 hour or until tender. Check that the water level is maintained throughout cooking.

Meanwhile, heat the oil and cook the garlic, ginger and onion for 3 minutes. Add the carrots, celery and mushrooms and cook for 3 minutes. Stir in the chilli powder, drained cooked beans, tomatoes and their juice, water and a little salt. Cook for 15 minutes until carrots are tender and the mixture fairly thick. Check seasoning and sprinkle with coriander leaves. Serve with natural yogurt (except for vegans).

■ COOK'S TIP

Fresh root ginger keeps well in the salad drawer of the refrigerator. Look out for smooth, plump ginger with a fine skin that shows it is young and tender.

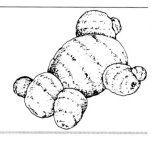

51 CHILLI BEAN TACOS

Preparation time:
15 minutes

Cooking time:
35 minutes

Oven temperature:
200 C, 400 F, gas 6

Serves 2-3

Calories:
505-335 per portion

YOU WILL NEED:
*100 g/4 oz frozen Mexican mix, or an
equivalent weight of fresh
vegetables including diced red and
green peppers, sweetcorn and
chopped onion*
*1 × 415 g/14½ oz can red kidney
beans, juice reserved*
½ teaspoon Tabasco sauce
2 garlic cloves, crushed
2 tablespoons tomato purée
6 Mexican taco shells
1 small lettuce, shredded
1 small onion, chopped
*50 g/2 oz vegetarian Cheddar cheese,
grated*

Place the Mexican mix or fresh vegetables in a medium saucepan with a small amount of boiling water. Bring back to the boil, reduce heat and cook for 10 minutes. Stir the kidney beans, Tabasco, crushed garlic, and tomato purée into the vegetables, then add enough of the reserved juice to make a thick sauce. Cook for another 10 minutes. Place the tacos on a baking tray and heat in a moderately hot oven for 10 minutes until hot.

Let guests fill their own tacos. First spoon a few tablespoons of the bean and vegetable mixture into the taco shells then top with the lettuce, onion and cheese.

52 GREEN PEA AND POTATO CURRY

Preparation time:
30 minutes

Cooking time:
20-30 minutes

Serves 4

Calories:
190 per portion

YOU WILL NEED:
50 g/2 oz butter or margarine
225 g/8 oz fresh or frozen peas
225 g/8 oz potatoes, peeled and diced
225 g/8 oz onions, diced
1 tablespoon garam masala
1 teaspoon ground turmeric
1 teaspoon chilli powder

Heat the butter or margarine in a pan, add all the ingredients and stir-fry for a few minutes to mix well. Cover and cook over a low heat for about 25-30 minutes or until the vegetables are tender. Stir occasionally during the cooking time to prevent sticking.

■ COOK'S TIP

*The tacos need to be eaten
with the fingers so have
plenty of paper napkins
available.*

■ COOK'S TIP

*When cooking with spices, it
is a good idea to use a
plastic cooking spoon
instead of a wooden spoon
which discolours and picks
up flavours easily.*

*Alternatively, if you prepare
spicy food frequently, then
set aside a special wooden
spoon for the purpose.*

53 BEAN AND PASTA CURRY

Preparation time:
20 minutes

Cooking time:
30 minutes

Serves 4

Calories:
405 per portion

YOU WILL NEED:
1 tablespoon vegetable oil
3 medium onions, chopped
2 garlic cloves, crushed
3 tablespoons curry powder
½ teaspoon ground cumin
½ teaspoon ground coriander
½ teaspoon chilli powder
2 teaspoons grated fresh root ginger (optional)
2 tablespoons wholemeal flour
900 ml/1½ pints vegetable stock
1 tablespoon lemon juice
salt (optional)
150 g/5 oz pasta shapes, such as quills or twists
2 × 415 g/14½ oz cans red kidney beans

To make the sauce, heat the oil in a pan with a lid and cook the onions and garlic gently for 5 minutes. Stir in the curry powder, cumin, coriander, chilli, ginger and flour. Cook for 1 minute. Pour in the stock and lemon juice, bring to the boil, cover and simmer gently for 25 minutes. Season. Cook the pasta in plenty of boiling salted water for about 10 minutes until 'al dente'. Drain and rinse. Drain the kidney beans, re-serving the liquid for thinning the sauce.

Add the pasta and beans to the sauce, stirring them in gently. Thin down with the reserved bean liquor if necessary. Reheat and serve piping hot.

▓ COOK'S TIP

The curry sauce can be prepared 24 hours in advance. Cover and keep in the refrigerator.

54 BEAN COBBLER

Preparation time:
20 minutes

Cooking time:
50 minutes

Oven temperature:
200 C, 400 F, gas 6

Serves 6

Calories:
390 per portion

YOU WILL NEED:
1 × 415 g/14 oz can red kidney beans
1 × 415 g/14 oz can butter beans
1 × 415 g/14 oz can flageolet beans
100 g/4 oz leeks, finely sliced
225 g/8 oz courgettes, finely sliced
300 ml/½ pint tomato juice
150 ml/¼ pint vegetable stock
1 teaspoon chilli powder
chopped parsley, to garnish
FOR THE SCONE TOPPING
225 g/8 oz self-raising flour
¼ teaspoon salt
2 teaspoons dried mixed herbs
2 teaspoons baking powder
50 g/2 oz margarine
6 tablespoons natural yogurt

Drain the kidney, butter and flageolet beans. Mix together with the leeks, courgettes, tomato juice, stock and chilli powder. Place in an ovenproof dish and bake for 20 minutes.

To make the scone topping, sift the flour, salt, herbs and baking powder into a bowl. Rub in the margarine until the mixture resembles fine breadcrumbs. Stir in the yogurt and mix gently. Turn on to a floured surface and knead very lightly. Roll out to about 1 cm/½ inch thick and cut out 12 rounds using a 5 cm/2 inch cutter. Place on top of the vegetables, return to the oven and cook for 30 minutes until golden and firm on top. The underside remains soft like a dumpling. Garnish with parsley.

▓ COOK'S TIP

When preparing sliced leeks for a dish, trim and slice the leeks, then place in a colander and wash thoroughly under cold running water.

55 WEST AFRICAN BEAN SALAD

Preparation time:
20 minutes, plus
overnight to soak

Cooking time:
45-60 minutes

Serves 4

Calories:
345 per portion

Suitable for Vegans

YOU WILL NEED:
*225 g/8 oz black-eyed beans, soaked
  overnight*
4-5 tablespoons peanut oil
*1 tablespoon lemon juice or wine
  vinegar*
1 garlic clove, crushed
salt and pepper
*1 medium red or white onion,
  chopped*
*225 g/8 oz large tomatoes, peeled and
  chopped*
*1 red chilli, deseeded and chopped
  (optional)*

Drain the beans and cover with fresh water. Bring to the boil, lower the heat and simmer for 45-60 minutes or until tender. Drain and rinse thoroughly. Transfer to a serving dish.

Blend the oil, lemon juice and garlic and add salt and pepper to taste. Pour over the warm beans and leave to cool.

When cool, mix in the onion, tomatoes and chilli, if using. Serve at once.

56 EGYPTIAN SALAD

Preparation time:
15 minutes, plus 36
hours to soak

Cooking time:
2 hours

Serves 4

Calories:
255 per portion

YOU WILL NEED:
*175 g/6 oz ful medames, soaked for 36
  hours or 1 × 400 g/14 oz can ful
  medames, drained and well rinsed*
salt
coriander leaves
2-3 eggs with light coloured shells
brown onion skins
3-4 tablespoons olive oil
1 tablespoon lemon juice
1 garlic clove, crushed
½-1 teaspoon ground cumin
2 tablespoons chopped parsley
coriander sprigs, to garnish

Drain the ful medames and cover with plenty of fresh water. Bring to the boil, skim, lower the heat and simmer for 1½ hours or until tender. Add salt to taste towards the end of the cooking time.

Place a coriander leaf on each egg. Wrap an onion skin around each egg and then wrap in absorbent kitchen paper to make a parcel. Tie each with cotton and cover with cold water. Bring to the boil, cook for 10 minutes and leave to cool. When cold, unwrap the eggs and set aside in the shells. Drain and rinse the beans with fresh water, then pop each bean out of its skin, if liked. Mix the olive oil, lemon juice and garlic; pour over the beans. Taste and adjust the seasoning. Transfer the beans to a serving dish and sprinkle with cumin and parsley. Garnish with coriander sprigs and serve, accompanied by the patterned hard-boiled eggs.

■ COOK'S TIP

The seeds of chillies are the hottest part, so always seed chillies unless a really hot flavour is required. Never touch lips or eyes while seeding them as a strong reaction occurs on the delicate skin.

■ COOK'S TIP

Ful medames are small, light brown/beige coloured dried beans like small broad beans. Available from health food shops, they must be soaked before cooking.

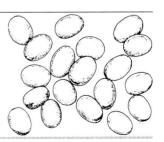

57 KIDNEY BEAN COLESLAW

Preparation time:
30 minutes

Serves 4-6

Calories:
210-140 per portion

YOU WILL NEED:
225 g/8 oz white cabbage, shredded
175 g/6 oz carrots, grated
½ small onion, chopped
1 dessert apple, cored and grated
1 × 415 g/14½ oz can red kidney
   beans, drained
4 spring onions, chopped
2 tablespoons chopped parsley
salt and pepper
50 g/2 oz vegetarian low-fat soft
   cheese
1 tablespoon lemon juice
2 tablespoons sunflower oil
2 tablespoons natural yogurt
watercress sprigs, to garnish (optional)

Mix the cabbage, carrots, onion and apple. Add the beans, spring onions and parsley then season to taste.

Mix the low-fat cheese with the lemon juice, oil and yogurt. Toss this dressing with the salad before serving.

A watercress garnish may be added, if liked.

58 COLOURFUL BEAN SALAD

Preparation time:
15-20 minutes

Cooking time:
15 minutes

Serves 4-6

Calories:
275-185 per portion

YOU WILL NEED:
450 g/1 lb green beans, topped and
   tailed
salt and pepper
pinch of grated nutmeg
3-4 tomatoes, quartered
575 g/1¼ lb new potatoes, scrubbed
   and cooked
1 onion, chopped
· 1 small bunch herbs (e.g. chives,
   parsley, thyme), chopped
2 tablespoons mayonnaise
6 tablespoons double or soured cream

Bring a large saucepan of water to the boil, add the beans with a little salt and the nutmeg. Bring back to the boil, then reduce the heat and cook gently for 10-12 minutes until tender. Drain, rinse under cold water, drain again and place in a serving bowl. Add the tomatoes and potatoes and toss well. Scatter the onion and herbs on top.

To make the dressing, blend the mayonnaise with the cream and salt and pepper to taste. Pour over the bean salad and toss well to mix.

■ COOK'S TIP

Sunflower oil is a polyunsaturated fat – a good choice for the health-conscious eater. Avoid blended oils, which may contain coconut or palm oil, *both high in saturated fatty acids.*

■ COOK'S TIP

Counting calories? Use low-fat yogurt in place of the double cream – you may need slightly less than the 6 tablespoons suggested above.

59 KIDNEY BEAN AND STILTON SALAD

Preparation time:
10 minutes

Serves 4

Calories:
192 per portion

YOU WILL NEED:
1 × 415 g/14½ oz can red kidney
  beans
225 g/8 oz French beans, finely sliced
  or 225 g/8 oz mangetout
juice of ½ lemon
100 g/4 oz cottage cheese
75 g/3 oz vegetarian blue Stilton,
  broken into small pieces
chopped parsley, to garnish (optional)

Drain the kidney beans. Mix together with the French beans or mangetout and the lemon juice. Spoon the cottage cheese on top and sprinkle over the crumbled Stilton. Garnish with parsley, if liked. Serve with hot garlic bread (see Cook's Tip).

60 RICE AND BEAN SALAD

Preparation time:
10 minutes

Serves 4

Calories:
285 per portion

YOU WILL NEED:
1 bunch of watercress
350 g/12 oz cooked rice
1 × 415 g/14½ oz can black eyed
  beans, drained
6 radishes, sliced
12 olives, stoned
1 tablespoon mayonnaise
½ teaspoon salt

Reserve a sprig of watercress for the garnish. Trim and separate the rest into small sprigs.

Mix together the rice, beans, radishes, olives, watercress, mayonnaise and salt. Serve immediately, garnished with the watercress sprig.

■ COOK'S TIP

To make garlic bread, beat a crushed garlic clove into butter and spread on French bread. Wrap in foil and heat through in the oven.

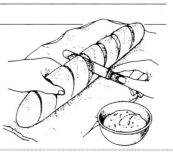

■ COOK'S TIP

To yield 350 g/12 oz cooked rice, prepare 100 g/4 oz raw rice. Instead of white or brown rice, try wild rice – dark, long thin grains which require more cooking.

61 FELAFEL IN PITTA POCKETS

Preparation time:
20 minutes

Cooking time:
20 minutes

Oven temperature:
110 C, 225 F, gas ¼

Serves 4

Calories:
520 per portion

YOU WILL NEED:

2 × 400 g/14 oz cans chick peas
1 medium onion, grated
1 garlic clove, crushed
1 teaspoon ground cumin
1 teaspoon ground coriander
¼ teaspoon ground chilli
½ teaspoon caraway seeds
salt and pepper
3 tablespoons chopped parsley
1 egg, beaten
75 g/3 oz wholemeal flour
vegetable oil for shallow frying
TO SERVE
4 wholewheat pitta breads
prepared salad ingredients

Drain the chick peas and reduce to a coarse paste in a liquidizer. Mix with the next eight ingredients.

Form the mixture into small balls then pat them into small flat cakes about 4 cm/1½ inch across. Dip into the beaten egg, then into the flour. Shallow fry in oil in batches for about 5 minutes until crisp and brown. Drain on absorbent kitchen paper. Warm pitta breads for 5 minutes, split along one side and fill the pockets with salad and the hot felafel.

62 BEAN PATE

Preparation time:
10 minutes

Cooking time:
5 minutes

Serves 4

Calories:
145 per portion

Suitable for Vegans

YOU WILL NEED:

1 medium onion, chopped
2 garlic cloves, crushed
1 tablespoon oil
1 tablespoon peanut butter, smooth or
    crunchy, or tahini
juice of 1 lemon
2 tablespoons chopped parsley
1 × 415 g/14½ oz can butter beans
dill sprigs, to garnish (optional)

Cook the onion and garlic in the oil until softened, about 5 minutes. Mix together the onion mixture, peanut butter or tahini, lemon juice and parsley. Drain the butter beans and add to the onion mixture. Mash with a fork or blend briefly in a liquidizer. Press into an oiled dish, cover and chill. Garnish with dill sprigs, if using.

▥ COOK'S TIP

For convenience, the uncooked felafel can be prepared up to 8 hours in advance and kept tightly covered with cling film to prevent the flavours *permeating the other foods in the refrigerator.*

▥ COOK'S TIP

This pâté looks good served in individual ramekin dishes. Place each on a saucer and garnish with wedges of lemon and parsley sprigs.

63 SPANISH CHICK PEAS

Preparation time:
20 minutes, plus
overnight to soak

Cooking time:
1½-2 hours

Serves 4

Calories:
320 per portion

YOU WILL NEED:
175 g/6 oz chick peas
900 ml/1½ pints cold water
1 tablespoon oil
1 teaspoon salt
25 g/1 oz butter
1 onion, chopped
1 garlic clove, crushed
1 green pepper, seeded and chopped
1 × 397 g/14 oz can chopped
    tomatoes
1 × 340 g/12 oz can sweetcorn,
    drained
2 green chillies, seeded and chopped
¼ teaspoon oregano
generous pinch of ground cumin

Soak the chick peas overnight in water to cover. Drain, dis-carding peas that have not absorbed any water. Place in a medium saucepan, add measured cold water, and oil and bring to the boil. Reduce the heat, cover the pan and simmer for 1-1½ hours, until the chick peas are tender, adding the salt towards the end of cooking. Drain and return the peas to the saucepan.

Melt the butter in a heavy-based frying pan and sauté the onion, garlic and green pepper until the onion is soft. Stir in the tomatoes, sweetcorn, chillies, oregano and cumin.

Add the sautéed onion mixture to the chick peas. Cover and cook gently, stirring frequently, for 20 minutes. Serve hot.

64 CREAMED LENTILS

Preparation time:
10 minutes

Cooking time:
30-35 minutes

Serves 4

Calories:
470 per portion

YOU WILL NEED:
25 g/1 oz butter
1 small onion, chopped
1 garlic clove, crushed
1 leek, sliced and washed
2 medium carrots, chopped
350 g/12 oz green lentils
1 litre/1¾ pints water
2 cloves
1 bay leaf
3 white peppercorns
3 tablespoons snipped chives
300 ml/½ pint soured cream
salt and pepper

Melt the butter in a saucepan and cook the onion, garlic, leek and carrots for 3 minutes, stirring frequently. Add the lentils and cook for 1 minute, stirring. Add the water, cloves, bay leaf and peppercorns, bring to the boil, cover, and cook very gently for 25-30 minutes or until the lentils are tender but still have some bite. Check that the mixture doesn't become too dry. Re-move the cloves and bay leaf. Turn into a warmed serving dish. Stir half the chives into half the soured cream and swirl through the lentils.

Swirl over the remaining soured cream and sprinkle with the remaining chives. Serve with wholewheat pasta or with brown rice.

▓ COOK'S TIP

Canned chick peas can be used instead of the dried variety. They should be drained and mixed with the sautéed mixture, then cooked as above.

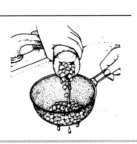

▓ COOK'S TIP

Dried flower buds of the Asian clove tree, cloves have a wonderful spicy fragrance. They are used in sweet and savoury dishes but extracted before serving to avoid the rather over powering effect of biting on them.

VEGETABLE DISHES

Packed with vitamins, minerals and fibre, fresh vegetables are a delight to cook with, not least because simple recipes are as successful at bringing out their natural flavours as more complicated ones, and are often more efficient in conserving nutritional content. Vegetables form a colourful accompaniment to a main course, contributing subtle or distinctive flavours.

65 POTATO AND CASHEW CURRY

Preparation time:
10 minutes

Cooking time:
55 minutes

Serves 4

Calories:
345 per portion

Suitable for Vegans

YOU WILL NEED:
450 g/1 lb potatoes, scrubbed
salt
3 tablespoons oil
1 teaspoon cumin seeds
1 teaspoon mustard seeds
1 teaspoon ground coriander
½ teaspoon chilli powder
½ teaspoon ground turmeric
1 × 227g/8 oz can tomatoes
600 ml/1 pint water
100 g/4 oz cashew nuts
chopped coriander, to garnish

Boil the potatoes in their skins in a pan of boiling salted water for 15 minutes. Drain the potatoes, allow to cool, then peel them and cut into small cubes.

Heat the oil in a pan and add the cumin and mustard seeds. As soon as the seeds begin to pop, add the coriander, chilli, turmeric, salt to taste and the tomatoes and their juices. Cook for a few minutes; then stir in the measured water.

Bring to the boil, reduce the heat and stir in the potatoes and nuts. Simmer for 30 minutes.

Garnish with coriander and serve.

66 CREAMED SWEDE DUCHESSE

Preparation time:
25 minutes

Cooking time:
45 minutes

Oven temperature:
200 C, 400 F, gas 6

Serves 4

Calories:
245 per portion

YOU WILL NEED:
675 g/1½ lb potatoes, peeled and cubed
350 g/12 oz swedes, peeled and cubed
salt and pepper
75 g/3 oz vegetarian low-fat soft cheese
25 g/1 oz butter
50 g/2 oz vegetarian low-fat hard cheese, grated
watercress sprigs, to garnish

Cook the potatoes and swede in boiling salted water until tender – about 20 minutes. Mash with seasoning, the soft cheese and butter. When cool enough to handle, pipe large vegetable rosettes on to a greased baking tray (see Cook's Tip). Bake for 20 minutes, until lightly browned. Sprinkle with the grated cheese and cook for a further 5-10 minutes until well browned. Serve at once, garnished with watercress.

▥ COOK'S TIP

Cover the pan when cooking the cumin and mustard seeds or they may pop right out of the pan.

▥ COOK'S TIP

For piping savoury foods like potato you will need a large star nozzle, sometimes called a potato pipe, and a large piping bag to hold the creamed vegetables.

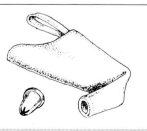

67 MEDITERRANEAN POTATOES

Preparation time:
5 minutes

Cooking time:
35 minutes

Serves 4

Calories:
335 per portion

YOU WILL NEED:
675 g/1½ lb potatoes
1 tablespoon oil
50 g/2 oz butter
1 garlic clove, crushed
1 medium onion, sliced
100 g/4 oz mushrooms, sliced
1 small green pepper, seeded and
    sliced
1 × 397 g/14 oz can tomatoes
2 teaspoons brown sugar
1 teaspoon mixed herbs
salt and pepper
50 g/2 oz fresh breadcrumbs
grated Pecorino or Parmesan cheese

Cut the potatoes into even-sized pieces and cook in enough boiling water to just cover, for 10-15 minutes or until just cooked.

Meanwhile, heat the oil and half the butter in a frying pan. Add the garlic, onion, mushrooms and pepper and cook for 5 minutes or until softened. Add the tomatoes and can juices, sugar, herbs and seasoning. Break up the tomatoes and cook for 10 minutes or until the onion is tender and the sauce not too runny. Melt the remaining butter in a small pan, add the breadcrumbs and fry until brown and crisp.

Place the drained potatoes in a warm dish, pour over the sauce and sprinkle with the breadcrumbs. Serve hot with Pecorino or Parmesan cheese handed separately.

68 ALMOND POTATOES

Preparation time:
10 minutes

Cooking time:
12-18 minutes

Serves 4

Calories:
320 per portion

YOU WILL NEED:
350 g/12 oz potatoes, cooked and
    mashed with milk and butter
plain flour seasoned with salt and
    pepper
1 egg, beaten
100 g/4 oz almonds, finely chopped
25 g/1 oz butter
1 tablespoon oil
parsley sprigs, to garnish

Divide the mashed potato into 12 pieces. Place the seasoned flour on a plate and shape each potato piece into a medallion shape, coating it with flour as you do so. Coat each medallion in the beaten egg and then the almonds.

Heat the butter and oil in a large frying pan and cook the medallions, a few at a time, for about 6 minutes, turning once, until golden. Drain on absorbent kitchen paper. Serve hot, garnished with parsley.

■ COOK'S TIP

A cheese mill, a cylindrical enclosed grater is useful for Parmesan. The cheese is stored in it and the lid is turned to grate it straight on to the food.

■ COOK'S TIP

These crunchy cakes can be frozen. Open freeze on trays lined with cling film, then pack in bags for storage. Cook from frozen, allowing time to heat through. They *are also good dotted with butter and baked.*

69 STIR-FRIED POTATOES

Preparation time:
15 minutes

Cooking time:
20 minutes

Serves 4

Calories:
225 per portion

YOU WILL NEED:

450 g/1 lb potatoes, grated and rinsed
    to extract starch
3 tablespoons oil
350 g/12 oz vegetables, finely chopped
1 tablespoon soy sauce
1 teaspoon ground ginger
salt and pepper

Suitable for Vegans

Use a cloth to squeeze the excess moisture from the grated potato. Heat the oil in a large non-stick pan or wok. Fry the grated potato for 5-10 minutes or until nearly cooked, stirring frequently. Add the chosen vegetables, soy sauce, ginger and salt and pepper and fry briskly for a further 5-10 minutes to cook vegetables yet keep them crisp. Serve hot.

70 POTATOES MADRAS

Preparation time:
15 minutes

Cooking time:
30 minutes

Serves 4-6

Calories:
380-255 per portion

YOU WILL NEED:

3 tablespoons oil or ghee
675 g/1½ lb potatoes, cut into large
    dice
225 g/8 oz cauliflower, cut into florets
1 large onion, sliced
2 garlic cloves, crushed (optional)
1 tablespoon curry powder
½ teaspoon ground ginger
100 g/4 oz red lentils
1 × 397 g/14 oz can chopped
    tomatoes
300 ml/½ pint vegetable stock
2 tablespoons malt vinegar
1 tablespoon mango chutney
salt and pepper
chopped parsley or coriander leaves,
    to garnish

Heat the oil in a large frying pan and quickly fry the potatoes, cauliflower, onion and garlic until just beginning to brown.

Stir in the curry powder and ginger. Continue to fry for a few minutes. Stir in the remaining ingredients except the parsley. Cover and simmer for about 20 minutes, stirring occasionally until the vegetables and lentils are tender. Garnish with parsley and serve.

▦ COOK'S TIP

Use a combination of the following: onion, cauliflower, peppers, runner beans, sweetcorn, broccoli, celery, courgettes, parsnip, mushrooms, cabbage, leeks.

▦ COOK'S TIP

This makes a colourful main dish for a dinner party. Serve with a selection of accompaniments such as poppadoms, slices of banana, chutney, yogurt and cucumber and desiccated coconut.

71 POTATO CAKE WITH CHEESE TOPPING

Preparation time:
15 minutes, plus 20
minutes to cool
potatoes

Cooking time:
35 minutes

Serves 4

Calories:
375 per portion

YOU WILL NEED:
675 g/1½ lb potatoes, scrubbed
75 g/3 oz butter
1 medium onion, chopped
salt and pepper
100 g/4 oz Danish Danbo or Havarti cheese, grated
sliced tomato to garnish

Boil the potatoes for 10 minutes. Drain and cool slightly, then peel and cool completely. Coarsely grate them into a large bowl. Melt 25 g/1 oz of the butter in a large frying pan and gently fry the onion for 5 minutes until softened. Remove the onion with a slotted spoon and gently stir into the potato.

Melt the remaining butter in the pan, add the potato mixture, sprinkle with salt and pepper and form into a 'cake'. Cook gently for 5-7 minutes until golden on the underside. Invert a plate over the pan and turn the 'cake' on to it, slide the 'cake' back into the pan and fry for a further 7-10 minutes.

Towards the end of the cooking time, heat a grill to moderate. Sprinkle the 'cake' with the cheese and grill until bubbling. Garnish with tomato slices and serve with a mixed salad.

72 EGG TATTIES

Preparation time:
15 minutes

Cooking time:
1 hour 25 minutes

Oven temperature:
200 C, 400 F, gas 6

Serves 2

Calories:
395 per portion

YOU WILL NEED:
2 large potatoes
3 eggs
1 tablespoon milk
salt and pepper
15 g/½ oz butter
2 tablespoons finely chopped chives
2 tablespoons thick Greek yogurt
watercress, to garnish

Clean the skins of the potatoes and prick at regular intervals with a fork. Bake in a moderately hot oven for about 1¼ hours, until tender. Just before the potatoes are ready, beat the eggs with the milk and seasoning to taste. Melt the butter and stir in the egg mixture; scramble lightly over a gentle heat, until the egg forms soft creamy flakes. Halve each potato lengthways and scoop out the cooked centre. Mix gently with the scrambled egg, half the chives and all of the yogurt then spoon back into the potato shells. Cover loosely with foil and return to the oven for a further 4-5 minutes. To serve, sprinkle with the remaining chives and garnish with watercress.

▓ COOK'S TIP

If you like, add an extra topping before the cheese – sliced tomatoes, chopped walnuts and mushrooms, cooked leeks, sweetcorn and peppers, for instance.

▓ COOK'S TIP

For a simple variation, why not add some diced vegetarian mozzarella cheese and chopped spring onions to the egg mixture. The filled potatoes can be topped with chopped cashew nuts or walnuts and a little extra diced mozzarella.

73 MUSHROOMS MONTEBELLO

Preparation time:
10 minutes, plus
overnight to
marinate

Serves 4

Calories:
130 per portion

Suitable for Vegans

YOU WILL NEED:
225 g/8 oz button mushrooms
4 tablespoons sunflower oil
1 garlic clove, crushed
pinch of dill
½ teaspoon oregano
2 tablespoons red wine vinegar
1 teaspoon lemon juice
salt and pepper

Combine all the ingredients in a bowl. Cover with cling film and leave to marinate in the refrigerator overnight. Serve to accompany rice or pasta dishes, as part of a salad buffet or as a starter.

74 STILTON-STUFFED MUSHROOMS

Preparation time:
10 minutes

Cooking time:
6-8 minutes

Serves 4

Calories:
310 per portion

YOU WILL NEED:
50 g/2 oz butter
8 medium flat mushrooms, stalks
  removed, wiped
4 small tomatoes, thinly sliced
175 g/6 oz vegetarian blue Stilton
  cheese, sliced
celery leaves, to garnish (optional)

Melt the butter in a sauté pan and cook the mushrooms open side uppermost for 3-4 minutes, until tender. Place in a flame-proof dish, top each one with slices of tomato and cheese, then brown under a hot grill until the cheese is melted and bubbling. Serve at once, garnished with celery leaves if liked.

◼ COOK'S TIP

These mushrooms make an excellent filling for an omelette. Add the drained mushrooms to the omelette when the it is half set and cook until firm.

◼ COOK'S TIP

Serve the mushrooms with ratatouille and baked potatoes for a tasty meal. For a starter or supper dish serve them on neat rounds of wholemeal toast.

75 CREAMED CHICORY AND MUSHROOMS

Preparation time:
15 minutes

Cooking time:
10 minutes

Serves 4

Calories:
200 per portion

YOU WILL NEED:
50 g/2 oz onion, chopped
40 g/1½ oz butter
275 g/10 oz chicory, sliced in half
100 g/4 oz button mushrooms, sliced
120 ml/4 fl oz vegetable stock
120 ml/4 fl oz double cream
salt and pepper
chopped parsley, to garnish

Soften the onion in the butter over a gentle heat, without browning. Add the chicory and mushrooms and cook for a few minutes. Pour in the stock and simmer, covered, for 5 minutes. Remove from the heat, add the cream, season well and reheat for a few minutes without boiling. Transfer to a warmed dish and sprinkle with chopped parsley.

76 MUSHROOM FONDUE

Preparation time:
15 minutes

Cooking time:
10-15 minutes

Serves 4

Calories:
665 per portion

YOU WILL NEED:
½ garlic clove
150 ml/¼ pint medium dry cider
1 teaspoon lemon juice
400 g/14 oz vegetarian Gouda cheese, grated
1 tablespoon cornflour
1½ tablespoons gin
100 g/4 oz button mushrooms, chopped
freshly ground black pepper
pinch of grated nutmeg
TO SERVE
1 stick French bread, cut into cubes
100 g/4 oz button mushrooms

Rub the inside of a fondue pot or flameproof casserole with the cut garlic, and place a little finely chopped garlic in the pot. Pour in the cider and lemon juice and heat slowly until nearly boiling. Gradually add the grated cheese, a little at a time, stirring continuously with a fork until all the cheese has melted. When the mixture is bubbling, blend the cornflour with the gin until smooth and add to the fondue, stirring well. Add the chopped mushrooms, pepper and nutmeg.

Serve the cheese fondue in the cooking pot at the table. There should be a fondue fork for each person, and the cubes of French bread and whole button mushrooms are speared with the fork and dipped into the fondue. This is delicious accompanied by an orange and cucumber salad.

■ COOK'S TIP

Frozen double cream is a useful item. Packed in neat sticks, just remove the number required for the dish and defrost at room temperature.

■ COOK'S TIP

If gin is not to your taste, substitute an equal amount of any of the following: Kirsch, whisky, brandy or dry sherry.

77 CELERY WITH MUSHROOMS

Preparation time:
15 minutes

Cooking time:
30 minutes

Serves 4

Calories:
175 per portion

YOU WILL NEED:
1 head celery, trimmed
salt and pepper
50 g/2 oz butter
1 medium onion, finely chopped
100 g/4 oz mushrooms, thinly sliced
coarsely grated rind of 1 lemon
75-100 g/3-4 oz vegetarian mozzarella cheese, cut into thin slivers

Cut the celery diagonally into 4 cm/1½ inch lengths. Blanch in a pan of boiling salted water for 5 minutes.

Melt the butter in a pan and fry the onion until soft. Add the celery and cook gently for 5-10 minutes until tender but still crisp. Add the mushrooms and fry for 5 minutes. Stir in the lemon rind and season to taste.

Transfer the mixture to a flameproof dish. Arrange the cheese slices over the vegetables and grill until golden.

78 CONTINENTAL-STYLE PANCAKES

Preparation time:
15 minutes

Cooking time:
15 minutes

Serves 4

Calories:
245 per portion

YOU WILL NEED:
1 × 283 g/10 oz packet frozen Continental stir-fry vegetables
50 g/2 oz vegetarian Cheddar cheese, grated
1 tablespoon finely chopped parsley
FOR THE PANCAKE BATTER
50 g/2 oz plain flour
pinch of salt
1 egg
150 ml/¼ pint milk
2 teaspoons melted butter
pinch of dried mixed herbs
oil for frying

First make the pancakes. Sift together the flour and salt. Beat to a smooth batter with the egg, half the milk and the melted butter. Stir in the remaining milk with a pinch of mixed herbs. Heat a little oil in a small frying pan and cook a quarter of the batter each time, to make four pancakes. Keep warm.

Cook the stir-fry vegetables according to the packet instructions. Divide between the pancakes and fold each one in half carefully. Place in a flameproof dish and sprinkle with the cheese. Place under a hot grill and cook until golden brown and bubbling. Sprinkle with chopped parsley and serve at once.

■ COOK'S TIP

Mozzarella is ideal for cooking as it does not become stringy when heated. Store in water in the refrigerator, and use as soon as possible.

■ COOK'S TIP

Do not worry if the pancake batter contains a few lumps. Simply press it through a fine sieve into a clean bowl.

79 CARROT AND MUSHROOM LOAF

Preparation time:
10 minutes

Cooking time:
1 hour 5 minutes

Oven temperature:
200 C, 400 F, gas 6

Serves 4

Calories:
200 per portion

YOU WILL NEED:
450 g/1 lb carrots, diced
40 g/1½ oz butter
2 teaspoons soft brown sugar
salt and pepper
300 ml/½ pint vegetable stock
100 g/4 oz button mushrooms, sliced
1 small onion, finely chopped
1 tablespoon chopped parsley
2 teaspoons chopped fresh or 1 teaspoon dried dill
3 eggs
25 g/1 oz vegetarian Cheddar cheese, grated
parsley sprig, to garnish

Cook the carrots in 25 g/1 oz of the butter until lightly browned, about 8 minutes. Sprinkle over the sugar and salt and pepper, then stir in the stock. Cook gently until the carrot is tender and the liquid has evaporated. Transfer the carrot mixture to a bowl. Heat the remaining butter and cook the mushrooms and onion until softened, about 5 minutes. Stir in the parsley and dill. Beat the eggs and stir into the carrot mixture. Stir in the mushroom mixture and the cheese. Spoon into a 450 g/1 lb loaf tin. Place the tin in a larger tin with enough warm water to come halfway up the sides. Cook for 30-40 minutes or until firm to the touch. Carefully turn out the loaf and garnish with parsley.

80 SPICED POTATOES

Preparation time:
30 minutes

Cooking time:
30-35 minutes

Serves 4

Calories:
355 per portion

Suitable for Vegans

YOU WILL NEED:
1 large onion, chopped
2 garlic cloves, crushed
2 tablespoons oil
1 kg/2 lb potatoes, cubed
2 teaspoons ground coriander
½ teaspoon turmeric
2 teaspoons ground cumin
1 bay leaf
1 × 397 g/14 oz can chopped tomatoes
150 ml/¼ pint water
salt and pepper
100 g/4 oz frozen peas
2 dessert pears or apples, peeled, cored and cubed
grated rind of ½ lemon
bay leaves, to garnish (optional)

Cook the onion and garlic in the oil until soft but not browned. Add the potatoes and stir in the spices. Add the bay leaf, tomatoes and water with seasoning to taste. Bring to the boil, cover and simmer for 15 minutes. Add the remaining ingredients and re-cover. Simmer for a further 5-10 minutes or until the potatoes are tender. Serve with brown or basmati rice. Garnish with bay leaves if you like.

▨ COOK'S TIP

Try other vegetables in this loaf to replace the carrots: cauliflower broken into tiny florets, parsnips, celeriac and swede, or a selection of vegetables.

▨ COOK'S TIP

Keep the potato cubes fairly large – dice them and they are liable to disintegrate, which spoils the appearance of this tasty dish.

81 VEGETABLE TERRINE

Preparation time:
25 minutes

Cooking time:
1 hour

Oven temperature:
180 C, 350 F, gas 4

Serves 4

Calories:
305 per portion

YOU WILL NEED:
450 g/1 lb carrots (peeled weight)
225 g/8 oz broccoli
350 g/12 oz cauliflower florets
salt and pepper
2 eggs
75 g/3 oz Danish Havarti cheese,
 grated
1 teaspoon mild mustard
100 g/4 oz fresh white breadcrumbs
75 g/3 oz Danish Buko soft cheese
 with garlic
¼ teaspoon ground coriander
sage leaves, to garnish (optional)

Line and butter a 900 g/2 lb loaf tin. Cook the vegetables separately in boiling salted water until just tender. Drain, rinse in cold water and cool separately. Purée the cauliflower in a liquidizer until smooth. Add 1 egg, the Havarti cheese, mustard, seasoning and 50 g/2 oz of the breadcrumbs. Turn into the prepared tin and smooth the surface. Arrange the broccoli in small florets on top. Liquidize the carrots until smooth. Add the remaining egg, seasoning, the garlic-flavoured cheese, coriander and the remaining breadcrumbs. Mix thoroughly. Spoon carefully over the broccoli and smooth the surface. Cover with buttered greaseproof paper and aluminium foil. Bake for 45-50 minutes or until firm. Remove from the oven and stand for 10 minutes. Turn out carefully, garnish and serve with a tomato sauce (see below).

82 STUFFED AUBERGINES

Preparation time:
10 minutes

Cooking time:
45-60 minutes

Oven temperature:
200 C, 400 F, gas 6

Serves 4

Calories:
305 per portion

YOU WILL NEED:
2 tablespoons oil
2 onions, chopped
2 garlic cloves, crushed
225 g/8 oz cooked haricot beans (or
 use canned beans)
2 tomatoes, chopped
1 teaspoon basil
1 teaspoon thyme
2 teaspoons tomato purée
salt and pepper
2 aubergines
1 × 397 g/14 oz can chopped
 tomatoes
225 g/8 oz vegetarian low-fat hard
 cheese, grated
watercress, to garnish

Heat the oil in a saucepan. Add the onions and garlic and cook until soft but not browned. Stir in beans, fresh tomatoes, herbs and tomato purée. Season well.

Cut the aubergines in half lengthways. Scoop out the flesh, chop this and add it to the beans; cook gently for 10 minutes. Meanwhile, parboil the aubergine shells for 5 minutes, drain well and fill with the bean mixture. Pour the tomatoes into a baking dish and arrange the aubergines on top. Sprinkle with cheese, cover with foil and bake for 20 minutes. Remove foil and cook for 15 minutes more. Garnish with watercress and serve with brown rice or potatoes.

■ COOK'S TIP

Tomato sauce: put 2 × 397 g/14 oz cans tomatoes and their juices in a pan. Add 50 g/2 oz butter, 2-3 teaspoons sugar, a few drops of Tabasco and salt and pepper and mash the tomatoes as the mixture comes to the boil. Cook for 8-10 minutes until thickened. Press through a sieve to remove seeds.

■ COOK'S TIP

A quick way of scooping out and chopping aubergines: cut in half and cut the middle criss-cross with a sharp knife. Scoop out the flesh carefully.

83 STUFFED MARROW RINGS

Preparation time:
15 minutes

Cooking time:
50 minutes

Oven temperature:
180 C, 350 F, gas 4

Serves 4

Calories:
325 per portion

YOU WILL NEED:
1 medium-sized marrow
1 medium onion, chopped
1 celery stick, sliced
25 g/1 oz butter
100 g/4 oz mushrooms, sliced
1 tablespoon tomato purée
100 g/4 oz mixed nuts, chopped
½ teaspoon ground cinnamon
½ teaspoon rosemary
50 g/2 oz vegetarian Danish Blue
    cheese, crumbled
75 g/3 oz fresh breadcrumbs
salt and pepper
1 egg, beaten
rosemary sprigs, to garnish

Peel the marrow and cut it into four. Scoop out the seeds. Cook in boiling water for 4-5 minutes until just starting to soften. Drain and place the rings in a lightly buttered ovenproof dish. Gently fry the onion and celery in the butter for 5 minutes until softened. Add the mushrooms, cover and cook for a further 2 minutes. Add the purée, nuts, cinnamon, rosemary, cheese, breadcrumbs, salt and pepper and the egg and mix well.

Fill the rings with the stuffing, placing any extra in a small ovenproof dish. Cover the stuffed marrow and bake for 40 minutes or until the marrow is tender. Cover the extra stuffing and bake at the same time (although it probably won't need quite as long). Garnish with sprigs of rosemary and serve with jacket potatoes.

■ COOK'S TIP

Try using peppers: select 4 squat ones (100-150 g/ 4-5 oz); blanch in boiling water for 4 minutes. Drain and cool in water. Cut a slice from the stalk end of each pepper. Discard the core and reserve the 'lids'. Seed and remove white pith. Fill with the stuffing, replace the 'lids' and bake as above.

84 CHEESE COURGETTES

Preparation time:
10 minutes

Cooking time:
40 minutes

Oven temperature:
180 C, 350 F, gas 4

Serves 2

Calories:
545 per portion

YOU WILL NEED:
4 large courgettes
salt and pepper
100 g/4 oz butter
1 large onion, finely chopped
1 tablespoon chopped parsley
50 g/2 oz vegetarian Cheddar cheese,
    grated

Trim the courgettes and cook whole in a saucepan of boiling salted water for 15 minutes or until just cooked. Drain. Cut the courgettes in half lengthways and carefully scoop out the flesh leaving a thin 'wall' all round. Chop the scooped-out flesh.

Heat the butter in a saucepan and fry the onion for 5 minutes until soft. Add the chopped courgette flesh and cook over high heat until pulpy. Stir in the parsley and half the cheese. Add salt and pepper to taste. Spoon mixture into courgette halves, place in an ovenproof dish, sprinkle with remaining cheese and bake for 20 minutes. Serve hot accompanied by a side salad.

■ COOK'S TIP

A parsley chopper is useful for chopping a variety of fresh herbs. Trim, wash and dry the herbs, place in a small mound on a board and roll away.

85 VEGETABLE BURGERS

Preparation time:
25 minutes, plus 10
minutes to stand

Cooking time:
20 minutes

Serves 4

Calories:
355 per burger

YOU WILL NEED:
225 g/8 oz leeks
350 g/12 oz celeriac, peeled and finely
    grated
225 g/8 oz carrots, finely grated
225 g/8 oz potatoes, grated
1 onion, finely chopped
2 garlic cloves, finely chopped
bunch of fresh parsley, finely chopped
2 eggs
100 g/4 oz wholewheat breadcrumbs
salt and pepper
about 6 tablespoons vegetable oil

Trim the leeks, cut a cross down through the green leaves to
the white part and wash. Cut across the leeks into thin slices
including about two-thirds of the green leaves. Place the
leeks, celeriac, carrots and potatoes in a tea towel and squeeze
well.

Place all the prepared vegetables and parsley in a bowl
and mix with the eggs and breadcrumbs to make a firm,
smooth and malleable mixture. Season to taste, cover and
leave to stand for 10 minutes.

With moist hands, shape the mixture into flat cakes or
burgers. Heat about half the oil in a frying pan. Fry the vegetable burgers, in two batches, over a high to moderate heat for
about 10 minutes, turning once. Add a little more oil to the
side of the pan, if necessary.

Serve hot, with a mixed salad.

■ COOK'S TIP

*Make the burgers half the
usual size and use with
salad as a filler for pitta
pockets, instead of the
traditional felafel. For
instructions on preparing*
*the pitta pockets, see recipe
61.*

86 VEGETABLE PARCELS

Preparation time:
20 minutes

Cooking time:
1 hour

Oven temperature:
180 C, 350 F, gas 4

Serves 2

Calories:
105 per portion

YOU WILL NEED:
2 large cabbage leaves
1 garlic clove, crushed
1 onion, chopped
75 g/3 oz long-grain brown rice,
    cooked
2 walnut halves, finely chopped
50 g/2 oz yellow pepper, seeded and
    finely chopped
1 stick celery, chopped
salt and pepper
300 ml/½ pint dry white wine or
    vegetable stock
2 tablespoons plain flour
3 tablespoons water
150 ml/¼ pint single cream

Blanch the cabbage leaves in boiling water for 1 minute, drain
and pat dry. Mix together the garlic, onion, rice, walnuts,
yellow pepper and celery, seasoning to taste. Divide this mixture between the cabbage leaves and roll up into parcels. Place
in an ovenproof dish and pour in the white wine or stock. Season with black pepper, cover, and bake in a moderate oven
for 1 hour.

Transfer the parcels to a serving dish and keep hot. Blend
the flour to a smooth paste with the water, add the cooking
juices from the parcels and pour into a saucepan. Bring to the
boil, stirring, then remove from the heat and add the cream.
Heat gently without boiling, season to taste and pour over the
parcels to serve.

■ COOK'S TIP

*Instead of cabbage leaves
you may like to stuff vine
leaves. Use packet or
canned leaves, allowing
about 4-6 instead of the
larger cabbage leaves.*

87 SAVOURY BAKE

Preparation time:
20 minutes

Cooking time:
45-50 minutes

Oven temperature:
180 C, 350 F, gas 4

Serves 4

Calories:
370 per portion

YOU WILL NEED:
1 large onion, sliced
50 g/2 oz butter
225 g/8 oz courgettes, thinly sliced
225 g/8 oz tomatoes, peeled and sliced
1 teaspoon dried mixed herbs
salt and pepper
40 g/1½ oz plain flour
450 ml/¾ pint milk
100 g/4 oz vegetarian Cheddar cheese, grated
50 g/2 oz fresh breadcrumbs
FOR THE GARNISH
tomato wedges
parsley sprigs

Cook the onion in 15 g/½ oz butter until just soft. Place half the courgettes in a 1.75 litre/3 pint ovenproof dish, cover with half the onion and the tomatoes. Sprinkle with the mixed herbs and seasoning, then top with the remaining onion and courgettes.

Meanwhile, make the sauce. Melt the remaining butter in a pan, stir in the flour and gradually add the milk, stirring continuously until the sauce thickens and boils. Season and add 75 g/3 oz of the cheese. Pour the sauce over the vegetables. Mix together the remaining cheese and the breadcrumbs and sprinkle over the sauce. Cook for 35-40 minutes until golden brown. Garnish with tomato wedges and parsley sprigs.

■ COOK'S TIP

When selecting courgettes, look for smooth-skinned, unblemished ones. They should be cooked and eaten as soon as possible after picking.

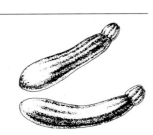

88 AUBERGINE LAYER

Preparation time:
20 minutes

Cooking time:
1 hour 12 minutes

Oven temperature:
180 C, 350 F, gas 4

Serves 4

Calories:
295 per portion

YOU WILL NEED:
2 medium aubergines, trimmed and sliced
salt and pepper
4 tablespoons vegetable oil
2 onions, sliced
4 tomatoes, peeled and sliced
50 g/2 oz walnuts, chopped
300 ml/½ pint tomato juice
½ teaspoon dried basil
FOR THE TOPPING
15 g/½ oz margarine or butter
¼ small onion, finely chopped
50 g/2 oz fresh wholewheat breadcrumbs
1 tablespoon grated Pecorino or Parmesan cheese
¼ teaspoon mustard powder

Place the aubergine slices in a colander set over a plate, sprinkle with salt and leave to drain for 30 minutes. Rinse and pat dry. Heat 3 tablespoons of the oil in a large frying pan, add the aubergines and fry until lightly coloured on both sides. Remove from the pan, add the remaining oil and fry the onions until softened. Layer all the vegetables and walnuts in an ovenproof dish. Season the tomato juice, add the basil and pour over. Cover and cook in a moderate oven for 45 minutes. Melt the margarine in a saucepan, add the onion and cook for 2-3 minutes. Stir in the remaining ingredients, use to top the vegetables and cook, uncovered, for 15 minutes. Serve at once.

■ COOK'S TIP

The reason for salting aubergines before cooking is to extract bitter juices which can spoil the flavour of the finished dish. In some recipes this is not an essential process. Make sure you rinse and dry the vegetables before using them or the dish will be very salty.

89 AUBERGINE FANS GEORGIA

Preparation time:	YOU WILL NEED:
20 minutes	2 medium aubergines
	175 g/6 oz vegetarian mozzarella
Cooking time:	cheese, thinly sliced
25-30 minutes	4 tomatoes, sliced
	50 g/2 oz salted peanuts
Oven temperature:	1 tablespoon groundnut oil
200 C, 400 F, gas 6	1 garlic clove, crushed
	1 tablespoon chopped parsley
Serves 4	1 teaspoon oregano
Calories:	salt and pepper
260 per portion	

Cut the aubergines in half lengthways. Place each half cut side down on a board and make slits at 1 cm/½ inch intervals from the stalk end down to the base, taking care not to cut right through. Fan out the aubergines and arrange them in a greased baking tin or individual dishes. Place cheese and tomato slices alternately in the cuts and sprinkle over the peanuts.

Mix the oil with the garlic, herbs and seasoning and brush evenly over the aubergines. Cover the tin with foil and bake in a moderately hot oven for 25-30 minutes, until the aubergines are tender. Serve hot.

90 MACARONI AND AUBERGINE LAYER

Preparation time:	YOU WILL NEED:
10 minutes, plus 30	350 g/12 oz aubergines, sliced
minutes to prepare	salt and pepper
aubergine	175 g/6 oz macaroni
	3 tablespoons oil
Cooking time:	1 onion, sliced
1 hour	1 garlic clove, chopped
Oven temperature:	150 ml/¼ pint natural yogurt
190 C, 375 F, gas 5	150 ml/¼ pint milk
	175 g/6 oz vegetarian low-fat hard
Serves 4	cheese, grated
Calories:	225 g/8 oz tomatoes, sliced
440 per portion	parsley, to garnish

Sprinkle the aubergine slices with salt and leave for 30 minutes. Cook the macaroni in boiling salted water for about 8 minutes, until tender but not soft, then drain.

Rinse and dry the aubergines. Heat the oil in a large frying pan. Quickly toss the aubergine and onion slices in the oil for 2-3 minutes. Add the garlic. Mix the yogurt, milk and two-thirds of the cheese. Layer the aubergine and onions, pasta and tomatoes in an ovenproof dish, seasoning the layers. Pour in the yogurt mixture and top with the remaining grated cheese. Bake for 45 minutes, until golden. Serve hot, garnished with parsley.

▮ COOK'S TIP

For simplicity, sprinkle the aubergine fans with spices, dot with butter and grill or bake. Lemon rind and Parmesan cheese make good toppings.

▮ COOK'S TIP

To make yogurt, heat milk to 50 C/100 F, then stir in 2-3 tablespoons natural live yogurt. Pour into a vacuum flask and leave overnight, until the yogurt has formed.

Remove from the flask and chill until required.

91 AUBERGINES BONNE FEMME

Preparation time:
20 minutes

Cooking time:
30 minutes

Oven temperature:
200 C, 400 F, gas 6

Serves 4-6

Calories:
295-200 per portion

YOU WILL NEED:
5 tablespoons olive oil
3 medium aubergines, cut in quarters
   lengthways, then in 2 cm/¾ in slices
1 large onion, coarsely chopped
2 garlic cloves, halved
250 g/9 oz tomatoes, roughly chopped
salt and pepper
1 teaspoon chopped fresh oregano
1 parsley sprig, chopped
50 g/2 oz Pecorino or Parmesan
   cheese, grated
1 tablespoon butter

Heat the oil in a saucepan, add the aubergines, onion and garlic and fry for 7-8 minutes. Remove and discard the garlic.

Add the tomatoes to the pan and season with salt and pepper to taste. Stir in the oregano and parsley. Cook for a few minutes then transfer the mixture to a shallow ovenproof dish. Sprinkle with the Pecorino or Parmesan cheese and dot with the butter. Cook in a moderately hot oven for about 20 minutes. Serve immediately.

92 AUBERGINE AND ONION GRATIN

Preparation time:
20 minutes, plus 1
hour to prepare
aubergine

Cooking time:
50 minutes – 1 hour

Oven temperature:
200 C, 400 F, gas 6

Serves 4

Calories:
350 per portion

YOU WILL NEED:
4 medium aubergines
salt and pepper
2-3 tablespoons oil
225 g/8 oz onions, sliced
225 g/8 oz vegetarian Cheddar cheese,
   grated
chopped parsley, to garnish

Slice the aubergines and layer in a colander, sprinkling each layer with salt. Set aside for 1 hour.

Rinse the aubergine slices under cold running water, then pat dry. Heat the oil in a frying pan and fry the aubergine slices, a few at a time, for 2-3 minutes on each side. Drain on absorbent kitchen paper. Fry the onions in the pan until soft.

Arrange the aubergine and onion slices in layers in a greased ovenproof dish, seasoning each layer. Sprinkle with the cheese. Cook in a moderately hot oven for 40 minutes. Garnish with parsley and serve.

▌COOK'S TIP

*Serve this delicious dish
accompanied by salad,
French bread and a French
red wine.*

▌COOK'S TIP

*If preferred, courgettes can
be used in place of the
aubergines in this recipe.
Courgettes do not need to
be salted prior to cooking
but you will need the*

*equivalent weight to the
aubergines.*

93 SUNFLOWER OKRA WITH MUSHROOMS

Preparation time:
10 minutes

Cooking time:
18-20 minutes

Serves 4

Calories:
130 per portion

YOU WILL NEED:

2 teaspoons vegetable oil
2 tablespoons sunflower seeds
350 g/12 oz okra, topped and tailed
25 g/1 oz butter
100 g/4 oz button mushrooms, halved
salt and pepper

Heat the oil in a small pan and cook the sunflower seeds for 1-2 minutes until brown. Drain on absorbent kitchen paper and set aside.

It is best to cook the okra whole but, if any are too large, cut them in half lengthways.

Melt the butter in a frying pan or wok and stir-fry the okra quickly for 3-4 minutes. Add the mushrooms and cook for a further 3-4 minutes. Sprinkle with salt and pepper, cover the pan and leave to cook for about 10 minutes until the mushrooms are soft and the okra crisply tender.

Remove the lid and cook quickly for 1-2 minutes to reduce the liquid in the pan. Spoon into a hot dish and sprinkle with the sunflower seeds.

94 LEEKS AU GRATIN

Preparation time:
10 minutes

Cooking time:
45 minutes

Oven temperature:
180 C, 350 F, gas 4
then
200 C, 400 F, gas 6

Serves 6

Calories:
280 per portion

YOU WILL NEED:

1 kg/2 lb leeks, trimmed and cut into
   2 cm/3/4 inch thick rings
15 g/1/2 oz butter
1 garlic clove, halved
300 ml/1/2 pint milk
pinch of grated nutmeg
1/2 teaspoon dried tarragon
salt and pepper
150 ml/1/4 pint double cream
100 g/4 oz vegetarian Gruyère cheese,
   grated

Rinse the leeks and drain thoroughly. Place in a large oven-proof dish.

Heat the butter in a small saucepan and fry the garlic for a few minutes until golden. Remove the pieces of garlic from the pan with a slotted spoon and discard. Pour the butter over the leeks.

Heat the milk with the nutmeg, tarragon and salt and pepper to taste, until almost boiling. Stir in the cream and pour over the leeks. Cover the dish tightly with greased foil and cook in a moderate oven for 20 minutes. Remove the foil and sprinkle with the cheese. Increase the oven temperature to moderately hot and bake for a further 15-20 minutes until the cheese is golden and bubbling. Serve immediately.

■ COOK'S TIP

Make sure the okra you buy are fresh, with no damaged ridges or brown patches.

■ COOK'S TIP

This dish can make a filling main course when served with jacket potatoes.

95 CIDERED HOTPOT

Preparation time:
15 minutes

Cooking time:
1 hour 45 minutes –
2 hours 15 minutes

Oven temperature:
200 C, 400 F, gas 6

Serves 4

Calories:
465 per portion

YOU WILL NEED:
225 g/8 oz swede
225 g/8 oz turnips
75 g/3 oz butter
2 medium onions, sliced
2 leeks, sliced
225 g/8 oz carrots, sliced
40 g/1½ oz plain flour
450 ml/¾ pint dry cider
1 tablespoon tomato purée
salt and pepper
1 teaspoon yeast extract
450 g/1 lb potatoes, peeled and thinly sliced
oil for brushing
75 g/3 oz vegetarian Cheddar cheese, grated

Cut the swede and turnips into 2.5 cm/1 inch cubes. Melt the butter in a large frying pan, add the swede, turnips, onions, leeks and carrots and cook gently for 10 minutes until softened. Transfer the vegetables to an oiled ovenproof dish.

Mix the flour to a paste with a little of the cider in a saucepan, gradually stir in the remaining cider and bring to the boil, whisking all the time. Add the tomato purée, salt and pepper and yeast extract. Pour over the vegetables. Arrange the sliced potatoes on top. Brush the potato slices with oil and sprinkle over the cheese. Cover.

Bake for 1½-2 hours or until the vegetables are cooked. Uncover the dish for the last 30 minutes to brown the topping.

96 PARSNIP CASSEROLE

Preparation time:
10 minutes

Cooking time:
1 hour 5 minutes

Oven temperature:
160 C, 325 F, gas 3

Serves 4

Calories:
290 per portion

YOU WILL NEED:
about 675 g/1½ lb parsnips
75 g/3 oz butter
1 medium onion, chopped
50 g/2 oz vegetarian Cheddar cheese, grated
salt and pepper
a few drops of Tabasco sauce
300 ml/½ pint vegetable stock
2 tomatoes, thinly sliced
50 g/2 oz fresh breadcrumbs

Peel the parsnips and cut into chunks. Heat 50 g/2 oz of the butter in a large saucepan and cook the onion until softened, about 5 minutes. Remove the pan from the heat, stir in the parsnip, cheese, salt and pepper, Tabasco and stock. Spoon into a lightly greased ovenproof dish. Arrange the sliced tomatoes on top, (see picture). Bake in the oven, covered, for 45-50 minutes or until the parsnip is just cooked. Melt the remaining butter and stir in the breadcrumbs. Sprinkle over the tomatoes and press down.

Return to oven, uncovered, for 10 minutes. Serve hot.

■ COOK'S TIP

This delicious hotpot makes an excellent family meal. Serve chunks of crusty Granary bread with it. Vary the vegetables to suit the season.

■ COOK'S TIP

Use a matured Cheddar to give the parsnip plenty of flavour. Instead of parsnip you can use courgettes, marrow or pumpkin in this dish.

97 SPINACH, CAULIFLOWER AND COURGETTE BHAJI

Preparation time:
5 minutes

Cooking time:
35 minutes

Serves 4

Calories:
50 per portion

YOU WILL NEED:
225 g/8 oz frozen leaf spinach
225 g/8 oz frozen cauliflower florets
225 g/8 oz frozen sliced courgettes
100 g/4 oz frozen onion slices, or 1 small fresh onion, sliced
2 garlic cloves, crushed
½ teaspoon grated or very finely chopped fresh root ginger
¼ teaspoon garam masala
1-2 teaspoons black mustard seeds
1-2 tablespoons thick set natural yogurt

Put all the vegetables in a large saucepan with some water, garlic and ginger. Bring to the boil, then reduce heat and cook for about 20 minutes. Add the garam masala and mustard seeds and cook for a further 10 minutes, or until the vegetables are just tender.

Just before serving, stir the yogurt into the vegetables.

▌ COOK'S TIP

Try using frozen broccoli in place of the cauliflower. You could also use frozen mixed sliced peppers instead of the courgettes.

98 BROCCOLI RING

Preparation time:
15 minutes

Cooking time:
25-30 minutes

Oven temperature:
180 C, 350 F, gas 4

Serves 6

Calories:
330 per portion

YOU WILL NEED:
450 g/1 lb frozen chopped broccoli, defrosted
1 onion, finely chopped
2 garlic cloves, crushed
50 g/2 oz butter
50 g/2 oz plain flour
300 ml/½ pint milk
225 g/8 oz vegetarian mature Cheddar cheese
4 eggs, well beaten
salt and pepper
FOR THE GARNISH
tomato wedges
watercress sprigs

Oil a 1.4 litre/2½ pint ring mould. Drain the broccoli very well, and put into a large mixing bowl. Add the onion and garlic. Melt the butter in a saucepan, add the flour and cook for a minute. Gradually add the milk, stirring, and bring to the boil. Simmer gently for a few minutes, then remove from the heat. Grate half the cheese and add to the sauce with the eggs. Season, beat until smooth. Add to the broccoli and mix well. Pour into the ring mould.

Place the mould in a roasting tin filled with hot water to a depth of 2.5 cm/1 inch. Bake in a moderate oven for 25-30 minutes until set. Cool in the mould for 5 minutes, then turn out on to a warm serving platter. Slice the remaining cheese thinly and lay the slices over the top of the broccoli ring. Grill until golden and bubbling. Garnish as shown.

▌ COOK'S TIP

Fresh broccoli may be used instead of frozen. Trim stems, cutting into 2.5 cm/ 1 inch pieces and florets. Steam for 3 minutes, then proceed as above.

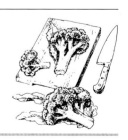

99 CHICORY IN MUSTARD SAUCE

Preparation time: 5 minutes	**YOU WILL NEED:** 8 small heads chicory
	150 ml/¼ pint salted water
Cooking time: 18 minutes	juice of 1 lemon
	15 g/½ oz butter
Serves 4	scant 1 tablespoon plain flour
	150 ml/¼ pint vegetable stock
Calories: 85 per portion	2-3 tablespoons single cream
	scant 2 tablespoons prepared mild mustard
	1 teaspoon sugar
	1 tablespoon chopped dill, to garnish

Rinse and drain the chicory and remove the thick stems. Bring the water and lemon juice to the boil. Add the chicory heads, lower the heat and cook for about 10 minutes. Drain and keep hot. Reserve cooking liquid.

Melt the butter in a small pan, stir in the flour and cook for 2-3 minutes. Gradually add the reserved cooking liquid and stock, stirring constantly.

Add the cream, mustard and sugar and bring to the boil, stirring constantly. Cook for 3 minutes, stirring. Arrange the chicory heads on a warmed serving dish, pour over the sauce. Sprinkle with the chopped dill. Serve immediately.

100 SPINACH WITH FLAKED ALMONDS

Preparation time: 10 minutes	**YOU WILL NEED:** 1 kg/2¼ lb leaf spinach
	50 g/2 oz butter
Cooking time: 20 minutes	½ onion, finely chopped
	salt
Serves 4	grated nutmeg
	4 tablespoons natural yogurt
Calories: 200 per portion	50 g/2 oz flaked almonds

Place the spinach in a sieve, rinse and drain thoroughly. Tear the leaves into manageable pieces. Melt half the butter in a large saucepan, add the onion and cook for 2-3 minutes until softened. Add the spinach, a little at a time, turning it in the butter to coat. Season with salt and nutmeg to taste. Cook over low heat for 10-15 minutes until tender, depending upon the thickness of the spinach leaves.

Stir the yogurt into the spinach mixture. Remove the spinach from the heat and transfer to a warmed serving bowl. Fry the almonds in the remaining butter, stirring, until golden. Fold the almonds into the spinach and serve.

■ COOK'S TIP

Look out for different mustards in delicatessens and health food shops. Try wholegrain varieties, those flavoured with herbs and continental types, such as *Swedish mustard which can be slightly sweet and very mild.*

■ COOK'S TIP

Freshly grated nutmeg gives the best flavour. Keep whole nutmegs in an airtight jar, then grate them as required on a special miniature, very fine grater.

101 CHINESE-STYLE STIR-FRY

Preparation time:
15 minutes

Cooking time:
5 minutes

Serves 4

Calories:
155 per portion

Suitable for Vegans

YOU WILL NEED:
4 tablespoons oil
175 g/6 oz Chinese leaves, shredded
175 g/6 oz Brussels sprouts, shredded
175 g/6 oz leeks, shredded
175 g/6 oz tiny cauliflower florets
salt and freshly ground black pepper
2 tablespoons soy sauce

Heat the oil in a wok or deep frying pan. Add the prepared vegetables and stir-fry for 4-5 minutes over a brisk heat. The vegetables should still be slightly crunchy. Sprinkle with salt and pepper and a generous quantity of soy sauce to taste. Serve immediately.

102 CRISPY VEGETARIAN NUGGETS

Preparation time:
25 minutes

Cooking time:
15-20 minutes

Serves 4

Calories:
600 per portion

YOU WILL NEED:
1 tablespoon vegetable oil
1 onion, finely chopped
225 g/8 oz mushrooms, finely chopped
175 g/6 oz long-grain rice, cooked
1½ teaspoons chopped fresh thyme
175 g/6 oz vegetarian Cheshire cheese, grated
salt and pepper
1 egg, beaten
2 tablespoons wholemeal flour
FOR THE COATING
2 tablespoons wholemeal flour
2 eggs, beaten
100 g/4 oz wholewheat breadcrumbs
2 teaspoons sesame seeds
oil for frying

Heat the tablespoon of oil in a sauté pan; fry the onion and mushrooms for 5 minutes, stirring occasionally. Mix with the remaining ingredients in a bowl and shape into 12 balls. Coat the balls in flour, then dip in beaten egg and finally roll in a mixture of breadcrumbs and sesame seeds. Heat the oil in the sauté pan and fry the balls until golden brown. Drain on absorbent kitchen paper and serve with a salad.

▊ COOK'S TIP

Stir-frying is an excellent method of cooking vegetables. They are cooked so quickly and in their own juices that very little of the nutritional content is lost.

▊ COOK'S TIP

Make a tasty soured cream sauce to accompany the nuggets. Mix 1 tablespoon grated onion and 2 tablespoons finely grated cucumber (with excess liquid drained off) with 150 ml/¼ pint soured cream. Season to taste and chill lightly before serving.

103 PARSNIP PATTIES

Preparation time:
20 minutes

Cooking time:
20-25 minutes

Serves 4-6

Calories:
360-240 per portion

YOU WILL NEED:
225 g/8 oz parsnips, peeled and
*   quartered*
225 g/8 oz potatoes, peeled, halved if
*   necessary*
salt
15 g/½ oz butter
50 g/2 oz walnuts, coarsely chopped
2 tablespoons plain flour
1 egg, beaten
75 g/3 oz dried breadcrumbs
oil for shallow frying

Cook the parsnips and potatoes in a pan of boiling salted water for about 15 minutes, until tender. Drain well.

Chop the parsnips coarsely and mash the potatoes. Mix together with the butter and walnuts. Shape into neat round cakes, or if you prefer, into cylindrical croquettes. Coat each cake in flour, then in beaten egg and finally in breadcrumbs.

Shallow fry the patties in hot oil for 3 minutes on each side until golden brown. Drain on absorbent kitchen paper, sprinkle with salt and serve immediately with a simple salad of tomatoes, onions and chopped parsley.

104 VEGETABLE CURRY

Preparation time:
20 minutes, plus 10 minutes to drain aubergine

Cooking time:
1 hour

Serves 4

Calories:
380 per portion

Suitable for Vegans

YOU WILL NEED:
1 aubergine, diced
salt and pepper
2 tablespoons oil
4 teaspoons mustard seeds
½ teaspoon ground turmeric
1½ teaspoons chilli powder
1 garlic clove, crushed
1 × 2.5 cm/1 inch piece fresh root
*   ginger, peeled and finely chopped*
1 small cauliflower, broken into florets
3 potatoes, peeled and diced
4 courgettes, thickly sliced
4 tomatoes, peeled and quartered and
*   seeded*
175 g/6 oz runner beans or French
*   beans, cut into 2.5 cm/1 inch*
*   lengths*
100 g/4 oz flaked almonds, toasted

Sprinkle the aubergine with salt, allow to drain in a colander for 10 minutes. Rinse and drain thoroughly.

Heat the oil in a heavy flameproof casserole or in a large heavy frying pan with a lid. Add the mustard seeds, turmeric and chilli powder and cook, stirring constantly, until the seeds begin to pop. Stir in the garlic and ginger and fry for a few seconds. Then stir in all the vegetables and seasoning. Cover and cook very slowly for 40-50 minutes until all the vegetables are tender. Taste for seasoning and stir in the almonds.

■ COOK'S TIP

Chill the patties in the refrigerator for 1-2 hours after coating in egg and breadcrumbs and they will hold their shape more satisfactorily when fried.

■ COOK'S TIP

To toast flaked almonds, distribute them evenly on a baking tray, then bake in a moderate oven (160 C, 325 F, gas 3), stirring frequently, until brown.

SALADS

Salads offer the perfect opportunity for mingling sweet and sour flavours, for incorporating protein-rich cheese and creating piquant new dressings – not omitting classics such as French dressing. In this chapter you will find salads crunchy with celery, apple and walnuts, juicy with grapes or pineapple, made into a meal with cheese, and dressings including herbs, nuts and yogurt. Creativity can flourish in salad-making.

105 CAERPHILLY BEAN SALAD

Preparation time:
20 minutes

Cooking time:
8 minutes

Serves 4

Calories:
470 per portion

YOU WILL NEED:
225 g/8 oz French beans
225 g/8 oz vegetarian Caerphilly cheese
1 small red pepper
FOR THE DRESSING
8 tablespoons salad oil
2 tablespoons red or white wine vinegar
salt, pepper and a little paprika
1 tablespoon single cream (optional)

Top and tail the French beans. Cook in boiling salted water until just tender. Drain, refresh with a little cold water, drain again and allow to cool.

Cut the cheese into neat pieces, either dice or thin strips. Discard the core and seeds from the red pepper and cut the flesh in thin rounds. Prepare the dressing by whisking all the ingredients together. Toss the cheese and beans in sufficient dressing to coat lightly, put in a salad bowl and scatter the rings of pepper over the top.

106 MUSHROOM AND LEICESTER SALAD

Preparation time:
15 minutes, plus 30 minutes to chill

Serves 4

Calories:
260 per portion

YOU WILL NEED:
225 g/8 oz very fresh cup or button mushrooms
4-6 tablespoons salad oil
salt and pepper
100 g/4 oz vegetarian Red Leicester cheese
1 tablespoon wine vinegar
1 tablespoon chopped parsley
2 teaspoons chopped chives (optional)

Trim and carefully wipe the mushrooms. Slice thinly and place in a wide bowl. Add enough oil to coat the mushrooms; season with salt and pepper. Cube the Leicester cheese or cut it into strips, add to the mushrooms with the vinegar and herbs. Toss all the ingredients together, put in a salad bowl, cover and chill briefly before serving.

■ COOK'S TIP

Substitute mangetout peas for the French beans. Top and tail and rinse them before boiling them briefly in salted water so that they retain a little bite.

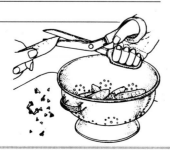

■ COOK'S TIP

Red Leicester adds colour to this nutritious salad. Red Windsor, a marbled cheese flavoured with elderberry wine or annatto berries, could be used instead.

107 SPINACH CHEESE SALAD

Preparation time:
15 minutes plus
20-30 minutes to
chill

Serves 4

Calories:
385 per portion

YOU WILL NEED:
1 kg/2 lb fresh spinach, washed
4 tablespoons salad oil
salt and pepper
wine vinegar or lemon juice (optional)
175 g/6 oz Derby cheese
2 tablespoons mayonnaise
chopped chives, to garnish (optional)

Blanch the spinach for 1 minute in boiling salted water. Drain and refresh with cold water. Press the spinach between two plates to remove excessive moisture. Place in a wide bowl.

Using two forks to help separate the leaves, dress the spinach with the salad oil, salt and freshly ground black pepper, adding a little wine vinegar or lemon juice if you like.

Cut the cheese into cubes, mix with the mayonnaise and extra seasoning, if necessary. Spoon on top of the spinach and serve lightly chilled. Add a garnish of chopped chives, if liked.

108 CHESHIRE SALAD

Preparation time:
10 minutes

Cooking time:
5 minutes

Serves 4

Calories:
115 per portion

YOU WILL NEED:
FOR THE DRESSING
4 tablespoons orange juice
1 teaspoon caster sugar
2 tablespoons oil
1 tablespoon white wine vinegar
1 tablespoon chopped parsley
1 tablespoon chopped chives
FOR THE SALAD
225 g/8 oz red cabbage
100 g/4 oz cooked beetroot
2 red-skinned apples
1 tablespoon lemon juice
4-8 lettuce leaves
225 g/8 oz vegetarian Cheshire cheese
parsley sprigs, to garnish

Whisk the dressing ingredients in a bowl. Shred the cabbage and blanch in boiling water for 2 minutes. Drain and toss into the dressing. Cool, mixing occasionally. Thinly slice the beetroot. Core and chop the apples; toss in the lemon juice. Arrange lettuce leaves on individual plates, top with cabbage and apple. Cube the cheese and scatter over the salad. Garnish with parsley and serve.

▓ COOK'S TIP

*Spinach has a very high
vitamin A content and is
rich in iron and vitamin C.
As it is low in calories it is
an excellent vegetable,
especially when served raw.*

▓ COOK'S TIP

*Although red wine vinegar
has an equally good flavour,
white wine vinegar is better
in salad dressings as red
wine vinegar can turn the
dressing pink.*

109 LIGHT CHEESE AND PINEAPPLE SALAD

Preparation time:
20 minutes, plus
20-30 minutes to
chill

Serves 4

Calories:
220 per portion

YOU WILL NEED:
175 g/6 oz vegetarian low-fat hard
  cheese, cubed
225 g/8 oz fresh pineapple, peeled and
  cubed
100 g/4 oz celery, chopped
100 g/4 oz apple, chopped
50 g/2 oz walnut pieces
3-4 tablespoons low-calorie
  mayonnaise
1 tablespoon chopped parsley
salt and pepper

Mix the cheese, pineapple, celery, apple and walnuts in a bowl. Coat with the mayonnaise and sprinkle with parsley. Season to taste and mix well. Chill the salad for 25-30 minutes before serving.

110 BLUE CHEESE AND MANDARIN SALAD

Preparation time:
15 minutes

Serves 6

Calories:
135 per portion

YOU WILL NEED:
1 × 298 g/10½ oz can mandarin
  orange segments in natural juice
75 g/3 oz vegetarian blue cheese
150 ml/¼ pint soured cream or
  mayonnaise
salt and pepper
450 g/1 lb white cabbage, finely
  shredded
lettuce, to serve

Drain the mandarins. Crumble the blue cheese into the mandarin juice then mix in the soured cream or mayonnaise. Season well before tossing with the cabbage and mandarins. Serve on a bed of lettuce.

■ COOK'S TIP

When selecting a pineapple, check for fragrance and ripeness. Discoloured, drooping leaves indicate the pineapple is not in peak condition.

■ COOK'S TIP

Blue cheese and mandarins form a highly successful combination. For an interesting starter, omit the cabbage and use the fruit and cheese mixture to fill *well-drained canned pear halves.*

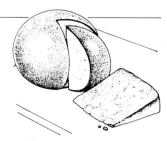

111 CRUNCHY BEANSPROUT AND CHEESE SALAD

Preparation time:
10 minutes

Serves 4

Calories:
305 per portion

YOU WILL NEED:
4 tablespoons natural wholenut peanut butter
4 tablespoons lemon juice
1 red pepper, seeded and cut into thin strips
175 g/6 oz beansprouts
175 g/6 oz vegetarian Double Gloucester cheese, cubed
½ crisp lettuce, shredded

Stir the peanut butter and lemon juice together until well mixed. Combine the remaining ingredients in a salad bowl, then stir in the peanut butter dressing just before serving.

112 TWO-CHEESE SALAD

Preparation time:
20 minutes

Serves 4

Calories:
485 per portion

YOU WILL NEED:
1 green pepper, seeded and cut into thin strips
1 red pepper, seeded and cut into thin strips
4 tomatoes, sliced
175 g/6 oz vegetarian blue cheese, cubed
175 g/6 oz vegetarian Edam or Gouda cheese, cubed
12 stuffed green olives
2 tablespoons olive oil
1 tablespoon lemon juice
1 cos lettuce
FOR THE SAUCE
300 ml/½ pint natural yogurt
salt and pepper
1 small avocado

Place the peppers, tomatoes, cheeses and olives in a bowl. Whisk the oil and lemon juice together until well blended, pour over the salad and toss lightly, to coat. Wash and prepare the lettuce and arrange it on a serving platter. Pile the cheese salad in the centre.

To make the sauce, mix the yogurt with plenty of seasoning. Peel and finely chop the avocado, then fold it lightly into the yogurt. Serve separately.

■ COOK'S TIP

If you have a grinder, making your own peanut butter is easy. Grind 100 g/4 oz roasted peanuts finely and mash them to a paste in a bowl, adding a little *vegetable oil if necessary. Hazelnuts, cashews and walnuts may also be used.*

■ COOK'S TIP

Vary the choice of cheeses here. Try smoked cheese with Cheshire cheese or Sage Derby with Edam. Strict vegetarians may prefer rennet-free varieties.

113 CREAMY WALDORF SALAD

Preparation time:
30 minutes, plus 1
hour to chill

Serves 6

Calories:
170 per portion

YOU WILL NEED:
2 tablespoons lemon juice
1 teaspoon caster sugar
1 tablespoon mayonnaise
3 green dessert apples
4 celery sticks
50 g/2 oz walnuts
100 g/4 oz green grapes
100 g/4 oz Danish Blue Castello
   cheese
6 tablespoons natural yogurt
salt and pepper
celery leaves, to garnish

Whisk the lemon juice, sugar and mayonnaise together in a large bowl. Core and dice the apples and mix into the lemon mixture. Set aside and turn occasionally while preparing the other ingredients. Thinly slice the celery, chop the walnuts, halve and seed the grapes. Add to the apple and stir to thinly coat with the lemon mixture.

Place the cheese in a bowl and beat to soften. Beat in the yogurt and seasoning to make a thick dressing. Alternatively, place the cheese, yogurt and seasoning in a liquidizer and blend until smooth. Pour over the apple mixture and turn gently with a fork until well mixed. Refrigerate for an hour then mix again. Turn into a serving bowl and garnish with celery leaves.

114 MUSHROOM SLAW

Preparation time:
15 minutes, plus
several hours to
chill

Serves 6

Calories:
235 per portion

YOU WILL NEED:
225 g/8 oz flat mushrooms, thinly
   sliced
225 g/8 oz white cabbage, shredded
50 g/2 oz sultanas
FOR THE DRESSING
150 ml/¼ pint mayonnaise
2 tablespoons lemon juice
2 tablespoons Dijon mustard
2 tablespoons single cream
2 tablespoons chopped chives
salt and pepper

Mix the mushrooms with the cabbage and sultanas. In a separate bowl combine the ingredients for the dressing, seasoning to taste. Pour the dressing over the salad and mix gently together. Cover and refrigerate for several hours. Toss together well before serving.

■ COOK'S TIP

If liked, fennel with its aniseed flavour and delicate feathery leaves may be finely chopped and substituted for the celery in this recipe.

■ COOK'S TIP

Make a bowl for the slaw from a Savoy cabbage; cut out the centre, wash, dry and use the outer leaves as a bowl. Use the centre, shredded, in the above recipe.

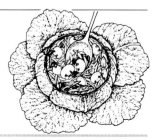

115 PASTA SLAW

Preparation time:
15 minutes, plus 30
minutes to cool

Cooking time:
13-15 minutes

Serves 4

Calories:
225 per portion

YOU WILL NEED:
75 g/3 oz pasta spirals
1 × 283 g/10 oz packet frozen whole
   French beans
75 g/3 oz white cabbage, finely
   chopped
½ green pepper, seeded and finely
   chopped
1 carrot, grated
4 spring onions, finely chopped
salt and pepper
parsley sprigs, to garnish (optional)
FOR THE DRESSING
4 tablespoons mayonnaise
2 tablespoons milk or cream
1 tablespoon wine vinegar
2 teaspoons sugar
salt and pepper

Cook the pasta in a large saucepan of boiling salted water for 10-12 minutes, until just tender. Cook the French beans in boiling salted water for 3-5 minutes. Refresh both under cold water, drain and allow to cool.

Meanwhile, mix together the remaining salad ingredients in a bowl. Combine the ingredients for the dressing and add to the salad bowl with the pasta and chopped French beans. Season to taste and garnish with sprigs of parsley to serve.

▮ COOK'S TIP

For additional fibre and B vitamins use wholemeal pasta in this recipe.

116 FRUIT COLESLAW

Preparation time:
25 minutes

Serves 4

Calories:
280 per portion

Suitable for Vegans

YOU WILL NEED:
½ medium white cabbage, finely
   shredded
4 celery sticks, cut into matchstick
   strips
2 red dessert apples, cored and
   chopped
50 g/2 oz raisins
50 g/2 oz walnuts, chopped
100 g/4 oz grapes, halved and seeded
1 tablespoon chopped chives
FOR THE DRESSING
4 tablespoons oil
1 tablespoon wine vinegar
pinch of mustard powder
1 teaspoon sugar
salt and pepper

To make the dressing, combine the ingredients in a screw-topped jar and shake well to blend. Place the cabbage in a large salad bowl and stir in sufficient dressing to just moisten. Add the celery, apples, raisins, walnuts, grapes and chives and toss well together.

▮ COOK'S TIP

To shred cabbage finely, choose a long-bladed, sharp knife, secure the cabbage with your fingers, moving them back as you shred.

117 CRUNCHY CABBAGE SALAD

Preparation time:
15 minutes

Serves 4

Calories:
260 per portion

YOU WILL NEED:
225 g/8 oz red cabbage, finely
   shredded
100 g/4 oz white cabbage, finely
   shredded
1 red pepper, seeded and chopped
50 g/2 oz sunflower seeds
100 g/4 oz salted peanuts
50 g/2 oz raisins
FOR THE DRESSING
1 tablespoon wine vinegar
1 teaspoon prepared mustard
2 tablespoons natural yogurt
2 tablespoons groundnut oil
1 tablespoon chopped parsley
salt and pepper

Place the red and white cabbage in a salad bowl with the pepper, sunflower seeds, peanuts and raisins. Mix well.

Place all the dressing ingredients in a small bowl and whisk with a fork until thickened. Pour over the salad and mix thoroughly. Serve immediately or cover and refrigerate until ready to serve.

118 DRESSED BEAN AND ONION SALAD

Preparation time:
15 minutes, plus 1
hour to chill

Cooking time:
5 minutes

Serves 4

Calories:
445 per portion

YOU WILL NEED:
50 g/2 oz butter or margarine
1 garlic clove, finely chopped
50 g/2 oz All-Bran cereal, crushed
¼ teaspoon salt
1 × 227g/8 oz can red kidney beans,
   drained
1 × 227g/8 oz can black-eyed beans
   or chick peas, drained
450 g/1 lb fresh or frozen green beans,
   cooked and sliced
onion rings, to garnish
FOR THE DRESSING
½ teaspoon salt
pinch of pepper
½ teaspoon dried basil
½ teaspoon mustard powder
3 tablespoons white wine vinegar
1 tablespoon clear honey
5 tablespoons oil

Melt the butter in a pan and sauté the garlic for 2 minutes. Stir in the cereal and salt and fry briskly for 2 minutes more. Leave to cool. Rinse the canned beans and drain well. Mix with the green beans in a salad bowl and chill. To make the dressing, combine the salt, pepper, basil, mustard, vinegar and honey in a bowl. Gradually beat in the oil. Stir the cereal mixture into the beans, then the dressing. Garnish with the onion rings and serve.

■ COOK'S TIP

Sunflower seeds are readily available in health food stores. As well as enhancing all kinds of salads, they provide a healthy nibble and are good toasted too.

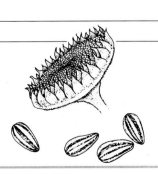

■ COOK'S TIP

Mixing pulse protein with cereal protein in this salad makes it a well-balanced dish which supplies a good combination of amino acids.

119 MUSHROOM AND MANGETOUT SALAD

Preparation time:
10 minutes, plus 20 minutes to cool

Cooking time:
4-5 minutes

Serves 4

Calories:
55 per portion

YOU WILL NEED:
175 g/6 oz mangetout
225 g/8 oz small button mushrooms, sliced
6 spring onions, chopped
150 ml/¼ pint natural yogurt
salt and pepper
snipped chives, to garnish

Cook the mangetout in boiling salted water for 4-5 minutes until just tender. Drain and cool. Combine the mushrooms, spring onions and yogurt with seasoning to taste.

Arrange the mangetout on a plate and top with the mushrooms. Sprinkle with chives and serve.

120 BROAD BEAN SALAD

Preparation time:
15 minutes

Cooking time:
10 minutes

Serves 4-6

Calories:
420-280 per portion

YOU WILL NEED:
350 g/12 oz fresh or frozen broad beans
salt
tarragon or parsley sprigs, to garnish
FOR THE HOLLANDAISE SAUCE
3 egg yolks
2 tablespoons lemon juice
175 g/6 oz unsalted butter, melted
salt and pepper

Cook the beans in boiling salted water for 5-10 minutes or until tender. Drain the beans, cool and pop the beans out of their outer skins, if liked (with young beans this will not be necessary.) Put the beans into a serving bowl.

To make the hollandaise sauce, blend the egg yolks and lemon juice together in a food processor for 30 seconds. Slowly pour in the hot melted butter to make a creamy sauce. Add salt and pepper to taste. Pour over the beans immediately and garnish with the tarragon or parsley. Serve warm or cool.

■ COOK'S TIP

The best way of preparing chives is to hold the washed bunch firmly and use a pair of scissors to snip them into a small basin.

■ COOK'S TIP

If using fresh broad beans, do not remove from the furry lined pods until just before cooking. There is no need to shell young, tender broad beans; top, tail, cut them up, then cook and serve in the pods.

121 MUSHROOM AND CUCUMBER SIDE SALAD

Preparation time:
15 minutes

Serves 4

Calories:
65 per portion

YOU WILL NEED:
¼ Webbs lettuce, finely shredded
100 g/4 oz button mushrooms, wiped and quartered
½ cucumber, diced
4 tablespoons low-calorie mayonnaise
2 teaspoons tomato ketchup
½ teaspoon lemon juice
paprika to sprinkle

Arrange the shredded lettuce in the base of four salad bowls. Mix together the mushrooms and cucumber and place over the lettuce. Combine the mayonnaise with the tomato ketchup and lemon juice and spoon over the salad. Sprinkle with a little paprika and serve at once.

122 MUSHROOM AND CELERIAC SALAD

Preparation time:
25 minutes, plus about 1 hour to chill

Serves 6

Calories:
315 per portion

YOU WILL NEED:
225 g/8 oz button mushrooms, halved if large
½ large celeriac root, coarsely grated
225 g/8 oz carrots, coarsely grated
chopped parsley, to garnish
FOR THE DRESSING
1 egg yolk
150 ml/¼ pint olive oil
2 tablespoons white wine vinegar
150 ml/¼ pint soured cream
salt and pepper

First make the dressing. Place the egg yolk in a small bowl and beat with 2-3 drops of the olive oil. Gradually whisk in the remaining olive oil, drop by drop, until pale and thick. Whisk in the vinegar, soured cream and seasoning to taste. Fold half the dressing into the mushrooms. Fold the rest of the dressing into the celeriac. Turn the celeriac on to a serving dish, top with the carrot and mushrooms, then sprinkle with parsley. Chill before serving.

COOK'S TIP

Choose lettuces with care, avoiding any with rust spots, wilted leaves or yellowing tips. Wash the leaves carefully and quickly (do not soak), dry between sheets of absorbent kitchen paper. Store in plastic bags in the refrigerator.

COOK'S TIP

For a substantial lunch or supper, serve this salad with a generous slice of quiche or flan.

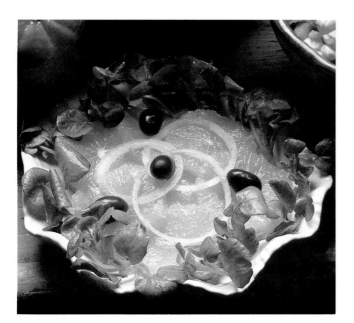

123 ORANGE AND WATERCRESS SALAD

Preparation time:	YOU WILL NEED:
15 minutes	*1 large bunch watercress, trimmed*
	3 oranges, peel and pith removed and thinly sliced into rounds
Serves 4	*1 onion, thinly sliced and separated into rings*
Calories:	*1 small green pepper, seeded, and thinly sliced into rings (optional)*
185 per portion	*6 tablespoons Vinaigrette dressing (see recipe 147)*
	black olives, to garnish.

Put the watercress in a salad bowl. Arrange the orange slices on top with the onion and pepper rings, if using. Pour on the prepared dressing and garnish with the olives.

124 BRUSSELS SPROUTS AND CARROT SALAD

Preparation time:	YOU WILL NEED:
20 minutes, plus 1 hour to chill	*450 g/1 lb Brussels sprouts*
	2 medium carrots, grated
	2 tablespoons sultanas
Serves 4	*1 tablespoon finely chopped onion*
Calories:	*FOR THE DRESSING*
170 per portion	*4 tablespoons oil*
	1 tablespoon wine vinegar
Suitable for Vegans	*1 teaspoon sugar*
	2 teaspoons Dijon mustard
	salt and pepper

Wash the sprouts. Remove and discard a slice from the base of each. Slice the sprouts thinly. Mix with the carrots, sultanas and onion in a large salad bowl. Combine the ingredients for the dressing and stir sufficient into the salad to moisten. Chill for at least an hour before serving.

▦ COOK'S TIP

For an attractive garnish, shape a tomato waterlily. Make zig-zag cuts around the middle of a tomato, through to the centre. Separate the two halves.

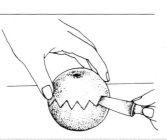

▦ COOK'S TIP

Brussels sprouts, although usually served hot, make an excellent base for a winter salad with their delicate colour and flavour. Nor are any of the valuable minerals and vitamins lost through cooking.

125 CHICORY AND SESAME SALAD

Preparation time:
15 minutes

Serves 4-6

Calories:
205-135 per portion

Suitable for Vegans

YOU WILL NEED:
3 heads of chicory
2 oranges
1 bunch of watercress
25 g/1 oz sesame seeds, roasted
4 tablespoons olive oil
1 tablespoon lemon juice
salt and pepper

Cut the chicory diagonally into 1 cm/½ inch slices and place in a mixing bowl. Remove the peel and pith from the oranges and cut the flesh into segments, holding the fruit over the bowl so that any juice is retained.

Divide the watercress into sprigs and add to the bowl with the sesame seeds.

Whisk together the oil, lemon juice and salt and pepper to taste, then pour over the salad and toss thoroughly. Transfer to a salad bowl to serve.

126 CARROT AND APPLE SALAD

Preparation time:
20 minutes

Cooking time:
5 minutes

Serves 4

Calories:
280 per portion

Suitable for Vegans

YOU WILL NEED:
350 g/12 oz carrots, coarsely grated
3 Cox's Orange Pippin apples, unpeeled, cored and sliced
1 tablespoon lemon juice
1 tablespoon sunflower seeds
3 tablespoons raisins
2 teaspoons vegetable oil
2 tablespoons cashew nuts
6 tablespoons French dressing (see recipe 146)
lettuce leaves, to serve

Put the grated carrot into a large bowl. Sprinkle the apple slices with lemon juice to prevent discoloration, then add to the bowl. Lightly mix in the sunflower seeds and raisins.

Heat the oil in a small pan and lightly brown the cashew nuts. Lift out and drain on absorbent kitchen paper, then add to the bowl.

Spoon the dressing over the salad and toss lightly. Serve on a bed of lettuce leaves.

■ COOK'S TIP

Sesame seeds have a nutty flavour which is released more fully when they are roasted in a moderate oven (180 C, 350 F, gas 4) for about 15 minutes. Stir them *frequently to prevent the seeds charring.*

■ COOK'S TIP

French dressing, without garlic and herbs, keeps well in a vinegar proof screw-topped jar or bottle. There is no need to refrigerate.

127 CELERY SALAD FLAVIA

Preparation time:
15 minutes, plus 30
minutes to chill

Serves 4

Calories:
140 per portion

Suitable for Vegans

YOU WILL NEED:
1 garlic clove, peeled and halved
1 head celery, cut into small strips
1 × 200 g/7 oz can artichoke hearts in
    brine, drained and halved
1 tablespoon black olives, stoned
1 tablespoon chopped parsley
3 tablespoons olive oil
1 tablespoon lemon juice
dash of Tabasco sauce
½ teaspoon prepared mustard
pinch of dried oregano
salt
few celery leaves, to garnish

Using the cut side of the garlic, vigorously rub the inside of a salad bowl, then discard. Add the celery, artichoke hearts, olives and parsley to the bowl.

To make the dressing, beat the olive oil with the lemon juice, Tabasco sauce, mustard, oregano and salt to taste.

Pour the dressing over the salad and toss well. Cover and chill for 30 minutes to allow the flavours to develop well.

Toss the salad again before serving and garnish with the celery leaves.

128 WINTER RADISH SALAD

Preparation time:
5 minutes, plus 10
minutes to stand

Serves 4

Calories:
90 per portion

YOU WILL NEED:
1 large winter radish
salt
150 ml/¼ pint soured cream
1 tablespoon snipped chives, to
    garnish

Scrub or thinly peel the radish. Grate or cut into very thin slices. Place in a bowl and sprinkle generously with salt. Leave to stand for 10-12 minutes. Rinse thoroughly and place in a salad bowl. Spoon over the soured cream, toss well and garnish with the chives.

■ COOK'S TIP

*To make this salad more
filling, garnish with a ring
of hard-boiled egg slices and
tomato wedges.*

■ COOK'S TIP

*It is important to rinse the
radish slices thoroughly to
remove all the salt. Dry
them as completely as
possible between sheets of
absorbent kitchen paper*
*before mixing with the
soured cream.*

129 TURKISH PEPPER SALAD

Preparation time:	YOU WILL NEED:
5 minutes, plus 15 minutes to plump raisins	2 tablespoons seedless raisins
	2 medium green peppers, seeded and cut into thin strips
Serves 4	2 spring onions, finely chopped
	25 g/1 oz pine nuts
Calories:	5 tablespoons olive oil
230 per portion	3 tablespoons lemon juice
	pinch of paprika
Suitable for Vegans	salt and pepper

Soak the raisins in a little warm water for about 15 minutes until plump. Drain well.

Mix together the green peppers, raisins, spring onions and pine nuts and place in a serving bowl.

Mix the oil, lemon juice, paprika and seasoning together and pour over the salad. Toss well to mix.

130 RADISH SALAD

Preparation time:	YOU WILL NEED:
20-25 minutes, plus several hours to chill	3 large bunches of radishes, washed, trimmed and thinly sliced
	1 small onion, thinly sliced and separated into rings
Serves 4-6	2 medium tomatoes, peeled and chopped
	1 teaspoon fresh mint, finely chopped
Calories:	1 lettuce, washed, dried and shredded
90-60 per portion	FOR THE DRESSING
	2 tablespoons olive oil
Suitable for Vegans	2 tablespoons lemon juice
	1½ teaspoons salt
	¼ teaspoon freshly ground black pepper

Put the radish slices, onion rings and tomatoes in a bowl and combine with the mint.

Whisk together the oil, lemon juice, salt and pepper. Pour over the salad ingredients and toss well.

Place on a bed of shredded lettuce and chill thoroughly before serving.

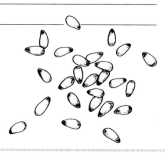

■ COOK'S TIP

Seeds of the Mediterranean stone pine, pine nuts are pale and oval and resemble miniature blanched almonds. Buy them in small quantities.

■ COOK'S TIP

For an extra zesty taste, use the large radishes that are often found during the summer months for this dish.

131 GRAPEFRUIT AND CHICORY SALAD

Preparation time:
15 minutes, plus 30
minutes to chill

Serves 4

Calories:
295 per portion

Suitable for Vegans

YOU WILL NEED:
2 heads of chicory, trimmed, washed
   and dried
2 grapefruit
FOR THE DRESSING
4 tablespoons olive oil
2 tablespoons white wine vinegar
salt and pepper
Tabasco sauce

Cut the chicory crossways into thin slices, and put in a salad bowl.

Squeeze and reserve the juice from half a grapefruit. Peel and remove pith from the remaining grapefruit and divide into segments. Cut each segment in half and mix with the chicory slices.

Combine the oil, vinegar and reserved grapefruit juice and season to taste with salt and pepper and a few drops of Tabasco. Pour over the salad, toss the ingredients together well and chill before serving.

132 ORANGE AND BEETROOT SALAD

Preparation time:
20 minutes

Serves 4

Calories:
80 per portion

YOU WILL NEED:
2 oranges
6 small beetroot, cooked and
   quartered
1 small onion, thinly sliced
FOR THE DRESSING
4 tablespoons natural yogurt
1 tablespoon clear honey
1 garlic clove, crushed
salt and pepper
freshly grated nutmeg

Grate the rind from one of the oranges and mix it with the beetroot, reserving a little for garnish, if liked. Peel both oranges and slice. Remove any obvious pips.

Combine the orange slices with the beetroot and place on a shallow serving dish or plate. Separate the onion slices into rings and sprinkle over the salad.

Place all the dressing ingredients in a bowl and blend thoroughly. Pour over the salad and serve.

▊ COOK'S TIP

This slightly sharp salad goes well with a variety of cheeses and French bread to make a tasty and quick supper.

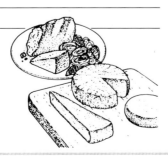

▊ COOK'S TIP

Honey can always be substituted for sugar in salad dressings to add a pleasing flavour and to complement other ingredients with its sweetness. Use this yogurt dressing for coleslaw or Waldorf and green salads.

133 GREEN SALAD WITH PEANUT DRESSING

Preparation time:
15 minutes

Serves 4

Calories:
210 per portion

YOU WILL NEED:
*selection of salad leaves, e.g. lettuce,
    endive, radicchio, watercress*
½ cucumber
1 avocado (optional)
FOR THE DRESSING
*25 g/1 oz salted peanuts, finely
    chopped*
1 teaspoon clear honey
1 tablespoon lemon juice
3 tablespoons groundnut oil
salt and pepper

Wash the salad leaves and dry well. Tear into pieces and place in a salad bowl. Mix together the peanuts, honey and lemon juice. Stir in the oil until well mixed then season with salt and pepper.

Just before serving, slice the cucumber and the avocado, if using, add to the salad and toss all well together with the dressing.

134 TOMATO RING SALAD

Preparation time:
15 minutes, plus
several hours to set

Cooking time:
25 minutes

Serves 4

Calories:
125 per portion

YOU WILL NEED:
*675 g/1½ lb tomatoes, roughly
    chopped*
1 onion, chopped
*150 ml/¼ pint vegetable stock or
    water*
*finely grated rind and juice of 1 orange
    or lemon*
1 small bunch fresh herbs
1 bay leaf
1 garlic clove, crushed (optional)
salt and pepper
2 teaspoons agar-agar
120 ml/4 fl oz water
1 teaspoon soy sauce
FOR THE GARNISH
cress
4 hard-boiled eggs

Cook the tomatoes and onion with the stock or water, orange or lemon rind and juice, herbs, bay leaf, garlic, if using, and seasoning in a covered pan for 20 minutes until pulpy. Remove bay leaf and rub sauce through a sieve to make a purée. Dissolve the agar-agar in the cold water in a small saucepan, then bring to the boil, stirring constantly. Stir into the purée, then add the soy sauce and salt and pepper to taste. Pour into a 600-900 ml/1-1½ pint ring mould, then chill until set. Unmould before serving and garnish.

■ COOK'S TIP

*In composing a green salad,
don't forget about the tiny
seedling cress, bought
growing in punnets and
adding a welcome piquancy
when sprinkled on top.*

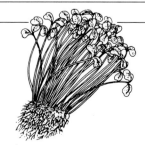

■ COOK'S TIP

*This is a perfect way to use
tomatoes that are too soft
for an ordinary salad.*

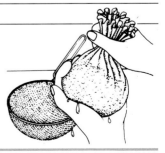

135 OKRA SALAD

Preparation time:
20 minutes

Cooking time:
2 minutes

Serves 4

Calories:
150 per portion

Suitable for Vegans

YOU WILL NEED:
450 g/1 lb okra
1 onion, chopped
FOR THE DRESSING
4 tablespoons sunflower oil
2 tablespoons lemon juice
1 garlic clove, crushed
1 teaspoon sugar
salt and pepper

Trim the ends off the okra and cut into short lengths. Select only the best okra for this salad – they must be in perfect condition. Drop the okra into a large pan of boiling water, bring back to the boil, then drain. Place the okra and onion in a salad bowl.

Mix all the remaining ingredients and toss into the okra, then transfer to a dish and serve at once.

136 TABBOULEH

Preparation time:
15 minutes, plus 1 hour to soak

Serves 4

Calories:
150 per portion

Suitable for Vegans

YOU WILL NEED:
75 g/3 oz bulgur wheat
40 g/1½ oz chopped parsley
3 tablespoons chopped mint
4 spring onions, chopped
½ cucumber, finely diced
2 tablespoons olive oil
juice of 1 lemon
salt and pepper

Soak the bulgur wheat in cold water for 1 hour. Line a sieve with muslin and tip the wheat into it. Lift out the muslin and squeeze out as much moisture as possible.

Place the wheat in a salad bowl and add the remaining ingredients, seasoning with salt and pepper to taste. Add more lemon juice if preferred. Toss thoroughly, then transfer to a shallow dish to serve.

■ COOK'S TIP

Cooked okra has a mucilaginous texture that not everyone appreciates. By merely blanching the pods, this problem is largely avoided.

■ COOK'S TIP

Bulgur wheat is available from health food stores and major supermarkets.

RICE & PASTA

Rice and pasta can be served with an infinite variety of sauces and ingredients and can form the main course of a meal, a tasty supper dish or lunch. The pasta recipes in this chapter are mostly based on the excellent dried packeted shapes, but do have a go at making your own pasta dough, with the added food value of eggs, then shaping it or cutting a ribbon pasta.

137 WHOLEMEAL PASTA SALAD

Preparation time:
5 minutes

Cooking time:
12 minutes

Serves 4

Calories:
310 per portion

YOU WILL NEED:
225 g/8 oz wholewheat pasta twists
3 tablespoons olive oil
1 tablespoon white wine vinegar
¼ teaspoon mustard powder
1 garlic clove, crushed
salt and pepper
2 spring onions, chopped
100 g/4 oz French beans, cooked
4 tomatoes, peeled, quartered and seeded
50 g/2 oz black olives, stoned

Cook the pasta in plenty of boiling salted water for 10-12 minutes or until just tender.

Mix together the oil, vinegar, mustard, garlic and salt and pepper until thickened. Pour over the hot pasta, mix well, cover and leave until cold. Stir in the spring onions, beans and tomatoes and mix well. Turn into a large salad bowl, scatter over the olives and serve.

138 MUNG BEAN AND FRESH HERB RISOTTO

Preparation time:
15 minutes, plus 6 hours to soak

Cooking time:
50 minutes

Serves 4

Calories:
835 per portion

YOU WILL NEED:
350 g/12 oz mung beans, soaked for 2 hours in cold water
25 g/1 oz butter
3 tablespoons vegetable oil
1½ large onions, chopped
450 g/1 lb long-grain brown rice
1.4 litres/2½ pints vegetable stock
6 tablespoons chopped mixed fresh herbs (parsley, thyme, basil, mint)
salt and pepper
4 tablespoons pumpkin seeds

Soak the beans overnight or for 4-6 hours in cold water. Drain the beans, rinse and drain again. Using a large saucepan with a well-fitting lid, heat the butter and 1 tablespoon of the oil and fry the onion for 3 minutes, then stir in the beans and rice. Add the hot stock and bring to the boil. Cover and simmer gently for 40 minutes until beans and rice are tender and all the stock has been absorbed. Add the herbs with salt and pepper and gently fork them through the mixture. Spoon the risotto into a serving dish and keep warm. Fry the pumpkin seeds rapidly in the remaining oil for 30 seconds (take care, as they jump about in the heat) then sprinkle over the risotto. Serve hot.

■ COOK'S TIP

If available, add some chopped fresh basil leaves to the spring onion, bean and tomato mixture.

■ COOK'S TIP

Mung beans will probably be most familiar in their sprouted form, as beansprouts. In dried form they may be bought whole, split and skinless.

139 RISOTTO WITH SPINACH AND HERBS

Preparation time:
15 minutes

Cooking time:
35 minutes

Serves 4-6

Calories:
775-520 per portion

YOU WILL NEED:
2 tablespoons olive oil
100 g/4 oz butter
1 onion, finely chopped
100 g/4 oz mushrooms, sliced
450 g/1 lb Italian risotto rice
  (Arborio)
1.5 litres/2¾ pints hot vegetable stock
225 g/8 oz cooked spinach, chopped
1 teaspoon dried oregano
1 garlic clove, crushed
salt and pepper
75 g/3 oz grated Parmesan or
  Pecorino cheese
lemon wedges, to garnish

Heat the oil and half the butter in a large saucepan. Add the onion and mushrooms and cook for a few minutes until the onions are lightly browned. Stir in the rice and cook for 5 minutes. Add the stock, spinach, oregano, garlic and salt and pepper. Stir well and cook for 20-25 minutes or until the rice is tender and has absorbed all the liquid. Stir in the remaining butter and the grated cheese. Serve the risotto garnished with lemon wedges.

140 RICE AND MUSHROOM BAKE

Preparation time:
10 minutes

Cooking time:
40-45 minutes

Oven temperature:
200 C, 400 F, gas 6

Serves 4

Calories:
415 per portion

YOU WILL NEED:
2 tablespoons vegetable oil
1 large onion, sliced
225 g/8 oz mushrooms, sliced
225 g/8 oz long-grain rice
1 teaspoon cumin powder
1 teaspoon mild chilli powder
1 teaspoon tomato purée
600 ml/1 pint vegetable stock
75 g/3 oz vegetarian Cheddar cheese,
  grated
40 g/1½ oz cornflakes

Heat the oil and cook the onion and mushrooms until softened, about 5 minutes. Add the rice and fry until golden brown. Stir in the spices, tomato purée and stock. Bring to the boil and stir once. Reduce the heat, cover the pan and simmer for 15-18 minutes, until the rice is tender and the liquid absorbed. Stir in half the grated cheese and transfer to an ovenproof casserole. Mix the remaining cheese with the cornflakes, sprinkle on top of the rice and bake in a moderately hot oven for 15-20 minutes, until golden brown.

■ COOK'S TIP

Parmesan and pecorino are both grainy, hard, grating cheeses. Straw-coloured Parmesan is made from cows' milk and pecorino from ewes' milk.

■ COOK'S TIP

Cumin, with its distinctive pungent flavour, is a spice worth investigating both as whole and ground seed. Popular in Mexico, North Africa and the East, it is sold by specialist grocers and supermarkets. Whole seeds keep their flavour longest and may be ground very easily in an electric coffee grinder.

141 RICE SALAD GADO GADO

Preparation time:
10 minutes, plus 30
minutes to cool

Cooking time:
15-18 minutes

Serves 4

Calories:
415 per portion

YOU WILL NEED:
225 g/8 oz long-grain rice
50 g/2 oz mushrooms, halved
600 ml/1 pint vegetable stock
100 g/4 oz beansprouts
2 tomatoes, peeled and quartered
2 hard-boiled eggs, quartered
FOR THE SAUCE
100 g/4 oz salted peanuts
4 spring onions, chopped
1 tablespoon soy sauce
1 teaspoon chilli powder

Put the rice, mushrooms and stock into a covered pan, bring to the boil and simmer gently for 15-18 minutes, until the rice is cooked and all the liquid is absorbed. Allow to cool then mix in the beansprouts, tomatoes and hard-boiled eggs.

Put the remaining ingredients in a liquidizer and blend thoroughly, adding enough water to make a smooth sauce. Pour over the rice salad and serve.

142 SPICED RICE AND COURGETTE SALAD

Preparation time:
15 minutes, plus 1
hour to chill

Cooking time:
40-45 minutes

Serves 4

Calories:
530 per portion

Suitable for Vegans

YOU WILL NEED:
225 g/8 oz long-grain brown rice
1 teaspoon each turmeric, curry
    powder, ground cumin and
    coriander
600 ml/1 pint water
100 g/4 oz courgettes, thinly sliced
2 tablespoons wine vinegar
5 tablespoons groundnut oil
salt
2 carrots, grated
1 onion, finely chopped
100 g/4 oz salted peanuts
1 dessert apple, unpeeled, cored and
    chopped

Place the rice in a saucepan with the spices and water. Bring to the boil then cover and simmer for 35-40 minutes, until the rice is tender and the liquid has been absorbed.

Meanwhile, blanch the courgettes in boiling salted water for 1 minute. Drain, refresh under cold running water and drain again. Turn the rice into a large salad bowl and stir in the vinegar, oil and salt to taste. Cool slightly then add the courgettes, carrots, onion, peanuts and apple. Mix well and chill thoroughly before serving.

■ COOK'S TIP

Made from fermented soya beans, soy sauce is used as extensively in Chinese cookery as salt is in the West. Most commonly dark and pungently flavoured, a more delicate – yet very salty – light soy sauce is also available.

■ COOK'S TIP

Flavourless peanut oil is a good choice for salad dressing. For extra flavour when cooking, first fry several slices of fresh root ginger or garlic in it.

143 VEGETARIAN GUMBO

Preparation time:	YOU WILL NEED:
10 minutes	4 tablespoons corn oil
	25 g/1 oz plain flour
Cooking time:	1 large onion, chopped
20-25 minutes	4 celery sticks, chopped
	1 small green pepper, seeded and
Serves 4	chopped
	225 g/8 oz okra, sliced
Calories:	1 × 397 g/14 oz can tomatoes
280 per portion	300 ml/½ pint vegetable stock
	1 teaspoon Tabasco sauce
Suitable for Vegans	salt and pepper
	350 g/12 oz hot cooked brown rice
	(100 g/4 oz uncooked weight)

Place half the oil in a small, heavy-based pan and heat gently. Add the flour and cook over a low heat, stirring frequently until the roux becomes a rich brown colour, but be careful not to let it burn.

In a large saucepan, heat the remaining oil and cook the onion until tender, about 5 minutes. Add the celery, green pepper and okra and sauté for 3 minutes. Stir the tomatoes, stock, Tabasco and roux into the mixture and simmer, covered, for 10 minutes. Season to taste and serve in individual bowls, topped with a portion of hot brown rice.

144 PASTA PESTO

Preparation time:	YOU WILL NEED:
15 minutes	350 g/12 oz wholewheat caramelli
	shells, or other pasta shapes
Cooking time:	salt and pepper
12 minutes	75 g/3 oz basil leaves
	4 tablespoons olive oil
Serves 4	3 garlic cloves, crushed
	50 g/2 oz pine nuts or blanched
Calories:	slivered almonds
600 per portion	50 g/2 oz Pecorino or Parmesan
	cheese, grated
	25 g/1 oz butter, softened
	grated Pecorino or Parmesan cheese,
	to serve

Cook the pasta in plenty of boiling, salted water for about 12 minutes, or according to the directions on the packet, until just tender. Drain, refresh in hot water and drain again, tossing to ensure that no water is trapped inside the caramelli. Keep hot.

To make the sauce, blend the basil, oil, garlic and nuts in a liquidizer. Remove the mixture to a bowl, beat in the cheese and butter and season with pepper.

Spoon the sauce over the hot pasta and serve at once, with Pecorino or Parmesan.

■ COOK'S TIP

Corn oil, made from the sweetcorn plant, or maize, is among the oils containing polyunsaturated fatty acids. Safflower, sunflower, and soya bean oil are others.

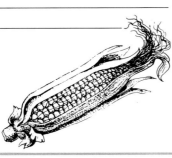

■ COOK'S TIP

It is very easy to grow your own basil in a pot. Basil is also excellent sprinkled on salads, particularly tomato.

145 MUSHROOM PASTA WITH PINE NUTS

Preparation time:
25 minutes

Cooking time:
40 minutes

Serves 4

Calories:
480 per portion

YOU WILL NEED:

1½ tablespoons vegetable oil
1 medium onion, sliced
450 g/1 lb flat open mushrooms, sliced
salt
1-2 teaspoons green peppercorns
1 tablespoon soy sauce
3 tablespoons water
2 tablespoons double or whipping
  cream
350 g/12 oz pasta shapes
2 tablespoons pine nuts
chopped parsley, to garnish

Heat 1 tablespoon oil in a medium saucepan and cook the onion for about 5 minutes. Add the mushrooms and cook for a further few minutes. Add the salt, green peppercorns, soy sauce and water. Cover the pan and simmer gently for about 20 minutes. Remove lid and cook quickly for 1 minute to reduce liquid. Pour into a liquidizer or food processor and blend very briefly, for just a few seconds. Return to the rinsed-out pan and stir in the cream.

Bring a large pan of salted water to the boil. Add the pasta and boil briskly for 10 minutes then drain.

Meanwhile, heat the remaining oil in a small saucepan and fry the pine nuts for 2 minutes until golden brown. Drain on absorbent kitchen paper. To serve, reheat the sauce without boiling and pour over the pasta. Sprinkle with the pine nuts and parsley.

■ COOK'S TIP

This mushroom sauce has a marvellous taste. Use the flat dark mushrooms for the best flavour. Pine nuts or kernels can be bought in health food shops.

146 BROWN RICE AND HAZELNUT SALAD

Preparation time:
20-25 minutes

Cooking time:
40 minutes

Serves 6-8

Calories:
245-185 per portion

Suitable for Vegans

YOU WILL NEED:

175 g/6 oz long-grain brown rice
salt
75 g/3 oz hazelnuts, chopped and
  toasted
1 red pepper, seeded and diced
6 spring onions, finely sliced
3 celery sticks, sliced (optional)
50 g/2 oz button mushrooms, sliced
6 tablespoons French dressing (made
  with 4 tablespoons oil and 2
  tablespoons vinegar, 1 teaspoon
  French mustard, salt and pepper
  and a a pinch of caster sugar)
3 tablespoons chopped parsley

Cook the rice in a saucepan of boiling salted water for 30-40 minutes until tender. Rinse and drain well.

Place in a salad bowl with the remaining ingredients. Add the dressing and toss thoroughly. Serve cold.

■ COOK'S TIP

Instead of the hazelnuts use toasted cashew nuts.

147 BROWN RICE SALAD

Preparation time:
10 minutes, plus 20
minutes to cool

Cooking time:
35 minutes

Serves 4

Calories:
395 per portion

Suitable for Vegans

YOU WILL NEED:
100 g/4 oz long-grain brown rice
salt and pepper
100 g/4 oz shelled peas or sliced beans
100 g/4 oz sweetcorn kernels
150 ml/¼ pint Vinaigrette dressing
  (made with 6 tablespoons oil, 2
  tablespoons vinegar, herbs and salt
  and pepper)
1 red pepper, seeded and diced
50 g/2 oz salted peanuts
1 small onion, grated

Cook the rice in a saucepan of boiling salted water for 30 minutes or until tender. Add the peas or beans and sweetcorn and simmer for a further few minutes until just tender. Drain thoroughly.

Transfer to a medium bowl and add half of the dressing while the rice and vegetables are still hot. Toss well to mix, then leave to cool.

Add the remaining ingredients and dressing. Mix well. Taste and adjust the seasoning just before serving. Serve cold with other salad dishes.

148 MACARONI SPECIAL

Preparation time:
5 minutes

Cooking time:
20 minutes

Serves 4

Calories:
570 per portion

YOU WILL NEED:
225 g/8 oz wholewheat macaroni
225 g/8 oz frozen mixed vegetables
25 g/1 oz butter
1 garlic clove, crushed
3 large tomatoes, peeled and chopped
225 g/8 oz mushrooms, sliced
3 tablespoons chopped parsley
  (optional)
300 ml/½ pint soured cream
50 g/2 oz vegetarian mozzarella
  cheese, coarsely grated
4 tablespoons grated Pecorino or
  Parmesan cheese
4 slices bread, crusts removed, cut
  into triangles and toasted

Cook the macaroni in plenty of boiling water for about 5 minutes, then add the frozen mixed vegetables and cook for a further 7 minutes. Drain.

Melt the butter in a saucepan, cook the garlic for 1 minute, stir in the tomatoes and mushrooms and cook for 3 minutes. Stir in the macaroni mixture, parsley, if using, soured cream and mozzarella and heat gently until mixture is hot and the cheese just melting. Stir in the Pecorino or Parmesan cheese and serve immediately, garnished with the toast triangles.

■ COOK'S TIP

Brown rice has more protein than polished (white) rice. It also has traces of iron, calcium and vitamin B. When cooked it retains much of its bite and is therefore an ideal basis for salads.

■ COOK'S TIP

A soured cream equivalent may be achieved by adding a few drops of lemon juice to fresh double cream.

149 PASTA WITH AUBERGINE

Preparation time:
5 minutes, plus 30
minutes to prepare
aubergine

Cooking time:
25 minutes

Serves 4

Calories:
355 per portion

YOU WILL NEED:
450 g/1 lb aubergine
salt and pepper
225 g/8 oz penne
1 medium onion, chopped
2 garlic cloves, crushed
4 tablespoons sunflower oil
1 teaspoon mustard powder
1 tablespoon tomato purée
1 × 397 g/14 oz can tomatoes
½ teaspoon oregano
1 tablespoon chopped parsley
grated Pecorino or Parmesan cheese to
serve

Cut the aubergine into cubes, place in a colander and sprinkle with salt. Leave for 30 minutes to extract some of the juices, rinse thoroughly and pat dry. Cook the pasta in plenty of boiling salted water for 10-12 minutes or until just cooked. Drain and keep warm. Meanwhile, cook the onion and garlic gently in the oil for 5 minutes until softened. Increase the heat, add the aubergine and cook, stirring, until lightly browned. Stir in the mustard, tomato purée, tomatoes and their juices, oregano, parsley and pepper to taste and simmer the mixture gently for 10 minutes until the aubergine is cooked, stirring occasionally. Pour the sauce over the pasta and serve at once, with Pecorino or Parmesan cheese.

150 SPAGHETTI WITH WALNUT SAUCE

Preparation time:
5 minutes

Cooking time:
20 minutes

Serves 4

Calories:
700 per portion

YOU WILL NEED:
450 g/1 lb spaghetti
salt and pepper
1 medium onion, chopped
2 garlic cloves, crushed
1 tablespoon oil
50 g/2 oz mushrooms, sliced
75 g/3 oz walnuts, finely chopped
bunch of watercress, chopped
300 ml/½ pint soured cream

Cook the spaghetti in plenty of boiling salted water for 10-12 minutes until just tender. Fry the onion and garlic in the oil for about 3 minutes until softened. Add the mushrooms and walnuts and cook for a further 3 minutes over moderate heat. Remove the pan from the heat, stir in the watercress, soured cream and salt and pepper to taste. Reheat very gently. Do not allow the sauce to boil.

Drain the spaghetti and place in a warm serving dish. Pour over the sauce and serve immediately.

■ COOK'S TIP

Be adventurous in selecting pasta shapes: rigatoni and mezze maniche (short sleeves) are other short, tubular ones; the latter is served with summer sauces.

■ COOK'S TIP

To eat pasta at its best, remember to drain it while it is al dente, which means while it still has a bit of bite to it. Test the pasta and remove it from the heat

before the core has become completely soft and it will be cooked to perfection.

151 SPINACH NOODLES

Preparation time:
10 minutes

Cooking time:
15 minutes

Serves 2-3

Calories:
780-520 per portion

YOU WILL NEED:
225 g/8 oz noodles
1 onion, chopped
50 g/2 oz butter
225 g/8 oz spinach, chopped
150 ml/¼ pint natural yogurt
*100 g/4 oz vegetarian low-fat soft
  cheese*
1 teaspoon lemon juice
salt and pepper
¼ teaspoon grated nutmeg

Cook the noodles in boiling salted water for about 12 minutes until tender.

Meanwhile, cook the onion in the butter until soft, but not browned. Add the spinach and continue to cook for 2-3 minutes. Stir in the yogurt, cheese, lemon juice, seasoning and nutmeg and stir over a low heat without boiling. Drain the noodles and add to the hot spinach sauce; toss well then serve immediately.

152 PASTA WITH RATATOUILLE SAUCE

Preparation time:
15-20 minutes

Cooking time:
35 minutes

Serves 4-6

Calories:
500-335 per portion

YOU WILL NEED:
1 large onion, chopped
1 garlic clove, crushed
450 g/1 lb courgettes, sliced
1 large aubergine, diced
1 green pepper, seeded and diced
*450 g/1 lb tomatoes, peeled and
  chopped*
1 tablespoon chopped oregano or basil
salt and pepper
*450 g/1 lb pasta (spaghetti, noodles,
  etc)*
1 tablespoon chopped parsley
*grated Pecorino or Parmesan cheese to
  serve*

Put all the ingredients, except the pasta, parsley and cheese in a large saucepan. Add enough water to cover the vegetables and cook gently for 30 minutes until the vegetables are tender and the juices have thickened slightly, stirring occasionally.

Meanwhile, cook the pasta in a large saucepan in plenty of boiling salted water until just tender (about 5 minutes for freshly made pasta and 15 minutes for dried). Drain and place in a warmed serving dish.

Taste and adjust the seasoning of the sauce, then pour over the pasta. Top with the parsley and grated Pecorino or Parmesan cheese. Serve hot.

■ COOK'S TIP

*For special occasions, use a
full-fat soft cheese such as
Roulé, which is made with a
blend of garlic and fine
herbs.*

■ COOK'S TIP

*This sauce can be served
cold as a starter, without
the pasta. Served in vol-au-
vents it makes an attractive
party snack.*

153 NUTTY RIBBON PASTA

Preparation time:	YOU WILL NEED:
5 minutes	*350 g/12 oz tagliarini or tagliatelli*
	300 ml/½ pint single cream
Cooking time:	*2 large egg yolks*
14-18 minutes	*freshly ground black pepper*
	4 sprigs fresh dill, chopped
Serves 4	*175 g/6 oz salted peanuts, roughly*
	chopped
Calories:	*chopped fresh dill, to garnish*
730 per portion	

Cook the pasta in boiling salted water for about 12-15 minutes, until tender but not soft. Meanwhile, combine the cream, egg yolks, black pepper and dill in a bowl. Stir in the peanuts. Drain the pasta and return it to the pan, then immediately add the cream mixture. Heat gently for 2-3 minutes, stirring to mix thoroughly. Serve immediately sprinkled with fresh dill.

154 PASTA AL POMODORO

Preparation time:	YOU WILL NEED:
10 minutes	*175 g/6 oz pasta bows*
	salt and pepper
Cooking time:	*2 tablespoons grated Parmesan or*
25 minutes	*other cheese*
	FOR THE SAUCE
Serves 2	*1 small onion, finely chopped*
	100 g/4 oz mushrooms, sliced
Calories:	*1 teaspoon sunflower oil*
430 per portion	*1 × 397 g/14 oz can tomatoes*
	1 tablespoon chopped fresh basil
	(optional)
	salt and pepper

Cook the pasta bows in a large pan of boiling salted water for 10-12 minutes. Drain and keep warm.

Meanwhile, make the sauce. Sauté the onion and mushrooms in the oil for 5 minutes, stir in the tomatoes and cook gently, uncovered, for 15 minutes to reduce the sauce. Add the basil, if using, and simmer for a further 5 minutes. Season to taste and serve with the pasta bows, topped with Parmesan and freshly ground black pepper.

▪ COOK'S TIP

The herb dill is especially delicious with eggs, so complements the eggs in this sauce. A herb omelette is another dish in which to use fresh dill.

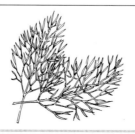

▪ COOK'S TIP

This simple dish is ideal for children, who will enjoy it even more if it is made with tri-coloured pasta – plain, spinach and tomato-flavoured.

155 PASTA WITH BOLINA CHEESE SAUCE

Preparation time:
10 minutes

Cooking time:
10-12 minutes

Serves 4

Calories:
435 per portion

YOU WILL NEED:
275 g/10 oz tagliatelle or pasta shells
125 g/4½ oz Danish Bolina cheese
25 g/1 oz butter
4 tablespoons single cream
2 tablespoons chopped parsley
salt and pepper

Cook the pasta in a large pan of boiling salted water for 10-12 minutes until just tender.

Meanwhile, place the cheese in a bowl. Break it up with a fork, add the butter and set over a pan of boiling water. Cook, stirring occasionally, until the ingredients have melted and blended together. Add the cream and parsley. Season to taste and heat through.

Drain the cooked pasta and place on a heated serving dish. Pour the sauce over the pasta and turn gently with two forks to coat. Serve immediately with a mixed salad and crusty Granary bread.

156 GRATIN OF PASTA

Preparation time:
15 minutes

Cooking time:
25 minutes

Serves 4

Calories:
380 per portion

YOU WILL NEED:
100 g/4 oz pasta shells
salt and pepper
25 g/1 oz butter
25 g/1 oz plain flour
300 ml/½ pint milk
100 g/4 oz vegetarian Cheddar cheese, grated
1 × 283 g/10 oz packet frozen Country stir-fry vegetables
2 tablespoons chopped parsley
2 hard-boiled eggs, sliced

Cook the pasta shells in a large saucepan of boiling salted water for 10-12 minutes, until just tender. Melt the butter, add the flour and cook for a minute. Remove from the heat and gradually stir in the milk. Return to the heat and bring to the boil, stirring continually until the sauce bubbles and thickens. Add the cheese, season to taste and leave to cool slightly.

Cook the stir-fry vegetables according to the packet instructions. Toss the cooked pasta shells in parsley and place in a flameproof serving dish. Sprinkle with the stir-fry vegetables and arrange the egg slices on top. Pour over the cheese sauce and brown under a hot grill, if preferred. Serve immediately.

■ COOK'S TIP

Using a big saucepan with plenty of boiling water to cook the pasta is important. The pasta swells and if it is cramped it will tend to clog together in lumps. Adding a *few drops of oil to the water helps to prevent this.*

■ COOK'S TIP

Pasta shells (conchiglie) are available in a range of sizes and in both plain and wholemeal varieties. They are particularly good with chunky sauces like this one.

157 MARROW LASAGNE

Preparation time: 35 minutes	**YOU WILL NEED:** 1 kg/2 lb whole marrow or squash
	2 tablespoons olive oil
Cooking time: 50 minutes	1 large onion, chopped
	4-6 cardamom pods
Oven temperature: 200 C, 400 F, gas 6	2 teaspoons black peppercorns
	1 teaspoon caster sugar
Serves 6	salt
	225 g/8 oz green lasagne, cooked
Calories: 300 per portion	225 g/8 oz goats' cheese, thinly sliced
	2 tablespoons cornflour
	2 tablespoons milk
	450 ml/¾ pint natural yogurt
	2 tablespoons grated Pecorino or Parmesan cheese

Scoop out the centre of the marrow, or squash, peel and slice the flesh. Cook in boiling water for 15 minutes, or until soft. Drain and mash coarsely.

Heat 1 tablespoon oil in a large pan and cook the onion until soft. Extract the seeds from the cardamom pods and crush with the peppercorns. Stir the ground spices, onion and sugar into the marrow and season. Brush the remaining oil over the base of a 20 × 28 cm/8 × 11 inch ovenproof dish. Layer the lasagne, marrow and goats' cheese in the dish, ending with a last layer of lasagne.

Mix the cornflour, milk and yogurt in a saucepan. Bring gently to the boil, stirring, and cook for 2-3 minutes. Pour over the lasagne and sprinkle with Pecorino or Parmesan. Bake in a moderately hot oven for about 35 minutes.

▧ COOK'S TIP

Green or white cardamom pods have lots of tiny black seeds inside, which should be shiny and highly aromatic. Buy from Indian and Pakistani food stores.

158 VEGETABLE LASAGNE

Preparation time: 10 minutes	**YOU WILL NEED:** 2 tablespoons oil
	225 g/8 oz French beans, chopped
Cooking time: 1½ hours	1 leek or onion, thinly sliced
	salt and pepper
Oven temperature: 180 C, 350 F, gas 4	1 × 397 g/14 oz can tomatoes
	100 g/4 oz lentils
Serves 4	300 ml/½ pint water
	pinch of oregano
Calories: 800 per portion using cream cheese 520 per portion using curd cheese	450 g/1 lb vegetarian cream or curd cheese
	2 eggs, beaten
	100 g/4 oz lasagne, cooked
	2 tablespoons chopped parsley
	2 tablespoons grated Pecorino or Parmesan cheese

Heat the oil in a saucepan and fry the beans and leek or onion for 5 minutes. Season to taste. Add the tomatoes, lentils, water and oregano and bring to the boil. Simmer for about 30 minutes or until the lentils are tender.

Mix together the cream or curd cheese and the eggs. Spread half the vegetable mixture in a 1.2 litre/2 pint ovenproof dish and cover with one-third of the lasagne. Spread half the cheese mixture over, then cover with another layer of lasagne. Make a layer with the remaining vegetable mixture, cover with the remaining lasagne and finally the remaining cheese mixture. Sprinkle over the Pecorino or Parmesan and bake for 40 minutes.

▧ COOK'S TIP

A very popular herb in Italy, oregano, like basil, perfectly complements the flavour of tomatoes. Aubergines and courgettes are also enhanced by its aromatic flavour.

159 SPINACH LASAGNE

Preparation time:
20 minutes

Cooking time:
45 minutes

Oven temperature:
200 C, 400 F, gas 6

Serves 4

Calories:
530 per portion

YOU WILL NEED:
salt and pepper
2 × 225 g/8 oz packets frozen
    spinach, defrosted and drained
¼ teaspoon grated nutmeg
25 g/1 oz pecan nuts, chopped
40 g/1½ oz butter
40 g/1½ oz plain flour
600 ml/1 pint milk
200 g/7oz mature vegetarian Cheddar
    cheese, grated
½ teaspoon prepared English mustard
175 g/6 oz wholewheat lasagne,
    cooked
paprika, to garnish

Season the spinach, add the nutmeg and stir in the nuts. Melt the butter in a saucepan over a low heat, then add the flour. Cook for 2 minutes, stirring. Gradually add the milk and bring the sauce to the boil, stirring constantly. Simmer gently for 2-3 minutes. Add 175 g/6 oz of the cheese and season with salt, pepper and mustard. Layer the spinach and lasagne in an ovenproof dish. Top with the sauce and sprinkle with the reserved cheese. Bake near the top of a moderately hot oven for 20-30 minutes until piping hot and brown on top.

Sprinkle with paprika and serve immediately.

160 COURGETTE AND CAULIFLOWER MACARONI

Preparation time:
30 minutes

Cooking time:
20 minutes

Serves 4

Calories:
605 per portion

YOU WILL NEED:
225 g/8 oz macaroni
salt
225 g/8 oz cauliflower, broken into
    small florets
225 g/8 oz courgettes, finely chopped
FOR THE SAUCE
450 ml/¾ pint milk
50 g/2 oz plain flour
50 g/2 oz margarine, cut up
175 g/6 oz vegetarian Cheddar cheese,
    grated
salt and pepper
paprika to garnish (optional)

Cook the macaroni in boiling salted water for 15 minutes, then drain. Cook the cauliflower in boiling salted water for 5 minutes, adding courgettes for the final 2 minutes. Drain well and reserve 150 ml/¼ pint of the water. Place the vegetables and macaroni in an ovenproof dish.

Whisk the milk, flour and margarine with the reserved vegetable water in a pan over low heat until boiling and thickened. Stir in most of the cheese with seasoning to taste. Pour over the macaroni, sprinkle with the remaining cheese and a little paprika, if using. Brown under a moderate grill, then serve piping hot.

■ COOK'S TIP

A roasting tin is the best container to use for cooking lasagne as it gives the pasta sheets plenty of room. When cooked, lift each sheet from the water separately with a fish slice and place in warm water. Keep the lasagne sheets in the warm water no longer than necessary, as they can absorb too much water.

■ COOK'S TIP

Chop a few sprigs of parsley and stir into the vegetable and macaroni mixture for additional flavour.

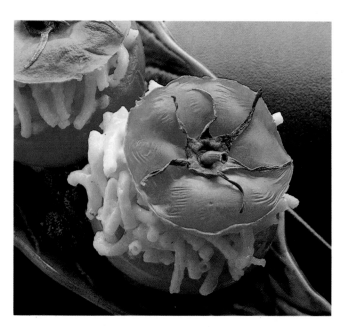

161 RAVIOLI

Preparation time: 40 minutes	**YOU WILL NEED:**
	225 g/8 oz frozen chopped spinach, cooked and drained
Cooking time: 5 minutes	100 g/4 oz vegetarian Cheddar cheese, grated
Serves 4	25 g/1 oz Pecorino or Parmesan cheese, grated
Calories: 720 per portion	1 egg plus 1 yolk, beaten
	¼ teaspoon grated nutmeg
	salt and pepper
	500 g/18 oz strong plain flour
	5 eggs
	½ beaten egg mixed with 1 tablespoon water for brushing

Mix the spinach, cheeses, whole egg and yolk, nutmeg and salt and pepper, cover and chill. Heap the flour on to a working surface and make a well in the centre. Break the 5 eggs into it and with a fork lightly beat them into the flour. Gradually work in all the flour. Knead the dough for 10 minutes until it becomes satiny smooth. Rest the dough for 5 minutes, covered. Halve the dough and roll out each portion thinly to equal size. Brush one with a little of the beaten egg wash, and top with rows of teaspoons of stuffing, about 2.5 cm/1 inch apart. Cover with the second sheet of pasta. Press together around the stuffing. Using pastry wheel, cut the dough into 2.5 cm/1 inch squares. Sprinkle lightly with flour.

Cook the ravioli in batches in boiling salted water for 5 minutes. Drain and serve with tomato sauce (see Cook's Tip 81) and grated Pecorino or Parmesan cheese.

162 MACARONI TOMATOES

Preparation time: 15 minutes	**YOU WILL NEED:**
	4 beefsteak tomatoes
Cooking time: 30 minutes	2 teaspoons oil
	1 small onion, finely chopped
	1 garlic clove, crushed
Oven temperature: 180 C, 350 F, gas 4	½ teaspoon mustard powder
	pinch of paprika
	2 drops of Tabasco sauce
Serves 4	salt and pepper
Calories: 255 per portion	100 g/4 oz vegetarian Cheddar cheese, grated
	100 g/4 oz macaroni, cooked and drained

Cut a lid off the tomatoes, scoop out the centres to leave a thin wall of flesh in each. Place the pulp in a small saucepan with the oil, onion, garlic, mustard, paprika, Tabasco and seasoning. Cover and cook over a low heat for 10 minutes until pulpy, then press through a sieve and mix with the cheese and macaroni. Divide the mixture between the tomatoes and place the 'lids' on top. Bake for 15-20 minutes until the tomatoes are soft and the macaroni is beginning to brown. Serve at once.

■ COOK'S TIP

If you want to go Italian replace the Cheddar cheese in the filling with soft ricotta cheese. You will need to double the quantity to 225 g/ 8 oz. Made from whey, ricotta is lighter in flavour and texture than cream cheese, but not tangy like curd cheese. Italian food stores, delicatessens, and supermarkets stock it.

■ COOK'S TIP

If you happen to grow rosemary in your garden, then snip off a sprig, chop finely and add to the tomato pulp and the other seasonings before cooking and sieving.

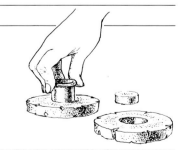

163 CORSICAN CANNELLONI

Preparation time:
15 minutes

Cooking time:
55 minutes

Oven temperature:
180 C, 350 F, gas 4

Serves 4

Calories:
275 per portion

YOU WILL NEED:

750 ml/1¼ pints boiling water
½ teaspoon vegetable oil
8 sheets 'No-need-to-precook' lasagne verde
225 g/8 oz frozen ratatouille mix
100 g/4 oz frozen broad beans
2 teaspoons chopped fresh mixed herbs
freshly ground black pepper
1 × 397 g/14 oz can chopped tomatoes
100 g/4 oz mature vegetarian Cheddar cheese, grated, to serve

Pour the boiling water into a suitably shaped large shallow ovenproof dish. Add a few drops of oil. Slide the sheets of lasagne into the dish and leave for 4-5 minutes to soften. Cook the ratatouille and beans in boiling water in a medium saucepan for about 10 minutes or until cooked. Drain well. Add the herbs and freshly ground black pepper to taste.

Lift out the lasagne sheets from the water and drain. Spread out on a clean working surface or large board. Divide the vegetable filling between the lasagne then roll up the strips. Place the cannelloni in a shallow ovenproof dish and spoon over the tomatoes. Cook in a moderate oven for 30 minutes. To serve, sprinkle with grated cheese and place under a preheated hot grill until brown.

164 TROPICAL SALAD

Preparation time:
15 minutes

Cooking time:
5 minutes

Serves 4

Calories:
475 per portion

Suitable for Vegans

YOU WILL NEED:

275 g/10 oz long-grain brown rice, cooked
50 g/2 oz dried coconut flakes
½ cucumber, unpeeled and cut into 1 cm/½ inch cubes
1 small ripe pineapple, peeled, cored and cut into 2.5 cm/1 inch pieces
1 tablespoon olive oil
1 teaspoon lemon juice
salt and pepper
2 teaspoons olive oil for shallow frying
50 g/2 oz whole blanched almonds
pineapple leaves, to garnish

Put the rice, coconut, cucumber and pineapple into a bowl. Add the oil and lemon juice and a little salt and pepper, taste and adjust the seasoning if necessary. Spoon the salad into a serving dish.

Heat the 2 teaspoons of oil in a small pan and quickly fry the almonds until golden brown. Scatter the almonds over the salad and garnish with the pineapple leaves.

■ FREEZER TIP

Cover the cannelloni with foil and freeze for up to 3 months. Reheat from frozen in a moderate oven (180 C, 350 F, gas 4) for about 30 minutes, then top with the cheese and place under a hot grill to brown.

■ COOK'S TIP

To remove the centre core from a slice of pineapple, stamp out with a small plain pastry cutter.

165 SZECHUAN NOODLES

Preparation time:
10 minutes, plus 15
minutes to prepare
cucumber

Cooking time:
8 minutes

Serves 4

Calories:
720 per portion

YOU WILL NEED:
½ cucumber, cut into 1 cm/½ inch
  dice
salt
small bunch of radishes, trimmed
1 spring onion, trimmed
450 g/1 lb fresh egg noodles or dried
  noodles
100 g/4 oz beansprouts
4 tablespoons peanut oil
3-4 tablespoons crunchy peanut butter
1 teaspoon sesame oil
25 g/1 oz salted peanuts, lightly
  crushed

Sprinkle the cucumber with salt and leave to drain for 15 minutes. Rinse and dry on absorbent kitchen paper. Slice a third of the radishes, leaving the remainder whole. Slice the spring onion diagonally. Meanwhile, cook the fresh noodles for 1 minute in boiling salted water, then drain thoroughly. Cook dried noodles as directed on the packet. Blanch the beansprouts in boiling water for 1 minute. Plunge into cold water, then drain thoroughly.

Fry the drained noodles quickly in 3 tablespoons of the peanut oil, stirring constantly. Transfer to a hot serving plate. Put the remaining oil into a pan with the peanut butter and sesame oil and heat gently. Pour over the noodles and mix lightly.

Arrange the prepared ingredients attractively on top and serve. Serve the remaining radishes in a bowl.

166 RICE AND BEANS

Preparation time:
10 minutes

Cooking time:
40 minutes

Serves 4

Calories:
475 per portion

Suitable for Vegans

YOU WILL NEED:
225 g/8 oz long-grain brown rice
750 ml/1¼ pints boiling water
3 tablespoons sunflower oil
1 tablespoon red wine vinegar
salt and pepper
4 spring onions, chopped
1 × 415 g/14½ oz can red kidney
  beans
50 g/2 oz button mushrooms, sliced
225 g/8 oz tomatoes
4 tablespoons French dressing (see
  recipe 146)
50 g/2 oz black olives
chopped parsley, to garnish

Cook the rice in the water for 40 minutes or until cooked and the water absorbed. Mix together the oil, vinegar and salt and pepper. Fluff up the rice with a fork and stir in the spring onions and oil and vinegar dressing. Cool.

Mix together the kidney beans and mushrooms. Slice the tomatoes and pour over the French dressing. Stir in the olives and salt and pepper to taste.

On a large serving plate, arrange a circle of rice salad round the edge, a circle of bean salad inside, and the tomato mixture in the middle. Scatter over the parsley to garnish.

▌ COOK'S TIP

*Peanut and sesame oil are
used in this recipe as they
add a distinctive flavour,
favoured by the Chinese.*

▌ COOK'S TIP

*The difference between
black and green olives is
that the black ones are ripe.
Black olives vary from
plump and succulent to
small and wrinkly.*

167 VEGETABLE RISOTTO

Preparation time:
15 minutes

Cooking time:
55-60 minutes

Serves 4

Calories:
465 per portion

Suitable for Vegans

YOU WILL NEED:
4 tablespoons oil
1 onion, chopped
175 g/6 oz long-grain brown rice
3 garlic cloves, crushed
450 ml/¾ pint water
1 teaspoon salt
2 celery sticks, thinly sliced
1 red pepper, seeded and diced
225 g/8 oz button mushrooms, sliced
1 × 415 g/14½ oz can red kidney beans
3 tablespoons chopped parsley
1 tablespoon soy sauce
50 g/2 oz cashew nuts, roasted
chopped parsley, to garnish

Heat 2 tablespoons oil in a pan, add the onion and cook until softened, about 5 minutes. Add the rice and 2 garlic cloves and sauté, stirring, for 2 minutes. Pour in the water, add salt and bring to the boil. Cover and simmer gently for 35-40 minutes, until all the water has been absorbed and the rice is tender.

Heat the remaining oil in a large frying pan, add the celery and red pepper and cook for 5 minutes, until softened. Stir in the mushrooms and remaining garlic and sauté for 3 minutes. Add the cooked rice, drained kidney beans, parsley, soy sauce and nuts. Cook, stirring to mix, until the beans are heated through. Garnish with parsley and serve with a green salad.

▌ COOK'S TIP

It is unnecessary to wash cultivated mushrooms, as well as being detrimental to their nutritional content. Simply wipe them with a damp cloth before use.

168 CREAMY CURRIED PASTA

Preparation time:
10 minutes

Cooking time:
15 minutes

Serves 4

Calories:
465 per portion

YOU WILL NEED:
225 g/8 oz pasta shapes
salt and pepper
3 tablespoons olive oil
1 tablespoon white wine vinegar
1 teaspoon chopped fresh mint
1 medium onion, finely chopped
4 tablespoons dry vermouth
2 teaspoons mild concentrated curry paste
2 teaspoons apricot jam
50 g/2 oz slivered or flaked almonds, toasted
150 ml/¼ pint soured cream
½ bunch watercress, chopped

Cook the pasta in plenty of boiling salted water for 10-12 minutes or until just tender. Drain.

Meanwhile, mix together the oil, vinegar, mint and salt and pepper to make a dressing. Pour over the hot pasta and leave until cold.

Place the onion and vermouth in a pan and bring to the boil. Simmer for 3 minutes, then cool. Stir the curry paste and jam into the pasta mixture. Stir in the onion mixture. Turn the mixture into a serving dish and scatter the almonds on top. Mix together the soured cream and watercress and serve separately with a salad.

▌ COOK'S TIP

Choose small, chunky shapes, such as orecchiette or conchiglie, which provide ideal surfaces for the dressing; or lumachine, which act like containers.

Suppers & Snacks

Choose a super-speedy snack when in a hurry, a gratin or bake for a satisfying supper dish. All are highly nutritious. The recipes in this chapter make good use of a large number of store-cupboard items, as well as incorporating plenty of fresh ingredients, such as vegetables, herbs, fresh cheeses and eggs.

169 CHEESE AND SEMOLINA BAKE

Preparation time:
10 minutes, plus 10 minutes to stand

Cooking time:
35 minutes

Oven temperature:
200 C, 400 F, gas 6
then
240 C, 475 F, gas 9

Serves 4

Calories:
335 per portion

YOU WILL NEED:
250 ml/8 fl oz vegetable stock
250 ml/8 fl oz milk
salt and white pepper
grated nutmeg
100 g/4 oz wholemeal semolina
2 eggs
150 g/5 oz vegetarian Gruyère cheese, grated
25 g/1 oz butter
2 tablespoons chopped mixed herbs

Bring the vegetable stock to the boil in a pan with the milk and a little salt, pepper and nutmeg. Remove the pan from the heat and gradually stir in the semolina. Cover the pan and leave to stand for about 10 minutes.

Beat the eggs with a fork until frothy. Stir into the semolina mixture with half the Gruyère. Grease a baking dish with a little of the butter. Fill with the semolina mixture and smooth the top. Bake in a moderately hot oven for 10 minutes. Increase the temperature to very hot. Bake for 10 minutes more.

Mix the remaining Gruyère with the herbs and spread over the dish. Dot with the remaining butter and bake for a further 10 minutes until the top is golden brown. Serve with a colourful mixed salad.

170 AUBERGINES AU GRATIN

Preparation time:
15 minutes, plus 15 minutes to prepare aubergine

Cooking time:
20 minutes

Oven temperature:
220 C, 425 F, gas 7

Serves 4

Calories:
290 per portion

YOU WILL NEED:
2 large aubergines, cut into large cubes
salt and pepper
3 tomatoes, sliced
1 courgette, sliced
1 bunch of mixed herbs (e.g. parsley, basil, rosemary), chopped
150 ml/¼ pint double cream
2 eggs, beaten
15 g/½ oz butter
1 garlic clove, peeled and halved
2 tablespoons dry white breadcrumbs

Sprinkle the aubergines with salt and leave to drain for about 15 minutes. Rinse and wipe dry with absorbent kitchen paper. Arrange alternate layers of aubergine, tomato and courgette in a greased ovenproof dish. Sprinkle with the chopped herbs.

Mix the cream with the eggs, add salt and pepper to taste and pour over the vegetable mixture.

Melt the butter in a small saucepan, add the garlic and fry for a few minutes until golden brown. Remove and discard the garlic. Add the breadcrumbs to the garlic-flavoured butter and cook for 1-2 minutes. Sprinkle over the vegetables in the dish. Cook in a hot oven for 12-15 minutes, or until golden brown. Serve hot.

■ COOK'S TIP

Semolina is a granular durum (hard) wheat flour rich in protein. It is often used with plain flour to increase the gluten content and so help pastries to hold their shape.

■ COOK'S TIP

Individual cloves of garlic vary enormously in size. When a recipe calls for 1 garlic clove, choose one about the size of the top joint on your little finger.

171 RED PEPPER MACARONI CHEESE

Preparation time:
20 minutes

Cooking time:
20 minutes

Serves 4

Calories:
740 per portion

YOU WILL NEED:
25 g/1 oz butter
25 g/1 oz plain flour
750 ml/1¼ pints milk
salt and pepper
½ teaspoon prepared English mustard
large pinch of cayenne
¼ teaspoon grated nutmeg
1 red pepper, seeded, cut into 1 cm/½
    inch dice and blanched
225 g/8 oz mature vegetarian Cheddar
    cheese, grated
175 g/6 oz wholewheat macaroni,
    cooked
2 tablespoons chopped parsley
12 triangles wholewheat bread, fried,
    to garnish

Melt the butter in a large saucepan over a low heat, then add the flour. Cook for 2 minutes, stirring. Gradually add the milk and bring to the boil, stirring constantly. Simmer for 2-3 minutes. Add salt, pepper, mustard, cayenne, nutmeg, red pepper and 200 g/7oz of the cheese. Add the macaroni and parsley, and heat through. Transfer to a flameproof dish, top with the remaining cheese and grill to brown. Garnish with the fried bread triangles and serve.

172 CRUMBLY NUT ROAST

Preparation time:
30 minutes

Cooking time:
1 hour 10 minutes

Oven temperature:
220 C, 425 F, gas 7

Serves 4

Calories:
535 per portion

YOU WILL NEED:
40 g/1½ oz butter
1 medium onion, chopped
1 celery stick, trimmed, scrubbed and
    chopped
225 g/8 oz mixed nuts (walnuts,
    brazils and hazelnuts in equal
    quantities), coarsely chopped
3 large tomatoes, peeled and chopped
175 g/6 oz fresh wholewheat
    breadcrumbs
salt and pepper
1 teaspoon mixed dried herbs
¼ teaspoon chilli powder
2 eggs, lightly beaten

Oil a 450 g/1 lb loaf tin and line the base with oiled grease-proof paper. Melt the butter in a large saucepan and fry the onion and celery gently for 5 minutes without browning. Add the nuts, tomatoes, breadcrumbs, salt and pepper, mixed herbs and chilli. Add the eggs and mix to a fairly soft consistency, then taste and adjust seasoning if necessary.

Spoon the mixture into the prepared tin, cover with oiled foil and bake in a hot oven for 50-60 minutes, or until set.

Ease off the foil and run a knife around the sides of the tin. Turn the loaf out on to a warm dish and serve with salad and buttered pasta, if liked.

■ COOK'S TIP

To add extra flavour, place a few tomato slices and some chopped fried onion on the base of the dish before adding the macaroni cheese.

■ COOK'S TIP

The uncooked nut roast mixture can be prepared up to 8 hours in advance and kept covered.

173 COURGETTE GRATIN

Preparation time:
20 minutes

Cooking time:
45 minutes

Oven temperature:
180 C, 350 F, gas 4

Serves 4

Calories:
320 per portion

YOU WILL NEED:
2 tablespoons oil
2 onions, sliced
1 garlic clove, crushed
350 g/12 oz courgettes, sliced
1 tablespoon chopped parsley
1 teaspoon chopped thyme
salt and pepper
4 large tomatoes, peeled and sliced
25 g/1 oz margarine
25 g/1 oz wholemeal flour
300 ml/½ pint milk
100 g/4 oz vegetarian Cheddar cheese, grated
1 tablespoon fresh wholewheat breadcrumbs

Heat the oil in a pan and cook the onions until softened. Add the garlic, courgettes, herbs and salt and pepper to taste, and cook for 5 minutes, stirring occasionally. Put half in an oven-proof dish and top with tomatoes, then spread the remaining mixture on top.

Melt the margarine in a saucepan over a low heat, then add the flour. Cook for 2 minutes, stirring. Gradually add the milk and bring the sauce to the boil, stirring constantly. Simmer gently for 2-3 minutes. Add half of the cheese, and salt and pepper to taste, then pour over the courgettes. Sprinkle with the breadcrumbs, then the remaining cheese. Bake in a moderate oven for 30 minutes until golden.

174 LEEK, POTATO AND CORIANDER BAKE

Preparation time:
15 minutes

Cooking time:
1¼ hours

Oven temperature:
200 C, 400 F, gas 6

Serves 4

Calories:
315 per portion

YOU WILL NEED:
450 g/1 lb leeks, trimmed and washed
1 kg/2 lb small potatoes, scrubbed and dried
1 tablespoon oil
25 g/1 oz butter
1 teaspoon black peppercorns
2 teaspoons coriander seeds
1 teaspoon sea salt

Slice the leeks into 2 cm/¾ inch rings and cut the potatoes into 1 cm/½ inch slices.

Put the oil and butter in a large shallow roasting tin and place in the oven until the butter is just melted. Add the leeks and potatoes, turning them over several times to coat them with the oil and butter. Crush the peppercorns with the coriander seeds in a pestle and mortar.

Put the crushed pepper and coriander in a small bowl and add the salt. Sprinkle evenly over the potatoes and leeks and stir through.

Cover the tin tightly with foil. Bake in a moderately hot oven for 45 minutes. Remove the foil, turn the potatoes and leeks over and put back near the top of the oven for a further 30 minutes until brown. Serve hot.

■ COOK'S TIP

To peel tomatoes, place them in a bowl and pour on freshly boiling water. Leave for 30-60 seconds, depending on ripeness, then drain and slit the skins which should slide off easily. Alternatively, hold a tomato on a fork over a gas flame until the skin splits. Turn the tomato slowly all the time.

■ COOK'S TIP

If you do not have a pestle and mortar, put the seeds and peppercorns between 2 double sheets of greaseproof paper and crush firmly with a rolling pin.

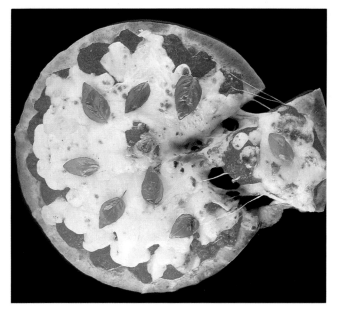

175 PROVENCAL EGGS

Preparation time:
10 minutes

Cooking time:
25 minutes

Oven temperature:
190 C, 375 F, gas 5

Serves 4

Calories:
235 per portion

YOU WILL NEED:
2 tablespoons oil
1 large onion, thinly sliced
1 garlic clove, crushed
1 red pepper, seeded and sliced
225 g/8 oz courgettes, sliced
1 teaspoon oregano
1 × 397 g/14 oz can tomatoes
salt and pepper
a few drops of Tabasco sauce
4 eggs
50 g/2 oz vegetarian Cheddar cheese,
  grated

Heat the oil in a large saucepan, add the onion and garlic and cook until softened, about 5 minutes. Add the pepper and courgettes and cook for 5 minutes. Stir in the oregano, tomatoes and their juices, salt and pepper and Tabasco and heat through. Pour mixture into a shallow ovenproof dish. Make four hollows in the mixture and break an egg into each. Sprinkle cheese over eggs. Bake for 12-15 minutes or until the eggs are just set. Serve hot.

176 PIZZA MARGHERITA

Preparation time:
35 minutes, plus
time to rise and
prove

Cooking time:
30 minutes

Oven temperature:
220 C, 425 F, gas 7

Serves 4

Calories:
360 per portion

YOU WILL NEED:
FOR THE DOUGH
225 g/8 oz strong plain flour
1 teaspoon salt
7 g/1/4 oz fresh yeast
150 ml/1/4 pint lukewarm water
FOR THE TOPPING
1 tablespoon oil
1 large onion, chopped
1 garlic clove, crushed
1 × 397 g/14 oz can tomatoes,
  chopped if liked
salt and pepper
100 g/4 oz vegetarian mozzarella,
  sliced
basil leaves, to garnish

To make the dough, put the flour and salt in a bowl. Blend the fresh yeast with water until dissolved, add to the flour and mix to a firm dough. Knead on a lightly floured surface for 10 minutes. Put the dough in a warm, greased bowl, cover with greased polythene and leave in a warm place until doubled in size.

Heat the oil in a saucepan. Add the onion and garlic and fry until soft. Add the tomatoes and seasoning. Knead the dough for 2 minutes, roll to a 23 cm/9 inch circle and place on a greased baking tray. Top with the tomato mixture and mozzarella slices. Leave to rise in a warm place for 15 minutes. Bake in a hot oven for 20-25 minutes. Garnish with basil leaves.

■ COOK'S TIP

Tabasco sauce gets its name from the part of Mexico which produced the peppers from which it was originally made. The peppers are pulped, salted and matured for 3 years, then mixed with distilled vinegar. After being clarified, the sauce is bottled. A fiery relish, a few drops are sufficient to impart a pleasing tang.

■ COOK'S TIP

Instead of fresh yeast use 1 teaspoon dried yeast. To prepare dried yeast dissolve 1/4 teaspoon sugar in the water, sprinkle in the yeast and set aside until frothy.

177 POTATO AND COURGETTE OMELETTE

Preparation time:	YOU WILL NEED:
5 minutes	450 g/1 lb potatoes, grated
	2 tablespoons olive oil
Cooking time:	225 g/8 oz courgettes, coarsely grated
20 minutes	1 garlic clove, crushed
Serves 4	6 eggs, beaten
	a few drops of Tabasco sauce
Calories:	salt and pepper
300 per portion	

Place the potatoes in a sieve and press out the excess moisture. Heat the oil in a large frying pan, add the potatoes and fry quickly until browned and almost cooked, about 10 minutes. Add the courgettes and garlic and cook gently for 5 minutes. Stir in the eggs, Tabasco and salt and pepper and cook gently until just set, about 5 minutes. Remove pan from heat, cut omelette into wedges and serve hot with a fresh mixed salad.

■ COOK'S TIP

Accompany each omelette with a simple side salad of tomato and basil, served with a vinaigrette dressing enlivened by a splash of soy sauce.

178 CAULIFLOWER OMELETTES

Preparation time:	YOU WILL NEED:
5 minutes	½ cauliflower, cut into florets
	salt
Cooking time:	2 tablespoons double cream
45 minutes	pinch of grated nutmeg
Serves 4	1 egg yolk
	1 tablespoon grated Pecorino or
Calories:	Parmesan cheese
310 per portion	pinch of dried basil
	6 eggs
	oil for frying
	75 g/3 oz vegetarian Gruyère cheese, grated
	FOR THE GARNISH
	tomato wedges
	parsley sprigs

Place the cauliflower florets in a medium saucepan. Add boiling water to cover and a pinch of salt. Bring to the boil, then lower the heat and cook for about 20 minutes.

Drain and blend in a liquidizer or pass through a fine sieve. Add the cream, nutmeg, egg yolk, Pecorino or Parmesan cheese and basil, mixing well.

Beat the eggs with a little salt. Heat a little oil in a frying pan. When hot, add one quarter of the egg mixture and cook for 2-3 minutes or until set.

Spread with one quarter of the cauliflower purée, fold over to enclose and sprinkle generously with one quarter of the Gruyère cheese. Place under a hot grill until the cheese melts; keep warm. Make three more omelettes in the same way. Garnish and serve.

■ COOK'S TIP

The oil should be very hot before the omelette mixture is added. Turn down the heat and as the omelette begins to cook draw the sides towards the centre.

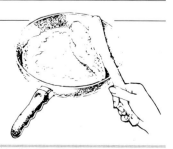

179 STUFFED PANCAKES

Preparation time:
50 minutes

Cooking time:
1 hour 5 minutes

Oven temperature:
200 C, 400 F, gas 6

Serves 5

Calories:
705 per portion

YOU WILL NEED:
FOR THE BATTER
100 g/4 oz plain flour
pinch of salt
1 egg, plus 1 yolk, beaten
300 ml/½ pint milk
1 tablespoon vegetable oil
50 g/2 oz lard or oil for frying
FOR THE FILLING
10 leeks, trimmed, slit and washed
FOR THE SAUCE
75 g/3 oz butter or margarine
75 g/3 oz plain flour
1 litre/1¾ pints milk
salt and pepper
125 g/5 oz Pecorino or Parmesan
    cheese, grated

To make the batter, place all the ingredients in a liquidizer and blend until smooth. Use to make 10 pancakes (see Cook's Tip). Set the leeks in a steamer over a pan of boiling water. Cover and cook for 10 minutes until tender. Set aside. To make the sauce, melt the butter or margarine in a saucepan over a low heat, then add the flour. Cook for 2 minutes, stirring. Gradually add the milk and bring the sauce to the boil, stirring constantly. Simmer gently for 2-3 minutes. Season to taste. Cool a little and add 100 g/4 oz of the cheese.

Place a leek and a little sauce on each pancake. Roll up and arrange in a greased ovenproof dish. Pour over remaining sauce and sprinkle with the 25 g/1 oz cheese. Bake in a moderately hot oven for 25-30 minutes.

■ COOK'S TIP

Oil a frying pan, heat slowly until very hot, then pour in a little batter. Tilt pan to cover the base, cook to set, turn the pancake and brown the second side.

180 FRITTATA

Preparation time:
15 minutes

Cooking time:
7 minutes

Serves 2

Calories:
310 per portion

YOU WILL NEED:
25 g/1 oz butter
4 eggs, beaten
275 g/10 oz spinach, cooked and
    lightly chopped, or 100 g/4 oz
    frozen spinach, cooked
3 firm tomatoes, peeled and coarsely
    chopped
100 g/4 oz cooked potatoes, diced, or
    75 g/3 oz cooked brown rice
salt and pepper
1 teaspoon chopped sage or ¼
    teaspoon dried sage
few drops of Tabasco sauce

Heat half the butter in a large frying pan until sizzling. Pour in the beaten eggs and stir for a few seconds. Allow the eggs to settle in the pan and then distribute the spinach, tomatoes, and potatoes or rice evenly over the surface. Sprinkle with salt, pepper, sage and Tabasco sauce. Cook gently for about 4 minutes until the underside is set and golden brown. Gently lift the edge with a fish slice to check. When the underside is done, tip the omelette out on to a large plate so that the cooked side is on top.

Add the remaining butter to the pan and melt, coating the base. Slide the omelette back into the pan and cook the other side for about 3 minutes. Cut the cooked Frittata into quarters and serve hot or cold.

■ COOK'S TIP

Butter burns more readily than oil and must be carefully watched while melting. To alleviate this problem, use a mixture of butter and oil.

181 AUBERGINE GALETTE

Preparation time:
20 minutes, plus 1
hour to prepare
aubergines

Cooking time:
1 hour 10 minutes

Oven temperature:
180 C, 350 F, gas 4

Serves 4

Calories:
460 per portion

YOU WILL NEED:
2 large aubergines
salt and pepper
150 ml/¼ pint olive oil
1 onion, chopped
1 garlic clove, crushed
450 g/1 lb tomatoes, peeled and
    chopped
1 egg
225 g/8 oz vegetarian ricotta or curd
    cheese
1 tablespoon sesame seeds, toasted
crusty wholewheat bread, to serve

Slice the aubergines, sprinkle with salt and leave in a colander
for 1 hour. Rinse well and dry on absorbent kitchen paper.
Heat 2 tablespoons of the oil in a pan and cook the onion
until softened. Add the garlic and tomatoes and simmer, uncovered, for 5-7 minutes.

Mix the egg with the cheese, adding salt and pepper to
taste. Heat the remaining oil in a frying pan and cook the
aubergine slices on both sides until golden. Drain on absorbent kitchen paper.

Arrange a layer of overlapping aubergine slices on the
base and sides of an 18 cm/7 inch springform cake tin. Cover
with half the tomato mixture, then top with half the cheese
mixture. Repeat the layers, finishing with aubergine. Cover
with foil and bake in a moderate oven for 40-50 minutes.
Turn out on to a serving dish and sprinkle with sesame seeds.

■ COOK'S TIP

*Toast sesame seeds under
the grill or in a dry frying
pan for 3-4 minutes,
shaking the pan
continuously. Alternatively,
roast the seeds in the oven.*

182 SPINACH AND POTATO PATTIES

Preparation time:
15 minutes

Cooking time:
20 minutes

Serves 3-4

Calories:
450-340 per portion

YOU WILL NEED:
1 tablespoon oil
1 onion, chopped
1 garlic clove, crushed
225 g/8 oz frozen chopped spinach,
    defrosted and drained
450 g/1 lb potatoes, boiled and
    mashed
¼ teaspoon grated nutmeg
100 g/4 oz vegetarian Cheddar cheese,
    grated
salt and pepper
wholemeal flour for coating
oil for shallow frying
watercress sprigs, to garnish

Heat the oil in a pan and cook the onion and garlic until softened. Squeeze the spinach dry and add to the pan with the
potato, nutmeg, cheese and salt and pepper to taste; mix
thoroughly.

Shape the mixture into eight balls, using dampened
hands, and flatten slightly. Place some flour in a plastic bag,
add the patties one at a time and shake to coat completely.

Fry the patties in hot oil for 2 minutes on each side until
golden brown. Garnish with watercress and serve with salad
and crusty bread.

■ COOK'S TIP

*The peppery flavour of
mineral-rich watercress is
the perfect foil for these
patties.*

183 CHEESY BANANA MUFFINS

Preparation time:
5 minutes

Serves 4

Calories:
210 per portion

YOU WILL NEED:
4 *wholewheat muffins, split in half*
and toasted
butter to spread
a little yeast extract, to spread
(optional)
75 *g/3 oz vegetarian low-fat hard*
cheese, grated
a little cress
1 *banana, thinly sliced*

Lightly spread the muffins with butter and spread four halves with yeast extract (if liked). Top the yeast-spread muffins with cheese, a sprinkling of cress and a few banana slices. Replace the muffin tops and serve at once with a selection of fresh salad ingredients.

184 TOFU CAKES

Preparation time:
15 minutes

Cooking time:
10-15 minutes

Serves 4

Calories:
210 per cake

YOU WILL NEED:
350 *g/12 oz tofu*
6 *spring onions, chopped*
2 *tablespoons chopped parsley*
3 *tablespoons finely chopped walnuts*
100 *g/4 oz fine wholewheat*
breadcrumbs
2 *tablespoons grated Pecorino or*
Parmesan cheese
salt and pepper
oil for shallow frying

Mix the tofu with the spring onions, parsley, nuts, breadcrumbs and Pecorino or Parmesan. Season to taste. Knead by hand to bind together and season to taste. Shape the mixture into eight round cakes.

Heat the oil for shallow frying and fry the cakes in batches until light golden brown, turning once. Drain on absorbent kitchen paper and keep hot while frying the remainder.

Serve with a crisp salad.

■ COOK'S TIP

For a school lunchbox treat, use bread rolls (untoasted) instead of muffins, wrapping them in foil to keep the filling in place.

■ COOK'S TIP

Caper cream sauce goes well with these tofu cakes. Simply stir 1 tablespoon chopped capers and 1 teaspoon tomato purée into 150 ml/¼ pint soured cream or *fromage frais. Serve the sauce as an accompaniment.*

185 CRUNCHY TOFU

Preparation time:
15 minutes, plus 1
hour to chill

Cooking time:
10-15 minutes

Serves 4

Calories:
280 per portion

YOU WILL NEED:
450 g/1 lb tofu
4 tablespoons plain flour
grated nutmeg
salt and pepper
1 egg, beaten
75-100 g/3-4 oz dry white
　　breadcrumbs
900 ml/1½ pints oil for deep frying
FOR THE SAUCE
1 large garlic clove, crushed
2 tablespoons tomato purée
4 tablespoons chopped herbs
150 ml/¼ pint double cream, lightly
　　whipped
FOR THE GARNISH
watercress sprigs
lemon wedges

Cut the tofu into slices. Mix the flour, nutmeg and seasoning. Coat the tofu in the seasoned flour, beaten egg and breadcrumbs. Chill. Mix the ingredients for the sauce and chill until required. Heat the oil for deep frying to 190 C/375 F. Fry the tofu until crisp and golden, then drain on absorbent kitchen paper. Garnish and serve piping hot with the chilled sauce.

186 SAVOURY WAFFLES

Preparation time:
10 minutes

Cooking time:
20-25 minutes

Makes 10-12

Calories:
195-160 per waffle

YOU WILL NEED:
100 g/4 oz wholemeal flour
2 teaspoons baking powder
pinch of salt
50 g/2 oz fine oat flakes
2 eggs, separated
50 g/2 oz butter or margarine
300 ml/½ pint milk
FOR THE TOPPING
225 g/8 oz vegetarian ricotta cheese
2 tablespoons toasted sunflower seeds
1 tablespoon sesame seeds
4 tomatoes, chopped
4 spring onions, chopped

Mix together the flour, baking powder and salt and stir in the oats. Combine the egg yolks with the butter or margarine and the milk, blending well. Make a well in the dry ingredients, pour in the milk mixture and beat until well blended. Whisk the egg whites until stiff and fold them into the batter.

Prepare a waffle iron, following the manufacturer's instructions. Pour in just enough batter to cover the plates, close the iron and cook quickly for 2 minutes or until the waffle is golden and crisp. Use the rest of the batter in the same way.

To make the topping, lightly mix all the ingredients together. For serving, place a spoonful of savoury cheese topping on each waffle.

■ COOK'S TIP

Tofu makes a creamy salad dressing. Mash 150 g/5 oz tofu with 2 tablespoons vegetable oil, 1 tablespoon cider vinegar, 1 teaspoon minced onion and season.

■ COOK'S TIP

The oats in these waffles add valuable fibre and a delicious flavour. Buckwheat flakes may be used instead.

187 CHINESE-STYLE TOFU

Preparation time:
10 minutes

Cooking time:
12 minutes

Serves 4

Calories:
250 per portion

YOU WILL NEED:

1 × 227 g/8 oz can bamboo shoots
    drained
350 g/12 oz tofu
4 tablespoons oil
1 garlic clove, peeled
175 g/6 oz mangetout, trimmed
4 tablespoons soy sauce
2 tablespoons roasted sesame seeds

Suitable for Vegans

Slice, then shred the bamboo shoots. Cut the tofu into 5 mm/¼ inch thick slices.

Heat the oil in a wok or large frying pan and crush the garlic into it. Add the tofu and fry the slices until crisp and golden, then remove them from the wok with a slotted spoon and drain on absorbent kitchen paper.

Add the mangetout and bamboo shoots to the wok and stir-fry for 5 minutes. Sprinkle the soy sauce and sesame seeds over them. Return the tofu to the wok and cook for a further minute before serving. A rice dish makes an ideal accompaniment for this dish.

188 TOFU WITH LEEKS

Preparation time:
15 minutes, plus 30
minutes to marinate

Cooking time:
20 minutes

Serves 4

Calories:
155 per portion

YOU WILL NEED:

300 g/11 oz tofu, cubed
4 tablespoons soy sauce
1 tablespoon dry sherry
1½ tablespoons wholemeal flour
2 tablespoons oil
225 g/8 oz leeks, washed and thinly
    sliced
1 garlic clove, finely chopped
120 ml/4 fl oz vegetable stock
white pepper
1 red pepper, seeded and diced
2 tablespoons chopped parsley
gomasio for sprinkling

Place the tofu in a bowl. Pour over the soy sauce and sherry and marinate for at least 30 minutes.

Drain the tofu, reserving the marinade, and coat in the flour. Heat the oil in a frying pan and fry the tofu until brown and crisp, stirring frequently. Remove and keep hot.

Add the leeks and garlic to the pan and fry over a moderate to high heat until coated in oil. Add the stock and tofu marinade. Bring to the boil, cover and simmer for 5-7 minutes.

Season to taste with pepper. Arrange the tofu on the vegetables and serve sprinkled with red pepper, parsley and gomasio (see Cook's Tip).

■ COOK'S TIP

Tofu, or bean curd, is made from ground, soaked soya beans. On its own it is tasteless and has a texture reminiscent of a chilled custard. It is high in food value (protein) and can be seasoned and flavoured in any number of dishes. Traditionally used in Chinese cooking, it is also used in vegetarian dishes.

■ COOK'S TIP

Salt substitute, gomasio or sesame salt, may be made at home: grind 4-5 parts roasted sesame seeds with one part salt. Keep in an airtight container 3 weeks.

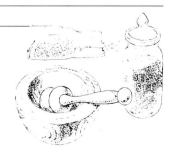

189 LEEK FLANS

Preparation time:
25 minutes

Cooking time:
45 minutes

Oven temperature:
200 C, 400 F, gas 6
then
190 C, 375 F, gas 5

Serves 4

Calories:
540 per portion

YOU WILL NEED:
FOR THE SHORTCRUST PASTRY
175 g/6 oz wholemeal or plain flour
75 g/3 oz butter
2-3 tablespoons cold water
FOR THE FILLING
2 medium leeks, halved
1 celery stick
25 g/1 oz butter
125 g/4½ oz Danish Bolina cheese
2 eggs, beaten
150 ml/¼ pint milk
salt and pepper
1 teaspoon grated nutmeg
15 g/½ oz flaked almonds (optional)

Place the flour in a bowl and rub in the butter until the mixture resembles fine breadcrumbs. Add enough water to make a stiff dough. Roll out on a lightly floured board and use to line 4 individual flan tins. Bake blind in a moderately hot oven for 10 minutes, removing the baking beans and greaseproof paper after 7 minutes. Reduce oven temperature.

Slice the leeks and celery. Melt the butter and cook the vegetables, covered, for 5-7 minutes until softened. Crumble the cheese into a bowl, beat to soften, then work in the eggs, a little at a time, to make a smooth mixture. Stir in the milk, seasoning and nutmeg.

Divide the vegetables between the flan cases, pour the cheese mixture over, scatter with the almonds, if using, and bake for 20-25 minutes.

■ COOK'S TIP

The flans make a superb summer starter; or make them a feature of a summer picnic basket – much more impressive than a pile of sandwiches!

190 CARROT AND CUMIN QUICHE

Preparation time:
20 minutes

Cooking time:
40 minutes

Oven temperature:
200 C, 400 F, gas 6

Serves 4

Calories:
510 per portion

YOU WILL NEED:
175 g/6 oz plain flour
pinch of salt
75 g/3 oz margarine
2 tablespoons cold water
FOR THE FILLING
175 g/6 oz cooked carrots
1 × 415 g/14½ oz can butter beans, drained
¾ teaspoon ground cumin
3 eggs
100 g/4 oz vegetarian Cheddar cheese, grated

Sift the flour and salt into a bowl. Cut the margarine into small pieces and rub into the flour until the mixture resembles fine breadcrumbs. Add enough water to mix to a dough. Roll out on a lightly floured board to line a 20 cm/8 inch flan dish or ring placed on a baking tray.

To make the filling, blend the carrots, beans, cumin and eggs in a liquidizer. Pour half the mixture into the flan case, sprinkle with half the cheese, cover with the remaining mixture and top with remaining cheese. Bake for 40 minutes. Serve hot or cold.

If liked, follow the attractive serving suggestion in the photograph by bordering the quiche on a serving plate with mixed salad leaves, for example, curly endive and radicchio.

■ COOK'S TIP

Choose bright orange carrots without splits. Best eaten raw, but if cooked whole, and scrubbed, not peeled, there will still be plenty of vitamin A.

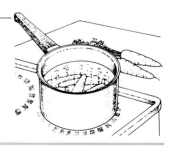

191 MUSHROOM PUFFS

Preparation time:
20 minutes

Cooking time:
3 minutes

Makes 18

Calories:
55 per puff, before
frying
Total for dressing
540

YOU WILL NEED:
225 g/8 oz frozen wholemeal puff
   pastry, defrosted
18 medium-sized button mushrooms
oil for deep frying
FOR THE DRESSING
100 g/4 oz vegetarian Stilton cheese,
   finely crumbled or grated
150 ml/¼ pint natural yogurt
2 tablespoons chopped coriander
   leaves or snipped chives

Roll out the pastry to a 30 cm/12 inch square. Cut the square into six 10 × 15 cm/4 × 6 inch strips. Cut each of these strips into 5 cm/2 inch squares (total 36).

Clean the mushrooms, remove the stalks and use for another recipe, and place each mushroom on a square of pastry. Dampen the edges with water and place a pastry square on top. Press the edges together to seal. Heat the oil to 180 C/360 F and deep fry the pastry squares a few at a time for 2-3 minutes or until puffed and golden. Drain on absorbent kitchen paper and keep warm while cooking the remainder.

To make the dressing, mash the Stilton with the yogurt until creamy. Stir in the coriander or chives. Serve the puffs hot or warm with the dressing.

192 CHEESE AND APPLE PIE

Preparation time:
10 minutes

Cooking time:
30 minutes

Oven temperature:
200 C, 400 F, gas 6

Serves 4

Calories:
700 per portion

YOU WILL NEED:
225 g/8 oz frozen puff pastry,
   defrosted
50 g/2 oz butter
1 large onion, finely chopped
450 g/1 lb cooking apples, peeled,
   cored and sliced
75 g/3 oz walnuts, chopped
225 g/8 oz Sage Derby cheese, sliced
salt and pepper
a little beaten egg or milk to glaze

Roll out the pastry on a lightly floured working surface until slightly larger than the top of a 1.2 litre/2 pint pie dish. Cut a strip from the edge and use to line the dampened rim of the dish. Melt the butter in a frying pan, add the onion and apple and cook for 5 minutes until slightly softened. Layer the onion and apple mixture with the walnuts and cheese in the pie dish, seasoning each layer. Dampen the pastry strip and cover with the pastry lid. Trim and flute the edges. If liked, use the pastry trimmings to decorate. Brush with beaten egg or milk and bake for 20-25 minutes until crisp and golden.

■ COOK'S TIP

*Do not add too many
pastry-coated mushrooms to
the oil at a time or the
temperature will drop and
the pastry will fail to puff
up properly.*

■ COOK'S TIP

*The combination of onion,
apple, walnuts and cheese
would be just as good in a
double crust pie and in that
form would be ideal for a
picnic.*

193 SUNFLOWER SNACKS

Preparation time:
20 minutes

Cooking time:
10-12 minutes

Serves 4

Calories:
285 per portion

YOU WILL NEED:
100 g/4 oz sunflower seeds, ground
100 g/4 oz wholewheat breadcrumbs
2 tablespoons grated Pecorino or
    Parmesan cheese
salt and pepper
1 garlic clove, crushed
1 large egg, lightly beaten
about 50 g/2 oz wholemeal flour
oil for deep frying

Mix together the ground sunflower seeds, breadcrumbs, Pecorino or Parmesan, a little salt and a pinch of pepper in a bowl. Stir in the garlic, then add the beaten egg and mix well to bind the ingredients together.

Using floured hands, roll the mixture into small balls. Season the flour with salt and pepper and dip each ball into the flour to coat thoroughly.

Heat the oil for deep-frying and fry the balls, in batches, until crisp and golden. Drain on absorbent kitchen paper.

194 NUTTY FRUIT SALAD

Preparation time:
5-10 minutes

Serves 2

Calories:
210 per portion

YOU WILL NEED:
2 medium dessert apples, cored and
    chopped
2 celery sticks, chopped
2 tablespoons sultanas
8 walnut halves, chopped
50 g/2 oz drained canned kidney
    beans
4 tablespoons natural yogurt
shredded crisp lettuce leaves
2 kiwi fruit, peeled and sliced, to
    decorate

Mix the apples, celery, sultanas, waluts and kidney beans, then coat with the yogurt.

Serve on a bed of shredded lettuce and kiwi fruit slices. This salad is ideal for a packed lunch.

■ COOK'S TIP

*Serve these irresistible
morsels as a cocktail party
snack. Supply plenty of
cocktail sticks with which
to spear them.*

■ COOK'S TIP

*Kiwi fruit came originally
from China and are now
largely grown in New
Zealand, hence the name.
They are rich in vitamin C.
Peel before cutting them.*

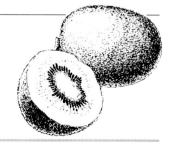

195 WALNUT DIP

Preparation time:
15 minutes, plus 1
hour to chill

Serves 6

Calories:
350 per portion

YOU WILL NEED:
*350 g/12 oz vegetarian Cheshire
   cheese, grated*
150 ml/¼ pint single cream
3 tablespoons milk
4 spring onions, chopped
salt and pepper
100 g/4 oz walnuts, finely chopped

Pound the cheese with the cream until well mixed, then beat
in the milk, onions, reserving a few rings for garnish if liked,
and seasoning until creamy. Add the walnuts, spoon into a
dish and chill for 1 hour before serving. Plain biscuits or toast,
celery and crisp apples make good accompaniments.

196 HUMMOUS

Preparation time:
5 minutes, plus
overnight to soak

Cooking time:
2¼ hours

Serves 8-10

Calories:
210-170 per portion

YOU WILL NEED:
*250 g/9 oz chick peas, soaked
   overnight*
150 ml/¼ pint tahini
3 garlic cloves, roughly chopped
juice of 1-2 lemons
salt and pepper
FOR THE GARNISH
*1 tablespoon olive oil blended with 1
   teaspoon paprika*
1 teaspoon chopped parsley

Drain the chick peas, place in a saucepan and cover with cold
water. Bring to the boil, cover and boil rapidly for 10 minutes,
then simmer gently for 1½-2 hours, until soft; the time will
vary depending on the age and quality of the peas. Drain, reserving 300 ml/½ pint of the liquid.

   Place the chick peas in a liquidizer or food processor, add
the remaining ingredients and season with salt and pepper to
taste. Add some of the reserved cooking liquid and blend to a
soft creamy paste.

   Turn into a shallow serving dish, drizzle over the blended
oil and spinkle with the parsley. Serve with pitta bread.

■ COOK'S TIP

*A white cheese with a
crumbly texture, Lancashire
has a mild flavour which
develops as it matures. It is
regarded as the perfect
cheese for toasting.*

■ COOK'S TIP

*This is a tasty starter. It will
keep for up to a week,
covered, in the refrigerator.
For speed, use canned chick
peas, which are already
cooked.*

197 TOFU AND AVOCADO SPREAD

Preparation time:
10 minutes

Serves 2

Calories:
320 per portion

YOU WILL NEED:
225 g/8 oz silken tofu
1 ripe avocado
2 tablespoons mayonnaise
½ teaspoon salt
1 teaspoon lemon juice
2 teaspoons finely chopped onion
4 drops of Tabasco sauce
a little cayenne

Break up the tofu with a fork. Halve the avocado, remove the stone and scoop out all the flesh. Mash it and add to the tofu together with the mayonnaise, salt, lemon juice, onion, Tabasco and cayenne to taste. Mix well and chill for about an hour. Serve with toast or wholewheat bread or rolls.

198 BREAKFAST SPECIAL

Preparation time:
10 minutes

Serves 8

Calories:
250 per portion

YOU WILL NEED:
225 g/8 oz rolled oats
50 g/2 oz wheatgerm
100 g/4 oz small dried apricots,
    chopped
175 g/6 oz sultanas
50 g/2 oz walnuts, roughly chopped
½ pear (per portion), peeled, cored
    and grated
brown sugar or honey, optional
milk or natural yogurt to serve

Mix the cereals, dried fruit and nuts together. Store in an airtight container. To serve, add grated pear to each portion, sprinkle with sugar or honey and serve with milk or yogurt.

■ COOK'S TIP

*What a combination!
Protein-rich tofu and
vitamin-packed avocado.
With wholewheat bread
providing carbohydrate, this
makes a well-balanced meal.*

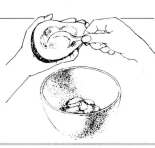

■ COOK'S TIP

*Seasonal fruits make a juicy
addition: fresh peach slices,
cherry halves, raspberries
and strawberries are among
the naturally sweet
possibilities.*

199 SPICED MUESLI

Preparation time:
5 minutes

Makes 575 g/1¼ lb muesli

Calories:
360 per 100 g/4 oz

YOU WILL NEED:
225 g/8 oz rolled oats
225 g/8 oz barley flakes or kernels,
  sesame and sunflower seeds, bran
  and wheatgerm, mixed according to
  taste
2 teaspoons cinnamon
1 teaspoon grated nutmeg
grated rind of 1 lemon
50 g/2 oz mixed nuts, chopped
50 g/2 oz seedless raisins and coarsely
  chopped dried fruit (apples,
  apricots, dates, figs), mixed
  according to taste

Put the oats in a bowl, then stir in all the remaining ingredients.

Store in a tin or another suitable airtight container and use as required. Serve with brown sugar or honey and milk, cream or yogurt. Seasonal fresh fruit may be added, if liked.

200 HAZELNUT TOASTS

Preparation time:
5 minutes

Cooking time:
3-4 minutes

Serves 1

Calories:
135 per portion

YOU WILL NEED:
1 tablespoon nutri-grain cereal (rye
  and oats with hazelnuts)
1 tablespoon vegetarian cottage cheese
½ small tomato, peeled and chopped
2 mushrooms, chopped
pinch of dried mixed herbs
1 slice wholewheat bread, toasted

Mix together the cereal, cottage cheese, tomato, mushrooms and mixed herbs. Spread this over the slice of toast, making sure it comes right to the edge. Heat under a moderate grill and cook until the topping is golden brown. Serve hot.

■ COOK'S TIP

*To get a good muesli base
make with a mixture of
different grains and seeds.
Bran is dry, wheatgerm has
a strong flavour and sesame
seeds are dry: use sparingly!*

■ COOK'S TIP

*For children cut the bread
into fancy shapes, using
large biscuit cutters.*

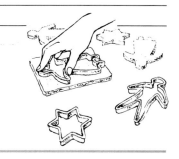

SPECIAL OCCASIONS

Many of the dishes in this chapter look very impressive when served to guests, although they do not necessarily involve complicated preparation processes. Without exception they are scrumptious to eat and will convert sceptical meat-eating friends!

201 TOMATO ROULADE

Preparation time:
30 minutes

Cooking time:
30 minutes

Oven temperature:
190 C, 375 F, gas 5

Serves 4

Calories:
200 per portion

YOU WILL NEED:
15 g/½ oz butter
450 g/1 lb tomatoes, peeled and finely
   chopped
25 g/1 oz wholemeal flour
salt and pepper
3 egg yolks
4 egg whites
FOR THE FILLING
50 g/2 oz vegetarian Cheddar cheese,
   grated
2 tablespoons chutney
½ teaspoon prepared mustard
2 tablespoons chopped watercress
salt and pepper

Line and grease a 23 × 30 cm/9 × 12 inch Swiss roll tin. Melt the butter in a pan, add the tomatoes and cook for about 4 minutes until pulpy. Stir in the flour and cook over a gentle heat for 1 minute. Remove from the heat, season and beat in the egg yolks. Whisk the egg whites until stiff and fold into the tomato mixture. Spread evenly into the prepared tin, making sure that the mixture reaches right to the edges. Cook in a moderately hot oven for about 20 minutes, until firm. Mix three-quarters of the grated cheese with the chutney, mustard, half the watercress and seasoning. Quickly turn the cooked roulade out on to a clean sheet of greaseproof paper and remove the lining paper. Spread the filling over the roulade and roll up. Place on an ovenproof dish, sprinkle with the remaining watercress and cheese; return to the oven for 2-3 minutes. Serve sliced.

202 SPINACH ROULADE

Preparation time:
30 minutes, plus 30
minutes to chill

Cooking time:
15-20 minutes

Oven temperature:
190 C, 375 F, gas 5

Serves 4

Calories:
310 per portion

YOU WILL NEED:
50 g/2 oz concentrated butter, melted
350 g/12 oz spinach, cooked
3 eggs, separated
salt and pepper
FOR THE FILLING
350 g/12 oz vegetarian cream cheese
1 bunch spring onions, chopped
175 g/6 oz broccoli, trimmed, blanched
   and drained
4 tomatoes, peeled

Line a 23 × 30 cm/9 × 12 inch Swiss roll tin with greaseproof paper and brush lightly with melted butter. Squeeze all the liquid from the spinach, chop finely or purée. Beat in the remaining butter, the egg yolks and seasoning to taste. Whisk the egg whites until just stiff and fold into the spinach. Turn into the prepared tin and cook in a moderately hot oven for 10-15 minutes.

Beat the cheese and spring onions together. Finely chop the broccoli. Halve the tomatoes, discard seeds and chop the flesh. Mix the broccoli and tomatoes into the cream cheese and season well.

Turn the cooked roulade out on to clean greaseproof paper. Carefully peel off the lining paper and trim the edges. Spread the filling evenly over three-quarters of the roulade and roll up from the unfilled end. Wrap paper tightly over the roulade and chill for 30 minutes.

■ COOK'S TIP

*Roll the roulade as you
would a Swiss roll, using the
greaseproof paper as a guide.
For a good roll, tuck the end
in neatly first to start the roll
off evenly.*

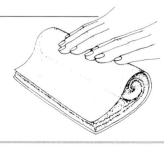

■ COOK'S TIP

*Serve this splendid roulade as
a dinner party starter with a
simple garnish or frilled
endive and radishes.*

203 COTTAGE PANCAKES

Preparation time:
10 minutes

Cooking time:
30-35 minutes

Oven temperature:
190 C, 375 F, gas 5

Serves 4

Calories:
385 per portion

YOU WILL NEED:
50 g/2 oz wholemeal flour
50 g/2 oz plain flour
1 egg
1 egg yolk
300 ml/½ pint water
salt and pepper
oil for frying
FOR THE FILLING
25 g/1 oz butter
1 small onion, finely chopped
225 g/8 oz vegetarian cottage cheese
50 g/2 oz salted peanuts, chopped
½-1 teaspoon dried rosemary, crushed

Mix together the flours, egg and egg yolk, stir in about a third of the water and beat to make a smooth batter. Stir in the salt and pepper and remaining water.

Heat a little oil in a 15 cm/6 inch frying pan. Pour in a little batter, so it just covers the base, and cook until the underside is golden. Turn and cook the second side. Remove and keep warm. Repeat with the remaining batter. To make the filling, heat the butter in a saucepan and fry the onion until softened, about 5 minutes. Stir in the cottage cheese, peanuts and rosemary.

Divide the filling between the pancakes and roll up. Place close together in one layer in an ovenproof dish. Cover with foil and heat through in the oven for 15-20 minutes. Serve the pancakes hot.

■ COOK'S TIP

Cottage cheese is made from skimmed milk curds which have been washed and rinsed. It is low in fat and therefore a good choice for slimmers.

204 PROVENCAL PANCAKES

Preparation time:
25 minutes

Cooking time:
50 minutes

Serves 4

Calories:
345 per portion

YOU WILL NEED:
50 g/2 oz buckwheat flour
50 g/2 oz plain flour
salt and pepper
1 egg, beaten
300 ml/½ pint milk
1 tablespoon vegetable oil
oil for cooking
2 tablespoons olive oil
1 onion, chopped
2 garlic cloves, crushed
1 green or red pepper, seeded and chopped
1 small aubergine, chopped
4 large tomatoes, peeled and chopped
1 tablespoon tomato purée
25 g/1 oz margarine, melted
2 tablespoons grated Pecorino or Parmesan cheese

Place the flours in a bowl, add salt and make a well in the centre. Add the egg, then gradually stir in half the milk and the vegetable oil. Beat until smooth; add the remaining milk. Use to make 12 small pancakes.

Heat the olive oil in a pan and cook the onion until softened. Add the garlic, pepper and aubergine and fry for 10 minutes, stirring occasionally. Add the tomatoes and tomato purée, cover and cook for 15 minutes. Season to taste. Fill the pancakes, roll up and place in an ovenproof dish. Top with the margarine and cheese; grill to brown.

■ COOK'S TIP

Pancakes can be made in advance. Place the stack of pancakes in a plastic bag and store in the refrigerator for 2-3 days.

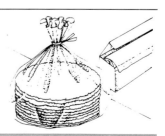

205 CHEESE MILLE FEUILLES

Preparation time:
30 minutes

Cooking time:
10-15 minutes

Oven temperature:
220-230 C, 425-450
F, gas 7-8

Serves 6

Calories:
500 per portion

YOU WILL NEED:
225 g/8 oz frozen puff pastry,
defrosted
cocktail gherkins, to garnish
FOR THE FILLINGS
225 g/8 oz vegetarian blue Stilton
cheese
75 g/3 oz butter
salt and pepper
2-3 tablespoons double cream, lightly
whipped
1-2 tablespoons milk
100 g/4 oz vegetarian Cheshire cheese,
grated
pinch of cayenne
pinch of mustard powder
1 tablespoon chutney, chopped

Roll out pastry to 25 × 35 cm/10 × 14 inch. Prick all over and bake in a hot oven for 10-15 minutes. Cool slightly, then cut lengthways into three even strips; crush trimmings and reserve.

Remove the rind from the Stilton. Cream the cheese with the butter and season well, adding a little cream.

Beat the milk into the Cheshire cheese, season and add the cayenne, mustard and chutney. If necesary, add a little cream to soften. Spread half the Stilton mixture over one pastry strip. Place the second strip on top, spread with the Cheshire cheese. Top with the last strip of pastry, press down gently before spreading with the remaining Stilton mixture. Mark with a knife and garnish, adding the crushed pastry as shown.

206 COURGETTE SOUFFLE

Preparation time:
20 minutes

Cooking time:
1 hour

Oven temperature:
180 C, 350 F, gas 4

Serves 6

Calories:
145 per portion

YOU WILL NEED:
350 g/12 oz courgettes, diced
salt and pepper
350 g/12 oz vegetarian low-fat soft
cheese
4 eggs, separated
½ teaspoon tarragon
pinch of cayenne

Cook the courgettes in boiling salted water until tender – about 5 minutes. Drain well, then sieve or blend in a liquidizer until smooth. Beat the soft cheese and egg yolks together. Stir in the courgettes, tarragon and cayenne. Whisk the egg whites until stiff and fold into the courgette mixture. Pour carefully into a 1.2 litre/2 pint soufflé dish and bake, without opening the oven, for about 45-55 minutes, until well risen and golden brown on top. Serve immediately with a green salad.

■ COOK'S TIP

To make gherkin fans, drain the gherkins and place them on a board. With a sharp knife, slice them lengthways, almost to the end. Ease the slices apart.

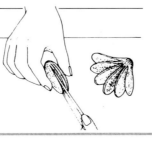

■ COOK'S TIP

It is the air incorporated in the egg whites during beating that makes a soufflé rise. Adding a pinch of salt will help to stabilise the mixture. Never beat eggs so stiffly that *they look dry – if this happens they will soon collapse.*

207 BLUE CHEESE SOUFFLE

Preparation time:
15 minutes

Cooking time:
30-35 minutes

Oven temperature:
200 C, 400 F, gas 6

Serves 4

Calories:
310 per portion

YOU WILL NEED:
40 g/1½ oz butter
25 g/1 oz plain flour
pinch of grated nutmeg
4 egg yolks
100 g/4 oz vegetarian Danish Blue
  cheese, crumbled
3 egg whites
salt and pepper

Melt the butter in a pan and use a little to brush the inside of a 1.4 litre/2½ pint soufflé dish. Stir the flour into the remaining butter; cook for 1 minute. Gradually stir in the milk, bring to the boil and cook for 2 minutes, stirring constantly. Add the nutmeg and allow to cool slightly. Beat in the egg yolks and cheese. Whisk the egg whites until stiff, lightly fold into the sauce and season to taste.

Turn into the prepared soufflé dish and cook in a moderately hot oven for 25-30 minutes until well risen and golden brown. Serve at once with green vegetables or a salad.

208 SURPRISE SOUFFLE

Preparation time:
20 minutes

Cooking time:
1 hour

Oven temperature:
190 C, 375 F, gas 5

Serves 4

Calories:
475 per portion

YOU WILL NEED:
4 large carrots, thickly sliced
3 large potatoes, peeled and cut into 1
  cm/½ inch dice
1 small turnip, cut into 1 cm/½ inch
  dice
1 large onion, chopped
salt and pepper
8 tomatoes, peeled and seeded
25 g/1 oz butter
25 g/1 oz plain flour
½ teaspoon mustard powder
300 ml/½ pint milk
3 eggs, separated
100 g/4 oz vegetarian Cheddar cheese,
  grated

Cook the carrots, potatoes, turnip and onion in a pan of boiling salted water for 15 minutes. Drain and season to taste, then place in a 1.75 litre/3 pint ovenproof soufflé dish. Purée the tomatoes with a little seasoning and pour this over the vegetables.

Melt the butter in a pan over a low heat, then add the flour and mustard powder. Cook for 2 minutes, stirring. Gradually add the milk and bring the sauce to the boil, stirring constantly. Simmer gently for 2-3 minutes. Allow it to cool slightly, then beat in the egg yolks and cheese. Whisk the egg whites until stiff and fold into the sauce. Pour the sauce over the vegetables in the soufflé dish. Bake in a moderately hot oven for about 40 minutes until risen and golden.

■ COOK'S TIP

When serving a soufflé use a large spoon to reach down to the lightly cooked mixture at the bottom of the dish. Each portion should also include some of the crust.

■ COOK'S TIP

The surprise in is this soufflé is the vegetable mixture at the bottom of the dish, which makes the soufflé sufficiently substantial to serve on

its own as a main course dish.

209 CHEESE FONDUE

Preparation time:
15 minutes

Cooking time:
10 minutes

Serves 4

Calories:
435 per portion

YOU WILL NEED:
1 garlic clove, halved
300 ml/½ pint dry white wine
1 teaspoon lemon juice
225 g/8 oz Danish Samsoe or Danbo
  Cheese, grated
225 g/8 oz Danish Havarti cheese,
  grated
2 tablespoons cornflour
freshly ground black pepper
pinch of grated nutmeg
1 tablespoon Kirsch or milk
TO SERVE
French bread
raw vegetables

Thoroughly rub the inside of a fondue pot or flameproof casserole with the garlic, then discard. Pour the wine and lemon juice into the pot and warm over a gentle heat. Add the cheese gradually and continue to heat gently, stirring until the cheese has melted. Blend the cornflour, pepper and nutmeg to a smooth paste with the Kirsch or milk and add to the melted cheese. Stir over the heat for a further 2-3 minutes. Place in the centre of the table. Serve at once with cubes of French bread and pieces of vegetables as dippers. Each guest is given a long fork with which to dip his bread and vegetables into the fondue pot. Keep the fondue warm over a spirit lamp or on a plate warmer.

210 FRUIT AND VEGETABLE KEBABS

Preparation time:
20 minutes, plus 1 hour to marinate

Cooking time:
11-14 minutes

Serves 4

Calories:
195 per portion

Suitable for Vegans

YOU WILL NEED:
8 button onions, peeled and left whole
1 small green pepper, seeded and cut
  into 8 pieces
1 small red pepper, seeded and cut
  into 8 pieces
16 button mushrooms
2 large bananas, peeled and cut into 8
  chunks
1 × 350 g/12 oz can pineapple cubes,
  drained
FOR THE MARINADE
6 tablespoons vegetable oil
1 tablespoon lemon juice
1 teaspoon grated orange rind
1 tablespoon finely chopped walnuts
salt and pepper

Blanch the onions and peppers in boiling water for 3 minutes so that they cook in the same time as the other ingredients. Drain and pat dry with absorbent kitchen paper. Thread all the ingredients on to eight kebab skewers. Lay the kebabs in a shallow dish while making the marinade. Stir the oil, lemon juice, orange rind, walnuts, salt and pepper together in a small bowl. Spoon the marinade over the kebabs and leave for about 1 hour. Grill for 8-10 minutes until evenly browned, brushing often with marinade.

■ COOK'S TIP

To make a change from bread, accompany the fondue with a selection of vegetables to dip. Try carrots, cauliflower, celery, courgettes and different coloured peppers all prepared and cut into bite-sized pieces.

■ COOK'S TIP

In the summer, cook these colourful kebabs over an outdoor barbecue.

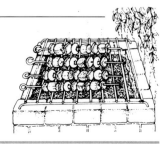

211 DANISH BLUE CHEESECAKE

Preparation time:
35 minutes, plus 3-4
hours to chill

Serves 8

Calories:
375 per portion

YOU WILL NEED:
FOR THE BASE
75 g/3 oz butter
175 g/6 oz wholewheat bran biscuits,
   crushed
FOR THE TOPPING
100 g/4 oz vegetarian Danish Blue
   cheese
100 g/4 oz vegetarian cream cheese
2 large eggs, separated
1 teaspoon French mustard
pinch of garlic salt
freshly ground black pepper
150 ml/¼ pint double cream
2 teaspoons agar-agar
6 tablespoons water
FOR THE GARNISH
cucumber slices
black grapes

Melt the butter and stir in the biscuit crumbs. Press firmly into
the base of a greased 20 cm/8 inch loose-bottomed cake tin
and chill. Soften both cheeses and beat together until creamy.
Beat in the egg yolks, mustard, garlic salt, pepper and cream.
Dissolve the agar-agar in the cold water in a small saucepan,
then bring to the boil, stirring constantly. Beat into the cheese
mixture and set aside. When on the point of setting, whisk the
egg whites until stiff but not dry and gently fold in. Pour over
the biscuit base and smooth the surface. Refrigerate for 3-4
hours. Garnish and serve.

■ COOK'S TIP

Another garnish is spring
onion curls. Trim the onion
to leave 2.5 cm/1 inch of
white stalk. Make cuts
down the green part. Place
in iced water to curl.

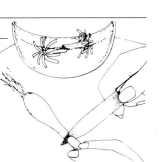

212 SPINACH AND FLAGEOLET LAYER

Preparation time:
25 minutes

Cooking time:
1 hour 10 minutes

Oven temperature:
180 C, 350 F, gas 4

Serves 4

Calories:
135 per portion

YOU WILL NEED:
450 g/1 lb fresh spinach
1 egg, beaten
1 × 415 g/14½ oz can flageolet beas
1 teaspoon French mustard
1 teaspoon curry powder
175 g/6 oz raspberries, puréed

Steam the spinach for 10 minutes. Keep about a quarter of the
leaves aside and chop the rest very finely or liquidize in a blender or food processor. Mix in the beaten egg. Oil a 450 g/1 lb
loaf tin and line with some of the reserved spinach leaves.

Drain and mash the flageolet beans. Mix with the mustard and curry powder and place in spinach-lined tin, top
with the spinach mixture. Arrange remaining spinach leaves
on top. Cover with foil. Place in a baking tin containing 2.5
cm/1 inch of water and cook in a moderate oven for 1 hour.

Leave to cool in the tin, turn out and serve with a sauce of
puréed raspberries (see Cook's Tip). Accompany with hot
garlic bread.

■ COOK'S TIP

To make the sauce or coulis,
simply purée fresh
raspberries and press
through a sieve to remove
the seeds. A little lemon juice
or gin maybe added, if liked,
to sharpen the flavour of the
sauce.

213 KOHLRABI WITH WALNUTS

Preparation time:
15 minutes

Cooking time:
18-20 minutes

Serves 4

Calories:
345 per portion

YOU WILL NEED:
1 kg/2 lb young, tender kohlrabi
1 tablespoon vegetable oil
2 shallots, peeled and finely chopped
salt and pepper
grated nutmeg
120 ml/4 fl oz double cream
2 tablespoons chopped basil or
    marjoram
100 g/4 oz walnuts, coarsely chopped

Trim the kohlrabi, cutting off the feathery leaves and reserving for garnish. Peel the kohlrabi, cut out any tough parts, wash and halve. Cut the halves first into 1 cm/½ inch slices and then into sticks.

Heat the oil in a frying pan and fry the shallots over a moderate heat until transparent, stirring continuously. Add the kohlrabi and stir until completely coated in oil.

Season with salt, pepper and nutmeg to taste. Add the cream, reduce the heat, cover and cook over low heat for 5-8 minutes until the kohlrabi is tender but still firm to the bite.

Rinse the kohlrabi leaves, pat dry and finely chop. Stir the basil into the kohlrabi mixture and transfer to a warmed serving dish. Sprinkle with the kohlrabi leaves and walnuts. Accompany with jacket-boiled new potatoes or brown rice.

214 WALNUT-FILLED FENNEL

Preparation time:
15-20 minutes

Cooking time:
1½ hours

Oven temperature:
180 C, 350 F, gas 4

Serves 2-4

Calories:
630-315 per portion

YOU WILL NEED:
4 large heads fennel
50 g/2 oz fresh breadcrumbs
75 g/3 oz walnuts, chopped
2 tablespoons clear honey
1 tablespoon snipped chives
1 tablespoon milk
salt and pepper
50 g/2 oz butter
FOR THE GARNISH
tomato wedges
parsley sprigs

Cut out the hard core of the fennel and discard. Remove and chop up a little more fennel, ensuring there is a reasonably large cavity to fill with stuffing.

Mix the chopped fennel, breadcrumbs, walnuts, honey, chives and milk, and season well with salt and pepper. Press this stuffing into the fennel cavities and place in an ovenproof dish.

Dot the surface with butter, cover tightly with foil and bake in a moderate oven for about 1½ hours, until the fennel is tender. Garnish with tomato and parsley.

■ COOK'S TIP

Kohlrabi looks like a large green turnip but is actually a member of the cabbage family. It is high in vitamins and low in calories.

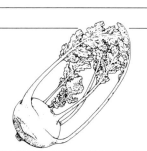

■ COOK'S TIP

Serve this dish as an interesting light main course. Alternatively, it can be offered as an accompaniment or an appetising starter.

215 BAKED GNOCCHI

Preparation time:
15 minutes

Cooking time:
40 minutes

Oven temperature:
200 C, 400 F, gas 6

Serves 4

Calories:
520 per portion

YOU WILL NEED:
450 ml/¾ pint milk
450 ml/¾ pint water
¼ teaspoon salt
225 g/8 oz semolina
100 g/4 oz grated Pecorino or
  Parmesan cheese
2 egg yolks
225 g/8 oz mushrooms, sliced
450 g/1 lb tomatoes, peeled and sliced
2 tablespoons chopped parsley
1 teaspoon oregano
50 g/2 oz stoned black olives, chopped
3 tablespoons melted butter

Bring the milk, water and salt nearly to the boil. Sprinkle in the semolina and cook, stirring, until it thickens to a purée consistency. Lower heat as much as possible and cook for 5 minutes. Remove the pan from the heat and stir in about two-thirds of the cheese and the egg yolks. Moisten a large roasting tin and press mixture into an even-sided oblong shape. Cut neatly into squares.

Place the mushrooms in a buttered ovenproof dish, cover with the tomatoes, sprinkle over the parsley, oregano and olives. Cover with the gnocchi squares, spoon over the melted butter and sprinkle with the remaining cheese. Bake for 25-30 minutes until the top is just beginning to brown.

216 SPINACH BAKE

Preparation time:
20 minutes

Cooking time:
35 minutes

Oven temperature:
200 C, 400 F, gas 6

Serves 4

Calories:
365 per portion

YOU WILL NEED:
2 tablespoons raisins
4 tablespoons apple juice
1 kg/2 lb fresh, or 450 g/1 lb frozen
  spinach
1 small onion, finely chopped
50 g/2 oz butter
salt and pepper
¼ teaspoon grated nutmeg
1 kg/2 lb potatoes, cooked, puréed
  with milk, butter and salt and
  pepper
150 ml/¼ pint soured cream
4 tablespoons fresh breadcrumbs
2 tablespoons grated Pecorino or
  Parmesan cheese

Soak the raisins in the apple juice. Wash the spinach several times in lukewarm water. Cook the spinach gently until soft. Drain in a sieve and press out any excess water. Cook the onion in the butter for 3 minutes until softened, add the spinach, raisins and apple juice, salt and pepper and nutmeg. Cook for 5 minutes over very gentle heat.

Meanwhile, pipe the creamed potato round the edge of an ovenproof dish. Turn the spinach mixture into the centre, spoon over the cream, sprinkle with the breadcrumbs and cheese and cook for 20-25 minutes until crisp and golden on top.

■ COOK'S TIP

A simple salad, such as Orange and Watercress (recipe 123) would be an excellent accompaniment to this dish.

■ COOK'S TIP

Soaking the raisins in apple juice plumps them up and adds flavour. Pear juice may be used instead, if preferred.

217 BARLEY CASSEROLE

Preparation time:
5 minutes

Cooking time:
1 hour

Serves 4

Calories:
510 per portion

YOU WILL NEED:
300 g/11 oz pearl barley
3 tablespoons olive oil
1 large onion, chopped
2 garlic cloves, crushed
1 medium carrot, chopped
600 ml/1 pint vegetable stock
350 g/12 oz mushrooms
1 tablespoon lemon juice
2 tablespoons chopped parsley
40 g/1½ oz ground almonds
3 tablespoons crème fraîche
salt and pepper
FOR THE GARNISH
watercress
lemon slices

Rinse the barley until the water runs clear; this removes the starch and stops the barley sticking. Heat 2 tablespoons of the oil in a saucepan and cook the onion and garlic for 3 minutes until softened. Add the carrot and cook for 2 minutes, stirring. Add the barley and stir to coat with the oil. Stir in the stock, bring to the boil, cover, and simmer for 45 minutes.

Meanwhile, slice the mushrooms and sprinkle with the lemon juice. Heat the remaining oil in a frying pan and cook the mushrooms for 6 minutes or until soft and the liquid has evaporated. Stir in the parsley, almonds and crème fraîche.

When the barley is cooked and the stock almost absorbed, stir in the mushroom mixture and check the seasoning. Serve on a warm dish and garnish with watercress and lemon slices.

■ COOK'S TIP

Crème fraîche is a cultured cream with a slight tang not as pronounced as that of soured cream.

218 STUFFED VINE LEAVES

Preparation time:
20 minutes

Cooking time:
1 hour

Serves 4

Calories:
460 per portion

YOU WILL NEED:
650 ml/22 fl oz vegetable stock
100 g/4 oz long-grain brown rice
20-25 vine leaves, in brine
1 bunch spring onions, chopped
100 g/4 oz ground almonds
salt and pepper
150 ml/¼ pint white wine
2 tablespoons cornflour
150 ml/¼ pint double cream

Bring 350 ml/12 fl oz of the stock to the boil in a saucepan, add the rice, cover, and cook over very low heat for 40 minutes or until tender.

Meanwhile, rinse the vine leaves in cold water. Drain. Mix the rice with half the spring onions, the ground almonds and a little salt and pepper.

Fill the vine leaves (see Cook's Tip). Place the rolls in a large, shallow pan and pour over the remaining stock, the remaining onions and the wine. Heat gently and simmer for 10 minutes. Drain off the liquid, blend the cornflour to a smooth paste with a little water, pour in some of the warm stock and return the liquid to a clean pan.

Bring the liquid to the boil. Pour over the cream and heat through. Do not boil. Transfer the rolls to a warm serving dish and spoon over a little of the liquid. Serve the remainder separately.

■ COOK'S TIP

To fill the vine leaves, spread them on a clean work surface and place a teaspoon of the rice mixture on each. Fold in the sides and roll up carefully.

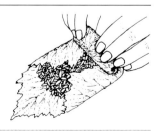

219 CORN FRITTERS

Preparation time:
10 minutes

Cooking time:
15 minutes

Serves 4

Calories:
235 per portion

YOU WILL NEED:
40 g/1½ oz wholemeal flour
225 g/8 oz canned sweetcorn, drained
2 tablespoons snipped chives
2 eggs, beaten
3 tablespoons water
25 g/1 oz butter
225 g/8 oz mushrooms, sliced
225 g/8 oz tomatoes, peeled and
   chopped
1 tablespoon chopped parsley
salt and pepper
vegetable oil for cooking

Put the flour in a bowl, stir in the sweetcorn and chives, re-serving a small quantity for garnish, and beat in the eggs. Add enough water to make a thick batter and transfer to a jug.

Heat the butter in a saucepan and cook the mushrooms for 3 minutes. Stir in the tomatoes, parsley and salt and pepper and set aside.

Heat a little vegetable oil in a heavy-based frying pan or griddle until hot. Pour spoonfuls of the batter on to the pan and cook quickly until golden underneath and just set on top. Turn over and quickly cook the other side. Drain on absorbent kitchen paper and keep warm while cooking the remaining batter.

Towards the end of cooking, return the mushroom mixture to the heat and warm through gently. Serve the fritters topped with the mushroom mixture and garnished with the reserved snipped chives.

220 VEGETABLE KEBABS

Preparation time:
15 minutes

Cooking time:
25 minutes

Serves 4

Calories:
270 per portion

Suitable for Vegans

YOU WILL NEED:
450 g/1 lb small new potatoes,
   scrubbed
1 medium green pepper, seeded
1 large aubergine, cubed
450 g/1 lb small onions
8 bay leaves
16 button mushrooms
4 tablespoons olive oil
juice of ½ lemon
1 garlic clove, crushed
1 teaspoon tomato purée
½ teaspoon oregano
salt and pepper

Cook the potatoes for 5 minutes in boiling water. Drain thoroughly. Cut the pepper into chunks. Thread the potato, pepper, aubergine, onions, bay leaves and mushrooms on to 8 skewers.

Mix together the oil, lemon juice, garlic, tomato purée, oregano and salt and pepper. Brush the kebabs all over with this mixture and cook them on a barbecue for about 10 minutes each side, basting with more of the oil mixture during cooking. Alternatively, cook the kebabs under a moderately hot grill for a similar time, turning once.

◾ COOK'S TIP

Only a little oil is needed for cooking the fritters, so either brush it on with a bristle brush or use a pad of absorbent kitchen paper to rub it on.

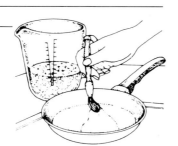

◾ COOK'S TIP

Serve the kebabs with a barbecue sauce. Sauté 1 onion and 1 garlic clove with 1 celery stick in a little oil. Add 175 g/6 oz canned chopped tomatoes, 1 tablespoon tomato purée, 1 teaspoon prepared mustard, 1 teaspoon soy sauce and 1 teaspoon brown sugar. Simmer for 20 minutes. Serve hot.

221 CARROT AIGRETTES

Preparation time:
15 minutes

Cooking time:
30 minutes

Serves 4-6

Calories:
415-315 per portion

YOU WILL NEED:
65 g/2½ oz plain flour
salt and pepper
pinch of cayenne
50 g/2 oz butter
150 ml/¼ pint water
2 eggs, lightly beaten
50 g/2 oz mature, vegetarian Cheddar
  cheese, grated
100 g/4 oz carrots, finely grated
50 g/2 oz hazelnuts, finely chopped
oil for deep-frying
grated Pecorino or Parmesan cheese

Sift the flour and seasonings on to a plate. Put the butter and water in a heavy-based saucepan and place over a low heat until the butter has melted, then increase the heat and bring to the boil. Remove from the heat and tip in all the flour mixture. Beat with a wooden spoon until the liquid has been absorbed. Continue to beat the mixture until it leaves the sides of the pan clean. Allow to cool.

Beat in the eggs, one at a time, until the mixture becomes shiny. Beat in the cheese, carrots and nuts.

Heat the oil for deep-frying. Drop in a few teaspoonfuls of the mixture at a time so that they have room to puff up. Fry in batches for 4-6 minutes until the aigrettes are puffy and golden brown. Remove with a slotted spoon and drain on absorbent kitchen paper.

Pile the aigrettes into a warmed serving dish and serve sprinkled with grated Pecorino or Parmesan cheese.

▪ COOK'S TIP

To test whether the oil is hot enough for the aigrettes, carefully drop in a cube of day old bread. It should turn golden in 1 minute.

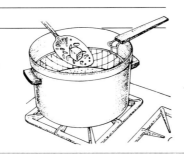

222 GOUGERE

Preparation time:
30 minutes

Cooking time:
1 hour

Oven temperature:
200 C, 400 F, gas 6

Serves 4

Calories:
425 per portion

YOU WILL NEED:
FOR THE CHOUX PASTRY
50 g/2 oz margarine
150 ml/¼ pint water
65 g/2½ oz wholemeal flour
2 eggs
50 g/2 oz vegetarian Cheddar, grated
FOR THE FILLING
2 tablespoons oil
1 onion, chopped
225 g/8 oz mushrooms, sliced
2 garlic cloves, crushed
1 tablespoon wholemeal flour
150 ml/¼ pint vegetable stock
75 g/3 oz walnuts, chopped
2 tablespoons chopped parsley

Melt the margarine in a large pan, add the water and bring to the boil. Add the flour all at once and beat until the mixture leaves the sides of the pan. Cool slightly, then add the eggs, one at a time, beating vigorously until glossy. Beat in the cheese. Spoon the pastry around the edge of a greased 1.2 litre/2 pint ovenproof dish. Heat the oil and cook the onion until softened. Add the mushrooms and garlic and fry for 2 minutes. Stir in the flour, then add the stock and bring to the boil, stirring. Cook for 3 minutes until thickened. Reserve 2 tablespoons of the walnuts and stir the remainder into the mushroom mixture, with the parsley and seasoning to taste. Pour the filling into the centre of the dish and sprinkle with the reserved walnuts. Bake for 40-45 minutes.

▪ COOK'S TIP

To avoid choux pastry collapsing, do not open the oven door to check the pastry until three-quarters of the cooking time is completed.

223 MUSHROOM VOL-AU VENTS

Preparation time:
20 minutes

Cooking time:
35 minutes

Oven temperature:
220 C, 425 F, gas 7

Makes 12

Calories:
130 per vol-au-vent

YOU WILL NEED:
12 frozen puff pastry vol-au-vent cases
beaten egg to glaze
FOR THE FILLING
1 tablespoon oil
1 onion, finely chopped
100 g/4 oz carrot, diced
225 g/8 oz mushrooms, sliced
2 tablespoons plain flour
200 ml/7 fl oz skimmed milk
¼ teaspoon dried sage
salt and pepper
75 g/3 oz sage Derby cheese, cubed
salad ingredients, to garnish

Place the vol-au-vent cases on a dampened baking tray. Brush with beaten egg and bake in a hot oven for 15-20 minutes, or as directed on the packet.

Heat the oil and cook the onion and carrot slowly in a covered pan for 5 minutes. Add the mushrooms and cook for a further 3 minutes. Stir in the flour and cook for 1 minute. Gradually add the milk and bring to the boil, stirring. Add the sage, seasoning and cheese. Spoon into the cooked vol-au-vent cases and serve at once, garnished with salad ingredients.

224 FETA PARCELS

Preparation time:
30 minutes

Cooking time:
35 minutes

Oven temperature:
180 C, 350 F, gas 4

Makes 6

Calories:
570 per portion

YOU WILL NEED:
150 g/5 oz butter
1 large onion, chopped
675 g/1½ lb frozen chopped spinach,
    defrosted and drained
225 g/8 oz vegetarian feta cheese
2 bunches spring onions, chopped
25 g/1 oz chopped parsley
1 tablespoon dill
salt and pepper
2 eggs, beaten
10 sheets filo pastry

Melt 25 g/1 oz of the butter and cook the onion for 5 minutes until softened. Place the spinach in a bowl, crumble the cheese over it, then stir in the spring onions, parsley, dill, seasoning and eggs and mix well.

Melt the remaining butter. Unwrap the filo pastry sheets. Place one on the work surface and brush with some of the butter, cover with a second sheet and brush with butter. Continue until 5 sheets have been brushed with butter. Brush the top sheet. (Cover any pastry not being used with a cloth.) Cut the layered pastry into three, widthways. Divide half of the spinach mixture between the strips leaving a 2.5 cm/1 inch border down the long edges. Fold in the long edges, brush with butter and fold up the short edges to make parcels 13 × 9 cm/5 × 3½ inch. Place on a baking tray, mark the tops and brush with butter.

Repeat with the remaining filo pastry sheets and spinach mixture. Bake for 25-30 minutes until golden.

■ COOK'S TIP

Don't save vol-au-vents for parties and weddings. With interesting fillings they make tasty suppers or quick starters for unexpected guests.

■ COOK'S TIP

Filo pastry is available in continental delicatessens and large supermarkets. If it's not to hand, the parcels may be made with puff pastry instead. Use 1 × 368-g/13-oz packet, defrosted. Cut it in half and roll each piece to a rectangle 30 × 37.5 cm/ 12 × 15 inch. The parcels will be slightly smaller.

DESSERTS

The final impression of a meal is made by the dessert, so always plan it with the preceding courses in mind. Follow a light main course with a substantial treat, like Gourmet bread and butter pudding, a luscious Chestnut roulade or Orange russe. Nectarine brûlée, on the other hand, provides the perfect, refreshing and quite light finish to a heavier main course.

225 ICED ORANGE CUPS

Preparation time:	YOU WILL NEED:
25 minutes, plus freezing time	*2 oranges*
	50 g/2 oz caster sugar
Serves 4	*120 ml/4 fl oz whipping cream*
	120 ml/4 fl oz thick Greek yogurt
Calories:	*50 g/2 oz raisins*
225 per portion	*2 glacé cherries, chopped*
	1 tablespoon brandy

Using a small sharp knife cut the oranges in half with zig-zag cuts. Scoop out the flesh with a teaspoon and press it through a sieve to extract the juice. Mix the juice with the sugar. Whip the cream until thick, then fold in the yogurt and orange juice. Pour into a shallow container and freeze until set 2.5 cm/1 inch in from the edges. Meanwhile macerate the raisins and cherries in the brandy.

Turn the mixture into a cold bowl and whisk to remove any large lumps. Stir in the raisin mixture and pour into the orange shells. Set these on a tray with absorbent kitchen paper underneath to keep them steady. Return to the freezer until firm, about 2 hours.

226 NECTARINE BRULEE

Preparation time:	YOU WILL NEED:
15 minutes	*450 g/1 lb nectarines, stoned and sliced*
Cooking time:	*4 tablespoons orange liqueur plus extra to flavour fruit*
15 minutes	*350 ml/12 fl oz soured cream*
Serves 6	*pinch of grated nutmeg*
	1 teaspoon vanilla essence
Calories:	*100 g/4 oz soft light brown sugar*
230 per portion	

Cover the nectarines with water in a saucepan, bring to the boil, then poach gently for 5-10 minutes or until soft. Drain and transfer to a flameproof casserole. Stir in a little of the orange liqueur to flavour.

Beat the soured cream, nutmeg, vanilla and remaining orange liqueur together until blended. Spoon the mixture into the nectarine slices then scatter the brown sugar over the top in a thick layer. Grill under a preheated hot grill for a few minutes until the sugar caramelises. Serve immediately.

■ COOK'S TIP

Pack crumpled greaseproof paper around the oranges to make quite certain that they do not fall over in the freezer.

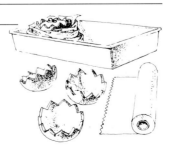

■ COOK'S TIP

Use fresh apricots, peaches or pineapple instead of nectarines. Double cream can be used instead of soured cream. Replace the nutmeg with cinnamon and the orange liqueur with rum, if preferred.

227 APRICOT AND ORANGE GLORIES

Preparation time:
20 minutes, plus 2
hours to set

Serves 4

Calories:
245 per portion

YOU WILL NEED:
2 × 185 g/6½ oz cans apricot halves
    in fruit juice
1 × 85 g/3½ oz packet vegetarian
    orange jelly crystals (see Cook's
    Tip)
150 ml/¼ pint boiling water
300 ml/½ pint natural yogurt
2 tablespoons clear honey
4 fresh cherries with stalks

Drain the juice from the apricots and make up to 300 ml/½ pint with water. Reserve four apricot halves and slice the remainder. Dissolve the jelly crystals in the boiling water then stir in the fruit juice. Pour into a shallow container and chill until set.

Turn the jelly out on to a work surface and with a wet knife chop it into small dice. Mix the yogurt and honey together, then layer the jelly, yogurt and apricot slices in four individual glass dishes. Top each with an apricot half, hollow side up and holding a cherry as a final touch.

228 FRUIT BASKETS

Preparation time:
30 minutes, plus
1½-2 hours to stand

Cooking time:
10 minutes

Oven temperature:
180 C, 350 F, gas 4

Serves 4

Calories:
315 per portion

YOU WILL NEED:
100 g/4 oz plain flour
100 g/4 oz icing sugar
3 egg whites
few drops of orange essence
25 g/1 oz flaked almonds
FOR THE SAUCE
2 slices fresh pineapple, peeled, cored
    and chopped
120 ml/4 fl oz pineapple juice
1-2 drops yellow food colouring
120 ml/4 fl oz natural yogurt
FILLING AND DECORATION
350 g/12 oz seasonal fruit
1 tablespoon icing sugar

Sift the flour and icing sugar, then beat in the egg whites until smooth. Stand for 1-2 hours. Stir in the essence and almonds. Mark four 18 cm/7 inch circles on baking trays lined with non-stick baking parchment. Spread the batter in the marked circles. Cook in a moderate oven for 8 minutes until pale golden. Allow to cool for about a minute, then ease off the baking trays with a palette knife and mould (see Cook's Tip). Simmer the pineapple, juice and colouring for 2 minutes then blend in the liquidizer. Chill then mix in the yogurt. Place each basket on a pool of pineapple sauce. Fill and decorate the biscuit baskets as shown.

■ COOK'S TIP

Vegetarian table jelly crystals are available in 85 g/3½ oz packets. To use, place the powdered crystals in a large bowl, pour in 200 ml/⅓ pint boiling water, stir briskly, then add the fruit juice. Proceed as in the recipe above.

■ COOK'S TIP

Shaping the biscuits: grease an orange with oil. Slide a biscuit off the tray and lift over the orange. Press gently and flute the edges. Lift off when cold.

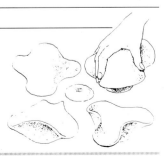

229 CRUNCHY PEAR LAYER

Preparation time:
10-15 minutes

Cooking time:
35 minutes

Oven temperature:
180 C, 350 F, gas 4

Serves 4

Calories:
305 per portion

YOU WILL NEED:

450 g/1 lb cooking pears, peeled,
   cored and quartered
3 tablespoons water
1-2 tablespoons ground ginger
150 g/5 oz demerara sugar
50 g/2 oz butter
50 g/2 oz fresh breadcrumbs
150 ml/¼ pint single cream, to serve

Cook the pears gently in the water with the ginger and 50 g/ 2 oz of the sugar until tender. Slice one of the poached pear quarters; reserve for decoration. Melt the butter in a frying pan and fry the breadcrumbs with the remaining sugar until crisp. Layer the pears and crunchy crumbs in a buttered oven-proof dish, finishing with a layer of crumbs.

Bake in a moderate oven for 30 minutes and serve hot or cold. Decorate with the reserved pear slices and serve with single cream.

230 WINTER FRUIT COMPOTE

Preparation time:
15 minutes, plus
overnight to soak

Cooking time:
30 minutes

Oven temperature:
190 C, 375 F, gas 5

Serves 4

Calories:
305 per portion

YOU WILL NEED:

225 g/8 oz dried apricots
100 g/4 oz stoned dried prunes
600 ml/1 pint unsweetened orange
   juice
2 oranges
100 g/4 oz raisins
2 small bananas, thickly sliced
natural yogurt, to serve

Place the apricots and prunes in a bowl and pour over the orange juice. Cover and leave to soak overnight.

Using a serrated knife, peel the oranges and remove all the pith. Cut in between the membranes to separate the orange segments. Stir into the fruit mixture with the raisins and bananas and turn into an ovenproof dish. Cover and cook in a moderately hot oven for about 30 minutes. Serve warm with natural yogurt.

■ COOK'S TIP

Use crushed ginger biscuits instead of the breadcrumbs, or try hazelnut biscuits for a delicious combination of flavours.

■ COOK'S TIP

To plump the fruit in a microwave: cook the apricots, prunes, raisins and orange juice, covered, 5 minutes on full power. Cool, add remaining fruit.

231 PLUM FLAPJACK CRUMBLE

Preparation time:
15 minutes

Cooking time:
30 minutes

Oven temperature:
180 C, 350 F, gas 4

Serves 4

Calories:
380 per portion

YOU WILL NEED:
1 kg/2 lb plums, halved and stoned
5 tablespoons apple juice
100 g/4 oz rolled oats
50 g/2 oz soft brown sugar
1 teaspoon mixed spice
50 g/2 oz soft brown sugar
1 teaspoon mixed spice
50 g/2 oz unsalted peanuts, roughly chopped
50 g/2 oz polyunsaturated margarine, melted

Place the plums in a covered pan with the apple juice and cook gently for about 10 minutes, until starting to soften. Transfer the plums with their juices to a greased 1.75 litre/ 3 pint ovenproof dish.

Mix together the oats, sugar, spice and peanuts in a bowl. Add the margarine and mix thoroughly. Spread evenly over the top of the plums, pressing down lightly with the back of a spoon. Bake in a moderate oven for 20 minutes, until the topping is crunchy and golden brown. Serve hot with thick Greek yogurt or vanilla ice cream, if liked.

232 CARNIVAL FIGS

Preparation time:
15 minutes, plus 1 hour to chill

Serves 4

Calories:
135 per portion

YOU WILL NEED:
8 fresh figs
1 × 142 ml/5 fl oz carton soured cream
4 tablespoons crème de cacao
grated chocolate or fig slices, to decorate

Place the figs in an ovenproof bowl, pour over boiling water to cover and leave for 1 minute. Drain thoroughly and peel off the skins. Cut each fig into quarters and place in a serving bowl.

Combine the soured cream and crème de cacao and pour over the figs. Decorate with grated chocolate or fig pieces or slices. Chill for at least 1 hour before serving.

■ COOK'S TIP

Instead of cooking fruits in sugar syrups, use natural juices. The edible leaves of herbs such as apple-scented geranium may be added to give a subtle flavour.

■ COOK'S TIP

Try using orange curaçao instead of crème de cacao, and decorate with grated orange rind.

233 ORANGE RUSSE

Preparation time:
30 minutes, plus
several hours to set

Serves 6

Calories:
350 per portion

YOU WILL NEED:
about 21 sponge fingers
grated rind and juice of 2 oranges
1 teaspoon lemon juice
2 teaspoons agar-agar
150 g/5 oz Blue Brie cheese
100 g/4 oz vegetarian curd cheese
50 g/2 oz caster sugar
2 egg whites
150 ml/¼ pint whipping cream
*few strips of blanched orange rind, to
    decorate*

Base-line an 18 cm/7 inch loose-bottomed cake tin. Trim the sponge fingers to 7.5 cm/3 inch lengths. Stand the fingers, trimmed side down and sugar side out, around the edge of the tin (see Cook's Tip).

Heat the orange and lemon juice to just below boiling, add the agar-agar and stir until dissolved. Set aside to cool. Thinly de-rind the Blue Brie. Beat with the curd cheese, sugar and orange rind until smooth. Gradually add the cooled agar-agar mixture. Leave until on the point of setting.

Whisk the egg whites until stiff but not dry, then whip the cream until it holds its shape. Fold just over half the cream into the setting cheese mixture, then add the egg whites. Pour into the biscuit-lined tin and level the surface. Refrigerate until set.

Remove from the tin to serve and decorate with the reserved cream and strips of blanched orange rind.

234 ST CLEMENT'S CHEESECAKE

Preparation time:
30 minutes, plus 1½
hours to chill

Cooking time:
5 minutes

Serves 8-10

Calories:
390-315 per portion

YOU WILL NEED:
75 g/3 oz unsalted butter
*175 g/6 oz digestive or gingernut
    biscuits, crushed*
FOR THE FILLING
2 eggs, separated
50 g/2 oz caster sugar
*350 g/12 oz vegetarian low-fat cream
    cheese, lightly creamed*
*150 ml/¼ pint whipping cream, lightly
    whipped*
*1 × 85 g/3½ oz packet vegetarian
    lemon jelly crystals (see recipe 227)*
200 ml/7 fl oz boiling water
FOR THE DECORATION
1 large peeled orange, segmented
1 small peeled lemon, segmented
sprig of fresh mint

Lightly grease a 20 cm/8 inch loose-bottomed cake tin. Melt the butter in a saucepan, mix in the crushed biscuits and press on to the base of the tin. Chill. Beat the egg yolks and sugar together until very thick and pale. Fold in the cheese and cream. Dissolve the jelly crystals in the boiling water. Cool, then stir into the cheese mixture. Whisk the egg whites stiffly, and fold into the mixture. Pour over the biscuit base and chill until firm.

Remove the cheesecake from the tin and decorate as shown.

▓ COOK'S TIP

*If the sponge fingers slither
sideways in the tin, stand
them upright and secure
each to the tin with a tiny
knob of butter.*

▓ COOK'S TIP

*If a loose-bottomed tin is not
available, grease and line a
20 cm/8 inch deep cake tin
and place double thickness
foil strips in a cross to lift
out the cheesecake when set.*

235 SPICED SULTANA CAKE

Preparation time:
30 minutes

Cooking time:
1 hour

Oven temperature:
180 C, 350 F, gas 4

Serves 8-10

Calories:
330-265 per portion

YOU WILL NEED:
FOR THE BASE
50 g/2 oz caster sugar
75 g/3 oz butter
1 egg
100 g/4 oz self-raising flour
½ teaspoon cinnamon
½ teaspoon mixed spice
FOR THE TOPPING
225 g/8 oz vegetarian cottage cheese,
 sieved
225 g/8 oz vegetarian low-fat soft
 cheese
2 eggs, separated
grated rind and juice of 2 lemons
50 g/2 oz caster sugar
2 tablespoons cornflour
150 ml/¼ pint low-fat double cream
50 g/2 oz sultanas

Beat the sugar and butter together until creamy, stir in the egg, flour and spices. Mix to a soft dough and press into the base of a greased 20-25 cm/8-10 inch round loose-bottomed tin. Beat the cheeses, egg yolks, lemon rind and juice, caster sugar and cornflour together. Whip the cream until it holds its shape and fold into the cheese mixture. Whisk the egg whites until stiff and add to the mixture, with the sultanas. Spoon over the base. Bake for about 1 hour, until the centre is firm to the touch. Partly cool in the tin and then remove to cool completely. Serve chilled.

■ COOK'S TIP

Thick and creamy mandarin yogurt may be used instead of the double cream if preferred. The cheesecake will not be quite so light, but it will taste delicious.

236 DANISH APPLE PUDDING

Preparation time:
15-20 minutes

Cooking time:
25-30 minutes

Serves 4

Calories:
455 per portion

YOU WILL NEED:
575 g/1¼ lb cooking apples, peeled,
 cored and sliced
75 g/3 oz butter
sugar to taste
75 g/3 oz granulated sugar
100 g/4 oz white breadcrumbs
FOR THE DECORATION
150 ml/¼ pint whipping or double
 cream, whipped
redcurrant jelly (optional)

Place the apples in a saucepan with a small amount of water and cook gently, until soft. Mash with a fork, adding 25 g/1 oz of the butter and sugar to taste. Cool completely.

Melt the remaining butter in a saucepan. Add the granulated sugar and the breadcrumbs. Cook gently for 20-25 minutes, stirring frequently, until the crumbs are golden. Cool completely.

Arrange alternate layers of apple and crumb mixture in a glass serving bowl, finishing with a layer of crumbs. Decorate the apple pudding with the whipped cream, and top with teaspoons of redcurrant jelly if desired.

■ COOK'S TIP

To prevent the breadcrumbs from becoming soggy, serve this traditional Danish cake as soon as it is assembled.

237 PAVLOVA

Preparation time:
30 minutes, plus 8
hours to cool

Cooking time:
1 hour

Oven temperature:
150 C, 300 F, gas 2
then
140 C, 275 F, gas 1

Serves 6

Calories:
360 per portion

YOU WILL NEED:
FOR THE MERINGUE
3 egg whites
200 g/7oz light soft brown sugar
1 teaspoon cornflour
1 teaspoon white wine vinegar
1 teaspoon vanilla essence
FOR THE FILLING
150 g/5 oz vegetarian Blue Brie cheese
300 ml/½ pint double or whipping cream
450 g/1 lb fresh fruit

Preheat the oven to the higher temperature. Draw a 23 cm/
9 inch circle on a piece of non-stick baking parchment then
place this paper, pencil side down, on a baking tray. Whisk
the egg whites until very stiff and dry. Gradually whisk in the
sugar. Mix together the cornflour, vinegar and vanilla and
whisk into the meringue mixture. Turn on to the prepared
baking tray and spread inside the marked circle, making a
slight wall around the edge. Place in the oven and immediately turn down the heat to the lower temperature. Bake
for 1 hour then turn off the heat and leave the meringue to
cool in the oven, preferably overnight.

    Thinly derind the cheese, place in a bowl and beat until
soft. Lightly whip the cream, add to the cheese and whisk
until stiff. Prepare the fruit, reserve some for decoration and
pile the remainder into the meringue case. Cover completely
with the cream and decorate.

■ COOK'S TIP

The mixture of cheese and
cream in the topping adds a
new dimension to this
popular dinner party dessert.
Assemble the Pavlova as
near to the time of serving it
as possible for best results.

238 APRICOT CHEESE FLAN

Preparation time:
25 minutes, plus
overnight to chill

Cooking time:
45 minutes

Oven temperature:
200 C, 400 F, gas 6
then
190 C, 375 F, gas 5

Serves 8

Calories:
320 per portion

YOU WILL NEED:
175 g/6 oz wholemeal flour
1 teaspoon ground ginger
75 g/3 oz margarine
50 g/2 oz demerara sugar
about 3 tablespoons water
1 × 411 g/14½ oz can apricot halves in natural juice, drained
225 g/8 oz vegetarian cottage cheese, sieved
225 g/8 oz vegetarian low-fat cream cheese
grated rind of 1 lemon
1 tablespoon cornflour
75 g/3 oz caster sugar
1 large egg, separated
150 ml/¼ pint soured cream

Mix the flour and ginger together. Rub in the fat, stir in the
sugar and add sufficient water to mix to a soft dough. Knead
the pastry until smooth and use it to line a 23 cm/9 inch fluted
flan ring. Chill for 20 minutes then bake blind at the hotter
temperature for 10 minutes. Remove paper and cook for a
further 5 minutes, then leave the case to cool. Reduce the oven
temperature. Arrange eight apricot halves around the edge of the
flan case, chop the remainder and pile in the centre.

    Beat the cheeses, lemon rind, cornflour, sugar and egg yolk
together. Stir in the cream. Whisk the egg white until stiff and
fold carefully into the mixture. Pour the filling into the flan case
and bake for 30 minutes or until the centre is just set. Cool, then
chill overnight.

■ COOK'S TIP

Try substituting 50 g/2 oz
ground almonds for an
equivalent amount of the
flour, and adding a drop of
almond essence to the filling.

239 CITRUS FLAN

Preparation time:
30 minutes, plus
several hours to
chill

Cooking time:
30 minutes

Oven temperature:
190 C, 375 F, gas 5

Serves 6-8

Calories:
480-360 per portion

YOU WILL NEED:
Wholemeal pastry (see recipe 189)
75 g/3 oz caster sugar
FOR THE FILLING
50 g/2 oz cake crumbs
2 tablespoons marmalade
1 large orange
1 grapefruit
50 g/2 oz cornflour
75 g/3 oz caster sugar
1 egg yolk
150 ml/¼ pint single cream
marmalade, warmed and sieved

Make the pastry, adding the sugar to the dry ingredients. Use two-thirds to line a 20 cm/8 inch fluted flan ring. Bake blind for 15 minutes. Remove the paper and cook for 5 minutes more. Roll out the remaining pastry thickly and trim to two 23 cm/ 9 inch long strips. Bake strips until brown, then use to divide flan case into four.

Mix the cake crumbs and marmalade together and spread in flan. Grate the rind of the orange and rind of half the grapefruit and keep separate. Squeeze the juice from half the orange and half the grapefruit and make up to 300 ml/½ pint with water. Slice remaining fruit. Blend the cornflour, sugar and egg yolk together in a small pan; gradually add the fruit juice and stir over a low heat until thick. Off the heat stir in the cream. Divide in half and stir orange rind into one half and the grapefruit rind into the other. Pour the custards into the sectioned flan case. Cool, then glaze with marmalade, decorate with the reserved fruit slices and chill.

■ COOK'S TIP

*Use a no-cook biscuit base
instead of pastry when time
is short. For extra flavour,
add 50 g/2 oz finely
chopped, toasted hazelnuts
to the pastry.*

240 CHESTNUT ROULADE

Preparation time:
30 minutes, plus
about 30 minutes to
cool

Cooking time:
20 minutes

Oven temperature:
160 C, 325 F, gas 3

Serves 6

Calories:
285 per portion

YOU WILL NEED:
50 g/2 oz wholemeal flour
1 tablespoon cocoa powder
4 eggs, separated
150 g/5 oz caster sugar
icing sugar to sprinkle
FOR THE FILLING
50 g/2 oz raisins
175 g/6 oz chestnut purée
25 g/1 oz soft brown sugar
120 ml/4 fl oz thick Greek yogurt
pinch of ground cinnamon

Sift the flour with the cocoa powder, adding back any bran left in the sieve. Whisk the egg whites until stiff, then whisk in half the sugar. Whisk the egg yolks with the remaining sugar in a large bowl until thick and pale, about 5 minutes. Carefully fold in first the flour mixture then the whisked egg whites. Turn into a greased and lined 23 × 30 cm/9 × 12 inch Swiss roll tin. Shake the tin gently to level the mixture and cook in a moderate oven for 20 minutes, until firm to the touch. Turn out on to a large sheet of greaseproof paper dusted with icing sugar and discard the lining paper. Roll up from one short end, rolling the clean greaseproof paper with the roulade, and leave until cold.

Beat together the raisins, chestnut purée and soft brown sugar. Fold in the yogurt and cinnamon. Carefully unroll the roulade and spread evenly with the filling. Re-roll, discarding the paper, and dust with icing sugar.

■ COOK'S TIP

*Before rolling up the just-
cooked roulade, trim off
any crusty edges with a
sharp knife, This will make
rolling much easier.*

241 FRUITY YULE PUDDING

Preparation time:
25 minutes

Cooking time:
3-4 hours, plus 2
hours on the day of
serving

Serves 8

Calories:
295 per portion

YOU WILL NEED:
100 g/4 oz self-raising wholemeal flour
100 g/4 oz fresh wholewheat
  breadcrumbs
1 teaspoon mixed spice
1 teaspoon ground cinnamon
1 teaspoon grated nutmeg
100 g/4 oz polyunsaturated margarine
75 g/3 oz light soft brown sugar
2 eggs, beaten
1 dessert apple, peeled, cored and
  grated
1 carrot, grated
225 g/8 oz raisins
grated rind and juice of 1 orange

Mix together the flour, breadcrumbs and spices. Beat the margarine with the sugar for about 5 minutes until soft and light, then beat in the eggs, apple, carrot, raisins, orange rind and juice. Stir in the flour mixture until evenly blended.

    Press lightly into a greased 1.2 litre/2 pint pudding basin and cover with double thickness greaseproof paper, tied down securely. Steam for 3-4 hours, topping up the water as necessary, then for a further 2 hours on the day of serving.

242 CHOUX RING

Preparation time:
45 minutes

Cooking time:
40-45 minutes

Oven temperature:
220 C, 425 F, gas 7
then
190 C, 375 F, gas 5

Serves 8

Calories:
435 per portion

YOU WILL NEED:
300 ml/½ pint water
100 g/4 oz butter
150 g/5 oz plain flour
3-4 eggs, lightly beaten
300 ml/½ pint double cream
1 tablespoon sweet sherry
1 × 225 g/8 oz can sweetened
  chestnut purée
a little cocoa powder

Make the choux pastry, using the first four ingredients and following the instructions in the Cook's Tip below. Transfer to a piping bag fitted with a large nozzle. Dampen a large baking tray and pipe a 25 cm/10 inch circle of paste on it. Pipe another circle immediately inside. Bake for 10 minutes at the higher setting, then reduce the temperature and cook for a further 35-40 minutes, until well puffed, crisp and brown. Split the choux ring in half immediately it is removed from the oven; cool.

    Whip the cream and sherry together and fold into the chestnut purée. Spread the choux base with the chestnut cream and cover with the choux top. Dust with cocoa.

■ COOK'S TIP

*Dried and fresh fruit
replaces much of the sugar
in this light Christmas
pudding; an ideal alternative
for the health and weight
conscious.*

■ COOK'S TIP

*Choux pastry: heat the water
and butter until the fat
melts, then bring to a rapid
boil. Off the heat, add all
the flour. Beat vigorously,
return to the heat and beat
until the mixture forms a
ball which leaves the sides
of the pan clean. Cool, beat
in enough egg to give a
piping consistency, then
beat till glossy.*

243 CHOUX BUN STAR

Preparation time:
25 minutes, plus 30
minutes to cool

Cooking time:
20-25 minutes

Oven temperature:
220 C, 425 F, gas 7

Serves 6

Calories:
280 per portion

YOU WILL NEED:
FOR THE CHOUX PASTRY
150 ml/¼ pint water
40 g/1½ oz concentrated butter
65 g/2½ oz plain flour, sifted
pinch of salt
2 eggs, beaten
FOR THE FILLING
350 g/12 oz strawberry fromage frais
FOR THE ICING
175 g/6 oz icing sugar, sifted
about 2 tablespoons warm water
pink food colouring

Make the choux pastry, adding the salt with the flour and following the instructions in Cook's Tip 242. Spoon into a piping bag fitted with a large star nozzle and pipe small stars on
to a greased and dampened baking tray. Cook in a hot oven
for 15-20 minutes until well risen and golden brown. Transfer
to a wire rack and cool.

When cool, split horizontally and fill with the fromage
frais. Place the icing sugar in a bowl with just enough water to
make a thick glacé icing. Add the colouring a few drops at a
time and mix to desired colour. Arrange the choux buns in a
star shape and drizzle the icing over the top.

244 CORINTH PANCAKES

Preparation time:
20 minutes

Cooking time:
45 minutes

Makes 8

Calories:
155 per portion

YOU WILL NEED:
100 g/4 oz wholemeal flour
1 egg, beaten
*150 ml/¼ pint unsweetened orange
  juice*
150 ml/¼ pint soda water
oil for frying
demerara sugar for sprinkling
FOR THE FILLING
*225 g/8 oz vegetarian low-fat soft
  cheese*
150 ml/¼ pint natural yogurt
1 tablespoon grated lemon rind
2 teaspoons lemon juice
100 g/4 oz currants
50 g/2 oz dried stoned dates, chopped

Place the flour in a bowl and beat in the egg. Gradually beat in
the orange juice and soda water.

Use the minimum of oil to grease a 20 cm/8 inch omelette
pan. When the pan is hot, pour in enough of the batter to
cover the base with a thin film. Cook until the pancake is
brown and bubbling on the underside. Flip or toss and cook
the other side. Keep the cooked pancake warm while making
seven more pancakes.

To make the filling, beat together the cheese, yogurt,
lemon rind and lemon juice. Stir in the currants and dates.
Spread the mixture over each pancake. Fold each one in half,
then in half again, so that they are wedge-shaped. Arrange in
a flameproof dish, sprinkle with sugar and grill to brown.

■ COOK'S TIP

*If preferred, fill the buns
with whipped cream and
drizzle melted chocolate
over the top.*

■ COOK'S TIP

*Soda water acts as a
leavener, keeping the
pancake batter lovely and
light. Add it immediately
before use or the effect will
be lost.*

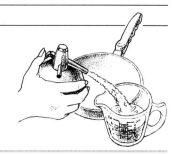

245 CAROB MOUSSE

Preparation time:
20 minutes, plus 4
hours to set

Cooking time:
10 minutes

Serves 4

Calories:
175 per portion

YOU WILL NEED:
1 × 100 g/4 oz carob bar
grated rind and juice of 1 small orange
2 eggs, separated
1 teaspoon agar-agar
4 tablespoons water
FOR THE DECORATION
strips of orange rind
carob curls

Place the carob in a medium heatproof bowl. Heat a medium saucepan of water until boiling, then reduce heat until simmering. Place the bowl on top and stir several times until the carob is melted. Remove from heat and stir in the orange rind and beat in the egg yolks.

Dissolve the agar-agar in the orange juice and water in a small saucepan, then bring to the boil, stirring constantly. Cool slightly and stir into the carob mixture. Whisk the egg whites to form stiff peaks and fold them into the carob mixture.

Divide between 4 individual ramekins and chill in the refrigerator until set. Decorate with the strips of orange rind and carob curls.

246 WALNUT PIE

Preparation time:
25 minutes

Cooking time:
55 minutes

Oven temperature:
180 C, 350 F, gas 4

Serves 6

Calories:
855 per portion

YOU WILL NEED:
1 quantity shortcrust pastry (recipe 189)
FOR THE FILLING
175 g/6 oz butter, softened
225 g/8 oz muscovado sugar
3 eggs
grated rind of 2 lemons
juice of ½ lemon
225 g/8 oz walnut halves

Make the pastry using wholemeal flour as instructed in recipe 189. Roll out on a floured surface and use to line a 20 cm/8 inch flan tin. Bake blind in a moderate oven for 10 minutes.

Cream together the butter and sugar. Carefully beat in the eggs, one at a time, then add the lemon rind, juice and walnuts. Mix well and turn the mixture into the flan case. Bake for 45 minutes until the filling has risen and turned golden brown. Eat warm or cold with cream.

■ COOK'S TIP

Carob tastes like chocolate and is available in health food stores. It comes from the carob bean and, unlike cocoa, it does not contain caffeine.

■ COOK'S TIP

Pecans, which are related to walnuts but have a milder flavour, may be used instead.

247 CITRUS APPLE PIE

Preparation time:
15 minutes, plus 30
minutes to chill
pastry

Cooking time:
40-45 minutes

Oven temperature:
200 C, 400 F, gas 6

Serves 6

Calories:
305 per portion

YOU WILL NEED:
225 g/8 oz plain flour
100 g/4 oz unsalted butter
25 g/1 oz caster sugar
2-3 tablespoons cold water
FOR THE FILLING
450 g/1 lb cooking apples, peeled,
*   cored and sliced*
1 orange, peeled and chopped
2-3 tablespoons water
sugar to taste
½ teaspoon ground cinnamon
*   (optional)*
FOR THE DECORATION
orange slices
apple slices brushed with lemon juice

Sift the flour into a bowl, then rub in the butter until the mixture resembles fine breadcrumbs. Mix in the sugar well and reserve 75 g/3 oz of this mixture. Add enough water to the remaining mixture to form a firm dough. Roll out and use to line a 20 cm/8 inch flan tin. Chill for 30 minutes.

Cook the apples and orange with the water for 5 minutes, until soft. Stir in sugar and cinnamon to taste.

Line the base of the flan with foil and dried beans and bake blind for 10 minutes. Remove the foil and beans, and bake for a further 5 minutes. Fill with the fruit and reserved flour mixture. Bake for a further 20-25 minutes, until golden. Decorate as shown and serve with cream.

248 PEAR FLAN

Preparation time:
25 minutes, plus 30
minutes to chill

Cooking time:
45 minutes

Oven temperature:
190 C, 375 F, gas 5

Serves 4

Calories:
350 per portion

YOU WILL NEED:
FOR THE PASTRY
100 g/4 oz plain flour
1 teaspoon ground cinnamon
50 g/2 oz butter, softened
25 g/1 oz walnuts, ground
25 g/1 oz caster sugar
1 egg yolk
2 teaspoons cold water
FOR THE FILLING
2 × 285 g/10 oz cans pear quarters in
*   fruit juice*
1 tablespoon each currants, sultanas
*   and chopped lemon peel*
1 tablespoon cornflour
1 tablespoon lemon juice
icing sugar to sprinkle

Sift the flour and cinnamon into a bowl, rub in the butter then stir in the walnuts and sugar. Bind with the egg yolk and water. Chill for 30 minutes. Drain the pear juice into a pan and add the currants, sultanas and lemon peel. Bring to the boil and simmer for 5 minutes. Mix the cornflour and lemon juice and stir into the mixture. Cook, stirring, until thickened. Roll out the pastry to line a 19 cm/7½ inch flan tin, reserving the trimmings. Prick the pastry and bake blind in a moderately hot oven for 15 minutes. Fill with the pears and thickened juice; top with a pastry lattice and bake for a further 20 minutes. Dust with icing sugar when cool.

▧ COOK'S TIP

To lift pastry into a flan tin, fold it over the rolling pin, then lift it loosely over the tin. Press in with fingertips.

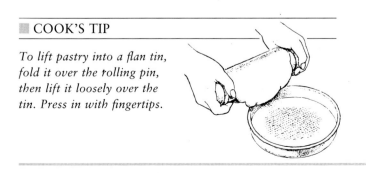

▧ COOK'S TIP

There are three ways to make a pastry lattice: the pastry slats may simply be placed on top of the filling with all the horizontal slats underneath and the vertical *ones on top; for a woven lattice the tops slats are threaded under and over the bottom ones; and in the twisted lattice the slats are turned.*

249 ORCHARD TART

Preparation time:
25 minutes

Cooking time:
35-40 minutes

Oven temperature:
200 C, 400 F, gas 6

Serves 6

Calories:
355 per portion

YOU WILL NEED:
FOR THE PASTRY
100 g/4 oz plain flour
50 g/2 oz concentrated butter,
  softened
50 g/2 oz ground hazelnuts
25 g/1 oz soft brown sugar
1 egg, beaten
FOR THE FILLING
4 large pears, peeled, cored and
  chopped
2 cm/3/4 inch piece fresh root ginger,
  peeled and chopped
2 tablespoons clear honey
100 g/4 oz demerara sugar
3 tablespoons water
4 dessert apples, peeled, cored and
  halved

Put the flour in a mixing bowl and rub in the butter until very fine. Add the hazelnuts and sugar, bind with the egg. Roll out to line a 20 cm/8 inch loose-bottomed flan tin.

Place the pears in a pan with the ginger, honey, sugar and water and cook over a moderate heat for 5 minutes. Remove the pears with a slotted spoon, drain well and place in the flan case, crushing them slightly. Slice the apple halves almost through but keeping in shape and arrange rounded side up over the flan. Reduce the pan juices until thick enough to coat then spoon over the apples. Bake in a moderately hot oven for 30 minutes and serve warm with cream.

■ COOK'S TIP

To slice apples not right through, place the halves cut side down in front of a board. Use a knife held horizontally so that the board halts the descending blade.

250 GOURMET BREAD AND BUTTER PUDDING

Preparation time:
15 minutes

Cooking time:
30-40 minutes

Oven temperature:
180 C, 350 F, gas 4

Serves 4

Calories:
455 per portion

YOU WILL NEED:
8 large slices white or Granary bread
50 g/2 oz concentrated butter, melted
50 g/2 oz demerara sugar
1/2 teaspoon mixed spice
100 g/4 oz sultanas
2 eggs, beaten
1 teaspoon vanilla essence
450 ml/3/4 pint milk
1 tablespoon sherry (optional)

Remove the crusts and cut the bread into fingers or desired shapes for one large (1.2 litre/2 pint) pudding or four individual (300 ml/1/2 pint) puddings.

Brush a little melted butter inside the ovenproof dishes and cover the base with bread. Mix the sugar, spice and sultanas together and sprinkle half over the bread, drizzle with a little of the melted butter and repeat the layers, finishing with bread and melted butter. Beat the eggs, vanilla, milk and sherry together and carefully pour over. Bake in a moderate oven for 30-40 minutes until set.

■ COOK'S TIP

The texture and flavour of this updated old favourite will be even better if the pudding is allowed to stand for 1 hour before cooking.

251 BLACKBERRY AND APPLE CRUMBLE

Preparation time:
15 minutes

Cooking time:
35-45 minutes

Oven temperature:
190 C, 375 F, gas 5

Serves 4

Calories:
350 per portion

YOU WILL NEED:
225 g/8 oz blackberries
450 g/1 lb cooking apples, peeled, cored and thinly sliced
25 g/1 oz unrefined sugar (golden granulated or molasses)
FOR THE CRUMBLE
100 g/4 oz wholemeal flour
75 g/3 oz polyunsaturated margarine
50 g/2 oz fruit 'n fibre cereal, lightly crushed
15 g/½ oz unrefined sugar

Mix together the fruit and sugar and place in a 1.2 litre/2 pint ovenproof dish.

Put the flour into a mixing bowl and rub in the fat. Stir in the cereal and sugar. Spread this topping evenly over the fruit and bake in a moderately hot oven for 35-45 minutes, until the crumble is crisp and the fruit is soft. Serve the crumble warm with custard.

252 AUTUMNAL PUDDING

Preparation time:
20 minutes, plus 2 hours to chill and set

Cooking time:
10 minutes

Serves 4

Calories:
225 per portion

YOU WILL NEED:
oil for brushing
8 thin slices wholewheat bread
150 ml/¼ pint apple juice
50 g/2 oz granulated sugar
juice of ½ lemon
2 dessert apples, peeled, cored and sliced
1 dessert pear, peeled, cored and sliced
75 g/3 oz blackberries
pinch of ground cinnamon
1½ teaspoons agar-agar
6 tablespoons water
FOR THE SAUCE
225 g/8 oz blackberries
3 tablespoons icing sugar
juice of ½ lemon
fresh fruit, to decorate

Brush the insides of four individual pudding basins with oil. Cut the bread into circles and fingers to line them.

Stir in the apple juice, sugar and lemon juice over low heat until dissolved. Add the apple and pear slices and poach gently for 4 minutes. Stir in the blackberries and cinnamon; cool. In a small saucepan, dissolve the agar-agar in the cold water, then bring to the boil, stirring constantly. Add to the cooled fruits. Spoon into the basins and chill. Poach the sauce ingredients gently, blend in a liquidizer and serve with the puddings, as shown.

■ COOK'S TIP

All berry fruits taste good with a crumble topping. Try cranberries, loganberries, tayberries or raspberries, varying the quantity of sugar as required.

■ COOK'S TIP

Agar-agar, which is derived from seaweed, is the preferred setting agent for many vegetarians.

BAKING

Home-baked cakes and breads are irresistible and their commercial counterparts cannot compete for texture and flavour. Among the teatime treats in this chapter are imaginative teabreads, such as Plum teabread and Banana and Honey teabread, moist cakes fruity, spicy and nutty, the exotic Brazilian ginger bran bread and Cheese and pineapple scones.

253 FRUIT TARTLETS

Preparation time:
20 minutes, plus 30 minutes to chill pastry and 20 minutes to cool pastry cream

Cooking time:
20-25 minutes

Oven temperature:
190 C, 375 F, gas 5

Makes 6 medium or 12 small tartlets

Calories:
630 per medium tartlet

YOU WILL NEED:
350 g/12 oz plain flour
pinch of salt
1 egg
225 g/8 oz butter or margarine
1 tablespoon caster sugar
FOR THE FILLING
50 g/2 oz caster sugar
3 egg yolks
2 tablespoons cornflour
300 ml/½ pint milk
2-4 drops vanilla essence

Line and grease 6 × 10 cm/4 inch or 12 × 5-7.5 cm/2-3 inch tartlet tins. Sift together the flour and salt into a large bowl. Make a well in the centre, drop in the egg and butter, and knead to form a soft, pliable dough. Wrap the dough and chill for 30 minutes. Roll out and use to line the tins. Prick the bases and bake blind for 10-15 minutes. Remove the beans and grease-proof paper. Bake for a further 5-10 minutes.

Mix together the sugar, egg yolks and cornflour. Heat the milk in a saucepan just to boiling point, cool slightly, then whisk into the egg mixture, return to the pan and slowly bring to the boil. Cover the surface of the mixture with dampened paper to cool. Fill the tartlets with the cold pastry cream and fruit.

◼ COOK'S TIP

To prevent oxidation or drying out, warm some jam or marmalade flavoured with either lemon juice or liqueur, sieve and brush carefully over the fruit.

254 BAKEWELL TART

Preparation time:
25 minutes

Cooking time:
20-25 minutes

Oven temperature:
180 C, 350 F, gas 4

Serves 4

Calories:
900 per portion

YOU WILL NEED:
75 g/3 oz plain flour
50 g/2 oz wholemeal flour
25 g/1 oz icing sugar
100 g/4 oz margarine
25 g/1 oz All-Bran cereal, crushed
1 egg
5 tablespoons jam
FOR THE FILLING
100 g/4 oz brown sugar
100 g/4 oz margarine
2 eggs
1 teaspoon vanilla essence
2 teaspoons almond essence
100 g/4 oz fresh breadcrumbs
100 g/4 oz All-Bran cereal
50 g/2 oz flaked almonds
icing sugar for dusting

Sift the flours and icing sugar together, adding any bran in the sieve to the mixture. Cut the margarine into small pieces and rub in until the mixture resembles fine breadcrumbs. Stir in the cereal and egg and mix to a dough. Knead, cover and chill.

To make the filling, cream the sugar and margarine together until light and fluffy. Gradually beat in the eggs. Stir in the essences, breadcrumbs, cereal and almonds until well mixed. Roll out the dough to line a 20 cm/8 inch round, loose-bottomed cake tin. Spread the jam over the dough. Top with filling and bake for 20-25 minutes or until the pastry is crisp and the filling set. Cool for 10 minutes, remove from the tin and dust the top with icing sugar. Serve warm or cold.

◼ COOK'S TIP

For a more elaborate effect, like that shown in the photograph, reserve one-third of the pastry, roll out the base thinly, then roll out the reserved pastry, cut into strips for the lattice and arrange over the filling. Decorate the tart by spooning a little glacé icing into the holes in the lattice. Add chopped cherries and nuts.

255 CHEESE SCONE RING

Preparation time: 15 minutes	YOU WILL NEED: *225 g/8 oz self-raising flour*
Cooking time: 15-20 minutes	*1 teaspoon baking powder* *50 g/2 oz butter* *50 g/2 oz vegetarian Danish Blue*
Oven temperature: 200 C, 400 F, gas 6	*cheese* *about 150 ml/¼ pint milk*
Makes 8 scones	
Calories: 180 per scone	

Sift the flour with the baking powder into a large bowl. Rub in the butter until the mixture resembles fine breadcrumbs. Crumble the cheese into this mixture and rub in. Using a fork, mix in enough milk to make a soft, but not sticky dough. Knead lightly.

Divide the mixture into eight equal pieces and shape each piece into a ball. Place one ball in the centre of a well buttered 20 cm/8 inch cake tin and arrange the remainder around the edge so that they are just touching. Brush with milk to glaze. Bake in a moderately hot oven for approximately 15-20 minutes, or until well risen and golden brown.

COOK'S TIP

At teatime spread the scones with blackcurrant or apricot jam, and for a lunch snack fill with sliced cucumber and slim wedges of Danish Blue cheese.

256 PASSION CAKE

Preparation time: 30 minutes	YOU WILL NEED: *175 g/6 oz plain flour*
Cooking time: 1¼ hours	*1 teaspoon bicarbonate of soda* *1 teaspoon baking powder* *1 teaspoon ground cinnamon*
Oven temperature: 160 C, 325 F, gas 3	*1 teaspoon mixed spice* *½ teaspoon salt* *2 large oranges*
Makes 1 cake	*175 g/6 oz light soft brown sugar* *3 eggs*
Total calories: 4835	*175 g/6 oz butter, melted* *225 g/8 oz carrots, grated* *100 g/4 oz walnuts, chopped* FOR THE TOPPING *100 g/4 oz vegetarian cream cheese* *50 g/2 oz unsalted butter, softened* *grated rind of 1 orange* *100 g/4 oz icing sugar, sifted* *15 g/½ oz walnuts, chopped, to* *decorate*

Sift together the first six ingredients. Pare away the zest only of half of one of the oranges. Cut into thin strips and blanch in boiling water. Grate the remaining orange rind. Beat the sugar, eggs and grated orange rind. Beat in the melted butter. Mix in the carrots, walnuts and flour mixture. Pour into a lined and greased 18 cm/7 inch square or 20 cm/8 inch round cake tin. Bake in a moderate oven for about 1¼ hours, until firm to the touch. Cool in the tin for 5 minutes, then cool on a wire rack. Beat the topping ingredients together, spread over the cake and decorate as shown.

COOK'S TIP

This lovely moist cake is almost irresistible. For a vanilla passion cake, substitute 1 teaspoon vanilla essence for the orange rind in the cake and omit the orange rind in the topping.

257 CARROT AND ORANGE CAKE ALABAMA

Preparation time:
20 minutes

Cooking time:
30-35 minutes

Oven temperature:
180 C, 350 F, gas 4

Makes 15 squares

Calories:
250 per square

YOU WILL NEED:
175 g/6 oz soft brown sugar
175 ml/6 fl oz groundnut oil
3 eggs, beaten
225 g/8 oz carrots, finely grated
100 g/4 oz raisins
75 g/3 oz peanuts, chopped
175 g/6 oz self-raising wholemeal flour
1 teaspoon bicarbonate of soda
1 teaspoon ground cinnamon
1 teaspoon finely grated orange rind
150 ml/¼ pint double cream, whipped
1-2 tablespoons chopped peanuts, to decorate

Mix together the sugar, oil and eggs in a large bowl. Stir in the carrots, raisins and peanuts. Mix the flour with the bicarbonate of soda, cinnamon and orange rind. Add to the bowl and mix lightly.

Turn into a greased and lined 18 × 25 cm/7 × 10 inch oblong tin and bake in a moderate oven for 30-35 minutes, until firm to the touch. Cool in the tin for 5 minutes, then turn out and cool on a wire rack. Cut into squares, then top with whipped cream and peanuts to serve.

258 BLACKCURRANT NUT CAKE

Preparation time:
15 minutes

Cooking time:
40-45 minutes

Oven temperature:
180 C, 350 F, gas 4

Makes 1 loaf

Total calories:
2610

YOU WILL NEED:
150 g/5 oz plain flour
2 teaspoons baking powder
½ teaspoon salt
75 g/3 oz All-Bran or Bran Buds cereal
100 g/4 oz butter
75 g/3 oz sugar
2 eggs
150 ml/¼ pint natural yogurt
100 g/4 oz chopped nuts
100 g/4 oz blackcurrants, fresh, frozen or canned

Line and grease a 1 kg/2 lb loaf tin. Sift together the flour, baking powder and salt. Stir in the cereal.

Cream the butter and sugar together until light and fluffy. Gradually beat in the eggs. Stir in the yogurt and then the flour mixture until just combined. Lightly stir in the nuts and blackcurrants (well drained, if canned). Spoon into the loaf tin; bake for 40-45 minutes. Insert a skewer in the centre of the cake; if it comes out clean the loaf is cooked. Cool for about 10 minutes before removing from the tin. Place on a wire rack to cool completely.

■ COOK'S TIP

In America, where this cake originated, it is traditional to serve it with a cream cheese topping. Beat 175 g/6 oz vegetarian cream cheese until soft and light and gradually add 450 g/1 lb icing sugar and 1 teaspoon vanilla essence. Beat in enough milk to give a spreading consistency, cover the cake and add-up the calories!

■ COOK'S TIP

This is the perfect cake for a picnic. Slice it just before setting out, reassemble the slices in the tin in which it was cooked, overwrap in foil and pack it in a box.

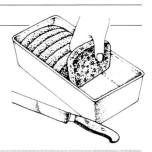

259 APPLE AND ALMOND LAYER CAKE

Preparation time:
20 minutes

Cooking time:
1½ hours

Oven temperature:
160 C, 325 F, gas 3

Makes 1 cake

Total calories:
3190

YOU WILL NEED:
150 g/5 oz soft margarine
2 large eggs, beaten
225 g/8 oz golden granulated sugar
1 teaspoon almond essence
225 g/8 oz self-raising flour, sifted
1½ teaspoons baking powder
350 g/12 oz cooking apples, peeled, cored and sliced
25 g/1 oz flaked almonds

Place the margarine, eggs, sugar, almond essence, flour and baking powder in a bowl and beat thoroughly until well combined. Alternatively use a mixer or food processor.

Spread half the cake mixture in the base of a greased 20-cm/8-in loose-bottomed cake tin. Cover with the sliced apples and put the remaining cake mixture on top of the apples in blobs. Sprinkle over the flaked almonds and bake in a moderate oven for about 1½ hours, until evenly golden and the edges shrink away from the sides of the tin. Turn out and cool on a wire rack.

260 CALIFORNIA CHRISTMAS CAKE

Preparation time:
30 minutes, plus 1 hour to macerate fruit

Cooking time:
2-2¼ hours

Oven temperature:
160 C, 325 F, gas 3

Makes 1 cake

Total calories:
4650

YOU WILL NEED:
350 g/12 oz raisins
50 g/2 oz glacé cherries, quartered
50 g/2 oz dried apricots, chopped
3 tablespoons sherry
175 g/6 oz margarine
175 g/6 oz light soft brown sugar
3 eggs, beaten
50 g/2 oz ground almonds
50 g/2 oz almonds, chopped
few drops of almond essence
225 g/8 oz self-raising wholemeal flour
1 teaspoon mixed spice
whole nuts for topping
clear honey to glaze

Soak the fruit in the sherry for 1 hour. Beat together the margarine and sugar until fluffy, beat in the eggs, then stir in the fruit mixture, ground and chopped almonds and essence. Fold in the flour and spice. Turn into a greased and double-lined 20 cm/8 inch round cake tin and smooth the top. Arrange rows of nuts over the top of the cake to completely cover it. Bake in a moderate oven for 2-2¼ hours, until firm to the touch and a skewer inserted in the centre of the cake comes out clean. Cool in the tin for 30 minutes, then turn out, remove the paper and cool on a wire rack. Brush the cake with melted honey when cold and fix a ribbon around the side.

COOK'S TIP

This is especially delicious served warm with whipped cream for dessert, though equally good as a lovely teatime cake.

COOK'S TIP

The easiest way to quarter the cherries is to use clean kitchen scissors. Vegetarians may prefer to use natural glacé cherries which do not contain cochineal.

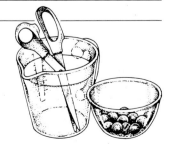

261 SPICED TEA BREAD

Preparation time:
10 minutes, plus
overnight to
macerate fruit

Cooking time:
1¼ hours

Oven temperature:
180 C, 350 F, gas 4
then
160 C, 325 F, gas 3

Makes 1 lb loaf

Total calories:
2005

YOU WILL NEED:
175 g/6 oz mixed dried fruit
grated rind and juice of ½ orange
1 teaspoon mixed spice
1 teaspoon ground cinnamon
freshly made tea
175 g/6 oz self-raising flour
50 g/2 oz wholemeal flour
2 teaspoons baking powder
50 g/2 oz caster sugar
1 egg, beaten
4 tablespoons oil
1 tablespoon chopped nuts

Place fruit, orange rind and spices in a basin. Make the orange juice up to 150 ml/¼ pint with tea and stir into the fruit. Leave overnight. Line and grease a 450 g/1 lb loaf tin. Mix the dry ingredients in a bowl. Beat in the egg, oil and macerated fruit mixture. Pour into the prepared tin and sprinkle the nuts on top. Bake at the hotter temperature for 45 minutes, then reduce the temperature for a further 30 minutes or until bread is firm and a skewer comes out clean. Leave for 5 minutes in the tin, then cool on a wire rack.

262 BANANA AND WALNUT LOAF

Preparation time:
20 minutes

Cooking time:
1 hour

Oven temperature:
180 C, 350 F, gas 4

Makes 1 loaf

Total calories:
2790

YOU WILL NEED:
100 g/4 oz soft margarine
175 g/6 oz light muscovado sugar
2 ripe bananas
2 eggs
225 g/8 oz self-raising flour
1 teaspoon baking powder
50 g/2 oz walnuts, chopped
2 tablespoons milk

Cream the margarine with the sugar until soft and light. Mash the bananas and mix in well. Break the eggs into the mixture and beat well. Gently fold in the sifted flour and baking powder, then stir in the walnuts and milk. Turn into a lined and greased 1 kg/2 lb loaf tin and bake in a moderate oven for 1 hour, until well risen and golden brown. Turn out and cool on a wire rack. Serve sliced, spread with butter if liked.

▨ COOK'S TIP

If a cake or loaf such as this one begins to brown too much before it is fully cooked, cover loosely with a piece of foil.

▨ COOK'S TIP

A great favourite with children, this, and so easy to make that even a relatively young child could attempt it with suitable supervision.

263 BRAZILIAN GINGER BRAN BREAD

Preparation time:
20 minutes, plus 2 hours to macerate fruit

Cooking time:
1¼ hours

Oven temperature:
180 C, 350 F, gas 4

Makes 18 slices

Calories:
145 per slice

YOU WILL NEED:
100 g/4 oz sultanas
100 g/4 oz raisins
100 g/4 oz currants
100 g/4 oz glacé cherries, washed, dried and halved
175 g/6 oz dark brown sugar
200 ml/7 fl oz strong black coffee
1 large egg
100 g/4 oz vegetarian cottage cheese, sieved
50 g/2 oz bran
200 g/7oz plain flour
2 teaspoons ground ginger
½ teaspoon bicarbonate of soda

Soak the fruits and sugar in the coffee for 2 hours. Base-line and grease a deep 20 cm/8 inch square cake tin. Beat the egg and cheese into the fruit mixture. Stir in the remaining ingredients, mixing thoroughly. Pour into the prepared tin and bake for 1¼ hours until well risen and firm. Cool in the tin for 5 minutes and then on a wire rack. Serve sliced, spread with butter.

264 PLUM TEABREAD

Preparation time:
30 minutes

Cooking time:
1¼ hours

Oven temperature:
190 C, 375 F, gas 5

Makes 12 slices

Calories:
180 per slice

YOU WILL NEED:
225 g/8 oz vegetarian cottage cheese
175 g/6 oz light soft brown sugar
2 large eggs
50 g/2 oz walnuts, chopped
175 g/6 oz plums, stoned
225 g/8 oz self-raising flour

Line and thoroughly grease a 900 g/2 lb loaf tin. Sieve the cottage cheese and beat in the sugar. Add the eggs and walnuts. Reserve two plums; chop the rest. Stir the chopped plums and flour into the mixture and spoon into the prepared tin. Bake for 30 minutes. Press four plum halves as decoration along the centre of the loaf and bake for a further 45 minutes, covering with foil if it over-browns, until cooked through. Cool on a wire rack and serve sliced, spread with butter.

◼ COOK'S TIP

Instead of spreading the slices of bread with butter, try using a light cream cheese. The flavours are wonderfully complementary.

◼ COOK'S TIP

For a more elaborate decoration on the top of this loaf, use almonds to transform each inverted plum half to a sunburst.

265 BANANA AND HONEY TEABREAD

Preparation time:
20 minutes

Cooking time:
1¼-1½ hours

Oven temperature:
180 C, 350 F, gas 4

Makes 1 large loaf

Total calories:
2830

YOU WILL NEED:
200 g/7oz self-raising flour
¼ teaspoon bicarbonate of soda
pinch of salt
75 g/3 oz butter
50 g/2 oz soft brown sugar
175 g/6 oz sultanas
100 g/4 oz walnuts, chopped
2 medium bananas, peeled
2 tablespoons clear honey
2 eggs

Line and grease a 900 g/2 lb loaf tin. Sift together the flour, soda and salt into a large bowl. Rub in the butter until the mixture resembles fine breadcrumbs. Stir in the sugar, sultanas and walnuts.

Mash the bananas in a bowl. Add the honey and eggs and whisk together. Add to the dry ingredients and mix well.

Pour into the prepared loaf tin and level the surface with the back of a metal spoon. Bake in a moderate oven for 1¼-1½ hours, or until a warmed skewer inserted into the centre comes out clean.

Allow to cool in the tin for 5 minutes. Turn on to a wire rack, remove lining paper and cool completely. Serve sliced and buttered.

266 APRICOT BARS

Preparation time:
20 minutes

Cooking time:
25-20 minutes

Oven temperature:
180 C, 350 F, gas 4

Makes 18

Calories:
125 per bar

YOU WILL NEED:
175 g/6 oz butter, softened
175 g/6 oz soft brown sugar
225 g/8 oz plain flour, sifted
½ teaspoon bicarbonate of soda
100 g/4 oz rolled oats
½ teaspoon salt
15 g/½ oz butter, melted
1 × 285 g/10 oz can apricot halves, drained
grated rind of 1 lemon
caster sugar, to decorate

Beat the softened butter with the sugar. Mix in the flour, bicarbonate of soda, oats and salt. Brush a 20 × 30-cm/8 × 12-in tin with the melted butter and spread over half the crumb mixture. Chop the apricots and mix with the lemon rind. Spread on to the crumb base and cover with the remaining mixture. Cook in a moderate oven for 25-30 minutes, cut into bars and leave to cool in the tin. Sprinkle over a little caster sugar.

■ COOK'S TIP

It is important to preheat the oven for at least 15 minutes before baking a cake. If the temperature is too low, the texture of the cake is liable to be coarse.

■ COOK'S TIP

To soften the butter, cut it into large cubes and place it in a bowl with cold (room temperature) water to cover. Stand for a few minutes, then pour off the water.

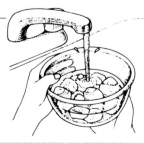

267 BLUE CHEESE LOAF

Preparation time:
20 minutes

Cooking time:
1 hour

Oven temperature:
190 C, 375 F, gas 5

Makes 1 loaf

Total calories:
1865

YOU WILL NEED:
100 g/4 oz self-raising wholemeal flour
100 g/4 oz self-raising flour
½ teaspoon baking powder
1 teaspoon mustard powder
½ teaspoon salt
50 g/2 oz butter
100 g/4 oz vegetarian Danish Blue cheese
2 celery sticks, finely chopped
50 g/2 oz walnuts, chopped
1 large egg
120 ml/4 fl oz milk
sesame seeds or poppy seeds (optional)

Sift the flours, baking powder, mustard and salt into a mixing bowl, adding back any bran left in the sieve. Rub in the butter until the mixture resembles fine breadcrumbs. Crumble the cheese and rub in. Mix in the celery and walnuts. Beat the egg and milk together, add to the dry ingredients and mix well to make a fairly stiff consistency.

Spoon the mixture into a lined and greased 450 g/1 lb loaf tin. Level the top and sprinkle with sesame or poppy seeds, if liked. Bake in a moderately hot oven for 1 hour, or until well browned. When cooked, a skewer inserted into the centre of the loaf will come out clean. Cool the loaf in the tin for 5 minutes, then turn out on to a wire rack, remove the lining paper and cool.

Serve warm or cold, sliced and spread with butter.

■ COOK'S TIP

To microwave: turn the mixture into a 900-ml/ 1½-pint rectangular dish. Microwave on full power 12 minutes then stand 10 minutes before cooling on a wire rack.

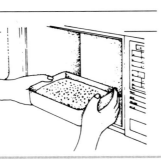

268 CARAWAY ROLLS

Preparation time:
25-30 minutes, plus time to rise and prove

Cooking time:
20 minutes

Oven temperature:
230°C, 450°F, gas 8

Makes 8

Calories:
170 per roll

YOU WILL NEED:
25 g/1 oz fresh yeast or 15 g/½ oz dried yeast (see Cook's Tip)
1 teaspoon sugar
250 ml/8 fl oz lukewarm water
15 g/½ oz butter or margarine
275 g/10 oz strong white bread flour
50 g/2 oz bran flakes, crushed
1 teaspoon caraway seeds
½ teaspoon salt

Blend the fresh yeast and sugar with a little of the water to form a smooth paste. Add the remaining water. Leave until frothy. Rub the butter or margarine into the flour and stir in the bran flakes, caraway seeds and salt. Add the yeast mixture and mix well to form a soft dough. Knead for about 10 minutes. Place the dough in a bowl and cover loosely with a large oiled plastic bag or cling film. Leave in a warm place until doubled in size. Turn the dough on to a floured surface and knead for a further 4 minutes. Shape into eight rolls, place on a greased baking tray and leave in a warm place until doubled in size. Brush with a little milk and bake in a hot oven for about 20 minutes.

■ COOK'S TIP

If using dried yeast, you will need 15 g/½ oz. Sprinkle the dried yeast over the water, stir in the sugar and leave until frothy, about 10 minutes.

269 SAVOURY CHEESE FLOWERPOT BREAD

Preparation time:
30 minutes, plus
about 3 hours for
rising

Cooking time:
45 minutes

Oven temperature:
200 C, 400 F, gas 6

Makes 1 × 675 g/
1½ lb flowerpot
loaf

Total calories:
1680

YOU WILL NEED:
350 g/12 oz strong wholemeal flour
¼ teaspoon salt
15 g/½ oz butter
1 sachet easy-blend dried yeast
25 g/1 oz walnuts, chopped
100 g/4 oz vegetarian low-fat hard
  cheese, finely grated
75 g/3 oz celery, chopped
150 ml/¼ pint warm water
beaten egg to glaze
1 tablespoon kibbled wheat

Mix the flour and salt together. Rub in the butter and stir in the yeast. Thoroughly mix in the walnuts, cheese and celery. Add the water to make a dough and knead for 10 minutes. Leave to rise in a large bowl, covered with a lightly oiled plastic bag, in a warm place, until double in size – about 2 hours.

Knock back, knead and shape to fit a well greased unused flowerpot measuring about 15 cm/6 inch in depth and width. Cover with plastic again and leave to rise for about 1 hour. Glaze and sprinkle with kibbled wheat. Bake for 45 minutes until golden. The bottom of the bread should sound hollow when tapped. Cool on a wire rack and serve sliced, lightly spread with butter.

270 PEANUT COOKIES

Preparation time:
10 minutes

Cooking time:
12 minutes

Oven temperature:
180 C, 350 F, gas 4

Makes 12

Calories:
95 per cookie

YOU WILL NEED:
50 g/2 oz butter, softened
50 g/2 oz soft brown sugar
50 g/2 oz salted peanuts, roughly
  chopped
½ teaspoon mixed spice
75 g/3 oz self-raising flour
1 tablespoon orange juice

Cream the butter and sugar together until light and fluffy, then stir in the peanuts, spice, flour and juice to form a soft, not sticky, dough. Break the mixture into 12 equal-sized pieces and roll each into a ball. Place well apart on greased baking trays, flattening them slightly with a fork. Bake for 10-12 minutes or until firming. Leave on trays until firm enough to transfer to a wire rack to cool completely.

■ COOK'S TIP

Season the flowerpot: brush
the inside with oil. Place
empty in a moderately hot
oven 15 minutes. Allow to
cool completely before use.

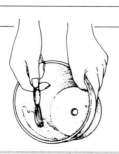

■ COOK'S TIP

Mixed spice usually includes
cinnamon, cloves and
nutmeg, but Jamaica pepper
or coriander may be added,
as well.

271 CHEESE AND PINEAPPLE SCONES

Preparation time:
20 minutes

Cooking time:
15 minutes

Oven temperature:
200 C, 400 F, gas 6

Makes 12 scones

Calories:
145 per scone

YOU WILL NEED:
275 g/10 oz wholemeal flour
4 teaspoons baking powder
pinch of salt
65 g/2½ oz butter
50 g/2 oz vegetarian low-fat hard
  cheese, finely grated
1 × 227g/8 oz can crushed pineapple,
  drained
3 tablespoons milk
1 large egg, beaten
milk to glaze

Mix the flour, baking powder and salt together. Rub in the butter until the mixture resembles fine breadcrumbs. Stir in the cheese and pineapple. Bind to a dough with the milk and egg.

Roll out 1 cm/½ inch thick and cut out 12 6 cm/2½ inch rounds. Place on a greased baking tray. Brush with milk and bake for about 15 minutes, until risen and golden. Cool on a wire rack. Serve split, spread with butter and pineapple jam.

272 NUT FLAPJACKS

Preparation time:
5 minutes

Cooking time:
40 minutes

Oven temperature:
160 C, 325 F, gas 3

Makes 12

Calories:
215 per flapjack

YOU WILL NEED:
100 g/4 oz vegetable margarine
4 tablespoons golden syrup
75 g/3 oz soft brown sugar
225 g/8 oz rolled oats
75 g/3 oz walnuts, chopped
grated rind of 1 orange
¼ teaspoon salt
FOR THE DECORATION
fromage frais or quark (optional)
orange slices (optional)

Grease a 19 cm/7½ inch square, shallow tin.

Put the margarine and syrup in a pan and melt over low heat. Remove from the heat and stir in the sugar, oats, walnuts, orange rind and salt until well mixed. Turn the mixture into the tin and bake for 40 minutes or until just starting to bubble at the edges. Cook for 5 minutes to firm up slightly. Cut into squares and leave until stiff enough to lift out on to a wire rack to cool completely.

Decorate as shown, if liked.

■ COOK'S TIP

Baking powder loses its potency if stored too long. To test for freshness, sprinkle 1 teaspoon baking powder into a little hot water. It should fizz.

■ COOK'S TIP

Coconut makes a very good addition to these flapjacks. Reduce the amount of oats by 75 g/3 oz and substitute desiccated coconut.

INDEX